JAPAN UNBOUND

JAPAN UNBOUND

A Volatile Nation's Quest for
Pride and Purpose

John Nathan

HOUGHTON MIFFLIN COMPANY

BOSTON   NEW YORK

2004

Library of Congress Cataloging-in-Publication Data

Nathan, John, date.
Japan unbound : a volatile nation's quest for pride and purpose /
John Nathan.
p. cm.
Includes bibliographical references and index.
ISBN 0-618-13894-3
1. Japan — Civilization — 1945– I. Title
DS822.5N376 2004
320.54'052 — dc22
2003060559

Book design by Melissa Lotfy

Printed in the United States of America

MP 10 9 8 7 6 5 4 3 2 1

Chapter 7, "Shintaro Ishihara: The Sun King," appeared as "Tokyo Story"
in *The New Yorker* in slightly different form.

Lines from "Vacillation": Reprinted with the permission of Scribner, an
imprint of Simon & Schuster Adult Publishing Group, from *The Collected
Works of W. B. Yeats, Volume I: The Poems, Revised,* edited by Richard J.
Finneran. Copyright © 1933 by The Macmillan Company; copyright re-
newed © 1961 by Bertha Georgie Yeats. Lines from "The Tower": Re-
printed with the permission of Scribner, an imprint of Simon & Schuster
Adult Publishing Group, from *The Collected Works of W. B. Yeats, Volume I:
The Poems, Revised,* edited by Richard J. Finneran. Copyright © 1928 by
The Macmillan Company; copyright renewed © 1956 by Georgie Yeats.

Publisher's Note
Some place names and personal names in "Chapter 2: The Family Cri-
sis" have been changed to avoid any unintended embarrassment. Spe-
cifically, the names of the Denda family (Ichiro, Hiroshi, and Masako), the
Kawatani family (Rikutaro, Izumi, Kazu, and Kanako), the Yano family
(Kazuya, Fumi, Masaichi, and Yumi), and Atsuko Matsuda are fictitious.

For Diane, Emily, and Tobias

Contents

JAPAN UNBOUND

Introduction

I FIRST WENT TO JAPAN in the fall of 1961, fresh out of Harvard with a joint degree in English literature and Far Eastern Languages, and remained there for seven years, until I returned to seek my fugitive identity at home. In those early postwar days, the Japanese were in the grip of a national conviction that no foreigner — the Japanese word translates more closely to mean "outsider" — could ever learn to use their language or understand anything about them. At Tokyo University, where I was admitted as an undergraduate in 1963, among the writers and artists I was beginning to meet, and certainly at home with my Japanese host family, it was conceded that I could speak and understand Japanese. This was a curious and unlikely phenomenon, but there it was. On the street, I was seen as just another foreigner, which meant that I was often unable to make myself understood. Rejection was eloquently communicated with a simple gesture: the rapid waggling of a hand in front of the nose, as if to fan away an unpleasant odor. "No!" it signaled. "I don't understand what you are saying and I want nothing to do with you." As I asked directions of passersby, or gave directions to a taxi driver, or purchased

tickets at a train station or stamps at a post office, or ordered from
a menu, all in Japanese increasingly close to fluent, people would
fan their noses in my face to indicate their refusal to understand.
If they spoke at all, it was not to reply but to whine aloud to no
one in particular that they failed to understand and had no access
to an interpreter. "You don't need an interpreter," I would protest.
"If you will just listen, you will hear that I am speaking Japanese."
The hands continued to wag.

I was obsessed with my study of Japanese, reading my way
through a one-hundred-volume set of modern Japanese fiction
and practicing words and phrases in front of a mirror at home for
hours every day, and this variety of rejection knifed intolerably
into my pride. I encountered it everywhere, even among intellectuals. A professor in my own department at Tokyo University told
a reporter for the school paper that he experienced my command
of Japanese as *usan-kusai*. I thought I knew what the word meant,
but it seemed such an unlikely thing to say that I consulted my
battery of dictionaries and discovered that it was even more of an
affront than I had realized. *Usan-kusai:* bizarre to the point of being suspicious, of doubtful wholesomeness, tainted. That week I
stayed home from class. I felt lonely and bitter.

Even so, I was aware of something comical and even charming
about Japanese parochialism. I also discovered that the astonish-
ment produced by rattling Japanese assumptions even a little
could work in my favor.

I got around on a motorcycle. In those days, the sight of a foreigner astride a Honda 250 cc "Sport" was sufficient to attract the
attention of the police, and if I exceeded the speed limit by a kilo-
meter, I was pulled over. The first time, when he had asked to see
my license and foreigner registration, the motorcycle cop noticed
the briefcase hanging from my handlebars and asked what was inside. "Books," I replied. "Books? What kind?" he inquired, as curious now as any four-year-old. I withdrew my copy of the eighth-
century *Chronicle of Ancient Matters,* the earliest Japanese mythol-

ogy, and opened it to show him. His eyes widened. "You can read that?" I nodded, sensing an advantage on the way. "Let's hear." I intoned a few lines: "So, thereupon, His-Swift-Impetuous-Male-Augustness said: 'If that be so, I will take leave of the Heaven-Shining-Great-August-Deity and depart.' With these words he forthwith went up to Heaven, whereupon all the mountains and rivers shook, and every land and country quaked." The policeman's eyebrows lifted and his gaze narrowed; into the mike on his shoulder, never taking his eyes off me, he called for backup. A patrol car drove up, and two more officers cautiously approached. "Read some more," the motorcycle cop ordered. Standing on the shoulder of the Tokyo beltway, I read aloud another passage. The policemen listened as though stunned. When I finished, they laughed together, like friends who have stumbled on something they are forbidden to see and are uncertain what to make of it. A little giddily, they waved me on with just a warning to observe the speed limit. Thereafter, I made sure my briefcase was always loaded with a Japanese literary classic when I climbed on my motorcycle. Sometimes I took *The Tale of Genji* or a collection of Basho's haiku. A newspaper would have served me just as well.

But such moments of comic relief were out of the ordinary. Day by day, my chagrin grew. In time, I devised a hustle that took advantage of the assumptions about me that I found most insulting. I would enter an *izaka-ya,* a Japanese version of a British pub, at an hour when it was crowded with company men on their way home from work, and would find an opportunity to mention in the course of a conversation at the bar that I not only spoke but could also read and write Japanese. Someone always asked, often in English, "You mean *kana,* Japanese alphabet!" "*Kana,* of course, but Chinese characters, too, just like you." Silence. "If you don't believe me, let's have a writing contest, a *kakikkura,* and to make it interesting we'll bet a little money on the side."

I would suggest a thousand yen (roughly $3 at the time) for round one, and my opponent — someone always took the bait —

would put money on the bar and write a Chinese character on a paper napkin. It was likely to be a simple four-stroke character, "tree" or "water" or "hand." I would read the character and produce another similarly basic word for my opponent to read.

For round two, I would up the stakes to five thousand yen. This challenge motivated my opponent to present me with a compound of two or more characters, such as "reality" or "landscape" or "capitalism." I would respond at the appropriate level of difficulty. Another draw.

By now we would have attracted a crowd, and they were hooked. For the final round, I would produce a ten-thousand-yen note, real money in those days. Sometimes my opponent would ask a friend to put up half his stake.

We had now arrived at the cunning part of the game. Encountering a foreigner who could read was so disorienting to my opponents that it never occurred to them that the kinds of words most likely to challenge me might be child's play for them. The truth was, anyone in the bar could have defeated me easily by selecting character compounds that were likely to be familiar to any Japanese — place names for example, which had not been disallowed — and unfamiliar to me, words that had to be known and could not be figured out. Instead, their choices were governed by what they expected would be difficult for native readers. The result was always a term that I had no trouble reading: "calumny," "garrulousness," "smithereen."

Then it was my turn to end the game. I carried around in memory for this purpose a list of Chinese characters with unlikely Japanese readings which had sent my learned Japanese landlord to his dictionary. I now produced one of these — an alternate character for "flying squirrel," or the name of a blind Buddhist angel who sits above the clouds playing his flute — and held it up for my opponent to see. As a precaution against claims that I had fabricated the character, I kept a dictionary in my bag, but I was never challenged. As the napkin was passed around, the men who had witnessed my victory observed me with surprise and confusion. It was gratifying to imagine that I had succeeded in shaking their view of the world if for only a moment.

I understood that the Japanese insistence on the impenetrability of their language was an assertion of their uniqueness. What I failed to see at the time was that the compulsion to assert uniqueness was the obverse side of a deep uncertainty about who they were, about what it meant to be Japanese in the modern world. Every society views itself as unique and has grounds for claiming uniqueness. Few societies are compelled to assert their uniqueness as loudly and insistently as the Japanese. Foreign students living in China report that their efforts to learn Chinese are welcomed and appreciated. With the exception of the French, whose arrogance about their culture reveals another variety of uneasiness, Europeans also tend to be pleased by foreigners' efforts to learn their languages. In America, the prevailing assumption is that American English is the only real language in the world. A corollary assumption is that anyone who happens to be in the United States will have a command of English; Americans in general are not conscious of a necessity to accommodate non-native speakers struggling with the language, nor do such efforts elicit either appreciation or resistance. An anecdote about a Texas governor is a striking confirmation of how airtight this assumption is. Angered by a grass-roots movement to elevate the Spanish language to parity with English in the Texas public school system, Governor John Connally declared at a press conference: "If English was good enough for Jesus Christ, it ought to be good enough for us Texans!" It is no coincidence that America is a society dramatically untroubled by uncertainty regarding national purpose or, for that matter, national identity.

Throughout their history, the Japanese have been prompted by familiar, troubling questions about identity to focus on their language as evidence of who they are and, more important, what makes them special. In a popular book written in 1985, *The Japa-*

nese Brain, an audiologist named Tadanobu Tsunoda argued that the Japanese language was not only evidence of Japanese uniqueness, but its source:

> My findings seem to provide an explanation of the uniqueness and universal aspects of Japanese culture. Why do Japanese people behave in their characteristic manner? How has the Japanese culture developed its distinctive features? I believe the key to these questions lies in the Japanese language. That is, the Japanese are Japanese because they speak Japanese. My investigations have suggested that the Japanese language shapes the Japanese brain function pattern, which in turn serves as a basis for the formation of Japanese culture.*

Since the late nineties, dozens of books promising to reacquaint readers with the expressive beauty and power of the Japanese language when it is used correctly have climbed to the top of the bestseller lists every year. The recent "Japanese language boom" is but one of many indications that Japanese society is once again in the grips of a need to reconfirm its uniqueness.

In fact, the Japanese have suffered recurrently from a tenuous hold on their cultural identity since long before the "modern" period. In *The Tale of Genji,* the eleventh-century romance that is the masterpiece of Japanese classical literature, Prince Genji insists that his son, Yugiri, study the Chinese classics despite objections from the boy's grandmother, an imperial princess: "The truth is, without a solid foundation of book learning [in the Chinese classics], this Japanese spirit about which we hear so much is not of any great use in the world." By "Japanese spirit," Genji intends both a code of valor and a poetics of life, an aesthetic sensibility that was neither borrowed nor derived from the treasure

---

* See Patrick Smith, *Japan: A Reinterpretation* (New York: Vintage Books, 1998), p. 199.

house of Chinese wisdom. But Genji is suggesting that "Japanese-ness" can bloom only after pollination by Chinese studies. The implication is that Japanese identity has its source, or at best is in some way contingent upon, China. For the female author of *Genji,* there was irony in this equation. Courtiers and poets of the day wrote their serious essays and kept their diaries in classical Chinese or in a hybrid version of that language cleverly evolved in Japan. Women at court were not encouraged to study the Chinese classics and language, and they wrote in pure Japanese that was unalloyed by Chinese constructions or vocabulary. It is no coincidence that most of the great literary works of the period were created by women, who were free to express themselves in their native language.

In the latter half of the eighteenth century, the nationalist scholar Motoori Norinaga rediscovered *The Tale of Genji* and used it as the basis of a Shinto revival. In a voluminous critique called *The Jeweled Comb,* Norinaga challenged the traditional reading of the book as a cautionary tale about good and evil animated by Buddhist and Confucian teaching. He argued that the *Genji* was instead a pure work of literary art whose subject was the nature and meaning of human existence, and that the wellspring of Lady Murasaki's invention was the quintessentially Japanese aesthetic and philosophical quality called *mono no aware,* a poignant consciousness of the evanescence of all things. In Norinaga's view, *The Tale of Genji* was thus a monumental and living elucidation of the "Japanese spirit," the essence of Japaneseness.

In the closing decades of the nineteenth century, the focus of Japanese learning and emulation shifted away from China to Europe and, increasingly, America. In 1853, Japan was pried open under threat from American gunboats after 250 years of isolation from the rest of the world under the feudal — Confucian — rule of the Tokugawa shoguns. Fifteen years later the feudal government had toppled, and the country embarked on a single-minded mission to transform itself into a modern state by borrowing from the West. The central figure in the national project to understand Western civilization was the philosopher-educator Yukichi Fuku-zawa (1834–1901), sometimes called the father of the Japanese en-lightenment. The son of a samurai, Fukuzawa received the tradi-tional education in Confucianism and the Chinese classics before he traveled to Osaka in 1851 to apply himself to *rangaku,* "Dutch studies," or the study of Western philosophy, mathematics, and medicine in the Dutch language. Three times he traveled to Eu-rope as a representative of the shogunal government. In 1868, he founded in Edo (Tokyo) a school of Western studies in Dutch and English which became Keio University. The translator of John Stuart Mill and author of *In Defense of* [Western] *Learning* and *A Theory of* [Western] *Civilization,* Fukuzawa held that Japan must turn its back on its Asian neighbors, on China in particular, and look to the West for models as it embarked on moderniza-tion. In the 1880s, he introduced the compound notion *wakon-yosai,* literally, "Japanese sensibility, Western knowledge." The tension between these two elements has never been resolved.

The challenge was not only understanding European political and social institutions and the worldviews they reflected, but adapting them to fit the contours of Japanese society. Establishing an authentic sense of national self and purpose in the modern world required the merging of two disparate and often irreconcil-able cultures, one native, inherent, grounded in history, the other founded on concepts such as individualism and intractably for-eign. This exercise in cultural synthesis continues to tax and trou-ble the Japanese imagination.

Throughout the twentieth century, Japanese intellectuals have expended inordinate energy on attempts to locate and define the quiddity of "Japaneseness" that Norinaga discovered in *The Tale of Genji.* In a society as homogeneous as Japan, the intensity of this effort is telling: it suggests, and there is abundant evidence to support the conclusion, that cultural ambivalence, the chronic sense of contingency on values and behaviors external to native traditions, has led to recurrent seasons of bewilderment and despair akin to a national identity crisis.

This issue is not generalized, conceptual, abstract: it comes down to an insubstantial sense of self that is experienced by individuals in the society with deep uneasiness as the emptiness of life. It will be clear in the chronicle of the current moment that is the subject of this book that Japan today is in the throes of just such a crisis.

The burden of balancing two cultures is brilliantly distilled in the writer-director Juzo Itami's 1986 film, *Tampopo* (the word means "dandelion," the name of a ramen shop). The film uses the ritual of preparing and enjoying Japanese noodles as a metaphor for nourishment and community. In two comic scenes, Itami dramatizes what I mean by cultural contingency and its perils. In the first, a group of senior business executives files into a private dining room in an affectedly French restaurant of the sort that is to be found in every posh Japanese hotel. The last man in, balancing a stack of briefcases in both arms, is an assistant who would have been played by Jerry Lewis in an American film. The poker-faced waiter hands the executive vice president a menu, which he glances at uncomprehendingly: it is written in French and English. He seeks safety in the one dish familiar to every Japanese businessman, sole meunière. His first course is consommé, another mainstay. Avoiding the imponderable wine list, he requests beer. Around the table the junior executives follow suit. At last, the pimply factotum contemplates the menu and inquires whether the boudin-style quenelles might be the same dish that is a specialty at Taillevent. The waiter acknowledges that the chef has trained at Taillevent. Unfazed by the flabbergasted stares now fixed on him, the assistant calls for escargot en croûte, an apple and walnut salad, and a glass of — rolling up his eyes and smacking his lips — Corton Charlemagne. The rest of the table is apoplectically silent.

In the second scene, a group of young ladies in Western party dresses are in the midst of a "charm school" class in the main dining room. Today's lesson is on the etiquette of eating spaghetti vongole. The chatelaine who is the instructor reminds her pupils that spaghetti must be enjoyed silently (unlike Japanese noodles, which are noisily inhaled from the bowl). As she lifts her fork daintily to her lips to demonstrate, there comes a clamorous slurping from across the room. All heads turn to discover a foreigner wolfing down his own plate of spaghetti. The girls are confused, the instructor outraged. Inevitably, the class abandons its tenuous hold on acquired table manners and, giving in to impulse, joins its mentor in attacking the vongole noisily, as if they were ramen.

The filmmaker's point is unmistakable: Western knowledge, as in the first scene, is the source of power and authority. Obversely, as in the second, the Japanese, in their frantic efforts to imitate the West, must continually look outside themselves for the source of authenticity and are as a consequence eternally subject to confusion about who they are.

The novelist Natsume Soseki, born in 1867 on the cusp of the old and the new order, was an impassioned critic of Japan's frantic efforts to Westernize, which he blamed for the emptiness at the center of his bleak vision of life. Soseki's personal encounter with Western culture tormented and disheartened him. In 1893, he became the second student to graduate from the newly established department of English literature at Tokyo Imperial University, where he would later teach briefly as a successor to Lafcadio Hearn. Soseki read deeply in Shakespeare, Sterne, Fielding, and Austen, and the more he read the more convinced he became of the futility of studying a "foreign" literature. In 1900, he was sent to England on a government stipend, and spent two wretched years in isolation in a London rooming house convincing himself that English life and letters were not merely beyond his comprehension but repugnant to his sensibility as a Japanese. This drove him into fits of depression that prompted a Japanese student to report back to the government, "Soseki has gone quite mad." In the preface to his 1906 *Theory of Literature,* he summarized his passionate and failed encounter with Western civilization:

> As a child I enjoyed studying the Chinese classics. Although the time spent in this kind of study was not long, it was from Chinese classics that I learned, however vaguely and obscurely, what literature was. In my heart, I hoped it would be the same when I read English literature, and that I would not necessarily begrudge giving my whole life to studying it, if that were required. What I resent, and the source of my agony, is that despite my study I never mastered it. I have been plagued by the disquieting feeling of having been somehow duped or cheated by English literature.

In a lecture he delivered at the newly created Peers' School in August 1911, "The Civilization of Modern-Day Japan," Soseki established an explicit connection between what he called "the loss of moral balance" and Japan's slavish emulation of the West:

> Simply stated, Western civilization (that is, civilization in general) is internally motivated, whereas Japan's civilization is externally motivated. Something that is "internally motivated" develops naturally from within, as a flower opens, the bursting of the bud followed by the turning outward of the petals. Something is "externally motivated" when it is forced to assume a certain form as the result of pressure applied from the outside . . .
> A nation, a people that incurs a civilization in this way, can only feel a sense of emptiness, of dissatisfaction and anxiety. There are those who gloat over this civilization of ours as if it were internally motivated, but they are wrong. They may think they represent the height of fashion, but they are wrong. They are false and shallow, like boys who make a great show of enjoying cigarettes before they even know what tobacco tastes like.

This is what the Japanese must do in order to survive, and this is what makes us so pitiful.*

The hero of Soseki's 1909 novel, *And Then,* predicted that equilibrium would not be regained until the doubtful day when "feeble Japan could stand shoulder to shoulder with the greatest powers of Europe." That day has come and gone, but the struggle to assimilate Western influence without losing balance continues. The novelist Kenzaburo Oe addressed this dilemma in the speech he delivered in English in Stockholm in December 1994 upon accepting the Nobel Prize:

> My observation is that after 120 years of its modernization since the opening of the country, present-day Japan is split between two opposite poles of ambiguity. This ambiguity, which is so powerful and penetrating that it divides both the state and the people, affects me as a writer like a deep-felt scar. The modernization of Japan was oriented toward learning from and imitating the West, yet our country is situated in Asia and has its own deep-rooted culture. The ambiguous orientation of Japan drove the country into the position of an invader in Asia, and resulted in its isolation from other Asian nations, not only politically but also socially and culturally. And even in the West, to which our culture was supposedly quite open, we have long remained inscrutable or only partially understood.

Like Soseki, Oe grew up at a time when Japan's connection to the values of its historical past was abruptly severed as a result of its defeat in World War II. The war effort had been fueled by a national mission that left no room for ambivalence or ambiguity, by Japan's traditional sense of itself as "the land of the gods" — but

---

* Natsume Soseki, *Kokoro and Selected Essays,* translated by Jay Rubin (Lanham, Md.: Madison Books, 1992), pp. 272, 279.

that comforting certainty was blown apart in August 1945. First there was the inferno of two atomic bombs. One week later, on August 15, Emperor Hirohito went on the radio for the first time and informed his subjects in his own voice that they must now "endure the unendurable" and lay down their arms. Oe later recalled listening to the emperor in his mountain village as a boy of ten: "The adults sat around their radios and cried. The children gathered outside in the dusty road and whispered their bewilderment. We were most confused and disappointed by the fact that the emperor had spoken in a *human* voice. . . . How could we believe that an august presence of such awful power had become an ordinary human being on a designated summer day?"

The disorienting possibility that Hirohito was a mortal man was reinforced by the unthinkable photograph of His Majesty standing alongside General Douglas MacArthur which appeared in the Tokyo morning newspapers of September 28, 1945. MacArthur had arrived in Japan from the Philippines on August 30; always strategic, he declined to visit the emperor at the palace, ordering Hirohito to pay his respects to him at the U.S. embassy. MacArthur chose to wear suntans with his collar open and no decorations or insignia of rank. In the photo, he stares straight at the camera, his face void of expression; one hand is thrust carelessly into his pocket; the other is on his hip. Alongside, reaching only to the general's shoulder, Hirohito stands ramrod-stiff in his coat and tails. The day after the photograph appeared, as if to underline the shocking disparity in power that it conveyed, MacArthur told the *Chicago Tribune*: "Japan has fallen to a fourth-rate nation. It will not be possible for her to emerge again as a strong nation in the world."

The recurrent uneasiness that afflicts postwar Japan has its most recent source in a constitution based on principles like democracy that had evolved in the West and were antithetical to the groupism at the heart of traditional society. Many Japanese are opposed to amending even the most controversial dictum in their constitution, Article 9, the war renunciation clause, but I have yet to meet anyone on the right or the left who refers to it with pride. In contrast to the resonant English of America's founding documents, even its language is foreign, a literal and wooden translation of the original English version.

Japanese history between 1950 and the early 1980s is principally about economic recovery. But even as Japan focused on outdoing America while embracing American values and the American way of life, there was evidence of longing to regain the defining sense of purpose and mission that had been lost at the end of the war.

Two historical moments in 1970 symbolized the fulfillment and the emptiness that are the defining paradox and dilemma of modern Japanese life. In March 1970, Japan marked its arrival on the global scene as a major world economy with the opening of Expo '70 in Osaka, a giant trade fair on which the government lavished $2 billion to attract participation from seventy-seven countries and which prompted the futurist Herman Kahn to predict that "the twenty-first century will be the Japanese century." And on November 25, the novelist Yukio Mishima committed ritual suicide by hara-kiri. At 10:50 in the morning, accompanied by four uniformed cadets from his private army, the Shield Society, Mishima paid a visit to the commandant of the Tokyo Battalion of the Self-defense Force on the pretext of showing him an antique Japanese sword. On a prearranged signal, the cadets seized and bound the commandant and Mishima ordered him to assemble the battalion in the courtyard below. Just before noon, he stepped onto the balcony and delivered a short speech appealing to the troops to join him and his cadets as true men and samurai warriors in a battle to the death in the name of the emperor against a postwar democracy that had deprived Japan of its army and robbed the nation of its soul. When the eight hundred soldiers began to boo and jeer, Mishima went inside and killed himself.

Mishima's suicide was driven in part by a longing for death —

specifically a martyr's death — that he had contemplated fearfully since his childhood. But we must not explain away the social significance of his act with a clinical diagnosis. As a young man during the Pacific War, he had tasted briefly the comforting certainty of identification with a transcendent ideal embodied by a divine emperor. Then, in 1945, following the defeat, he was expelled with the rest of his generation into a hollow postwar world that had been bereft of tradition and severed from historical continuity. During the 1950s, his response to what he described as "existential uneasiness" was to acquire a gaudy wardrobe of European and American styles and sensibilities and to wear them flamboyantly. When he built his house in 1958, he told his architect that he wanted to sit in a rococo chair in jeans and an aloha shirt. The result was a mélange of Greek statuary and French period furniture that looked like a movie set and made many Japanese who received invitations to his cocktail parties on Tiffany stationery desperately uncomfortable. Meanwhile, by his own account, beneath the masquerade he suffered from a growing feeling of emptiness.

Beginning in the early 1960s, Mishima turned his back on Western rationalism and the Greek ideals of symmetry and measure and embraced the dark, romantic, death-ridden aesthetics of ultranationalism. In July 1968, he published an elaborate disquisition on identity, "In Defense of Culture," in which he established the rationale for his final act. Mishima argued that the Japanese self could be discovered only in Japanese culture, and that authentic culture had its source only in the emperor. Specifically, His Imperial Majesty was the defining source of *miyabi,* a value in Japanese classical aesthetics that is usually defined as "courtly elegance," as epitomized in *The Tale of Genji.* In Mishima's singular definition, *miyabi* was "the essence of court culture and the people's longing for that essence . . . . If we Japanese ever hope to regain our connection to *miyabi,* the quality that defines us, we must protect the emperor at any cost."

Mishima was not alone in his suffering. If American democracy was proving to be a not entirely satisfactory substitute for wartime values, neither was the frantic pursuit of GNP that was being promulgated as the new national mission. By the late 1960s, the company man, the cog in the wheel of Japan's emerging economic miracle, was feeling tired and vaguely disillusioned. He was earning more money than his father had ever seen, and he had acquired the undisputed trophies of middle-class success known in the media as "the three Cs," an air conditioner, a car, and a color TV. But as he watched *Ben Casey* and *The Partridge Family* and *I Love Lucy* dubbed in Japanese on Sony Trinitrons, he observed Americans setting out for their lakeside cabins to try new motorboats and was troubled to realize that he had no place to go. In any event, he was too busy at work even to consider taking his annual weeklong vacation. Sundays, his one day off, he went shopping with his wife at the electronics bazaar in Akihabara or hit balls at a crowded driving range on the roof of a department store — real golf courses were still beyond his means. He was tired; his head ached from drinking with his boss and colleagues every evening; and he was beginning to wonder why life was affording him so little gratification despite his hard work: prosperity was not after all a goal worth living for. Asked what such a goal might be, he would hardly have answered a reconnection to *miyabi* achieved by a warrior's death. Nonetheless, the insubstantial sense of self that tormented Mishima was becoming endemic in Japan. There is no question that his suicide was personal and idiosyncratic, fully comprehensible only in the light of his lifelong erotic fantasies. At the same time, it should be understood as a lucid expression of a national affliction: the pain of cultural disinheritance.

The Mishima incident shocked the public — though many shared his dismay at the country's inability to find its own footing and its own voice — and angered and discountenanced the government, which was intent on demonstrating to the world that Japan was now a thoroughly modernized — Americanized — na-

tion. By 1980, except for a fringe element of Mishima worship-
pers on the extreme right, the writer had been marginalized as a
novelist and largely forgotten as a public figure. Recently, however, he has been rediscovered, and there is currently a full-scale
Mishima boom in progress. Between 1999 and 2002, thirty-seven
new books have been written about him, and every large book-
store in Japan today has a "Mishima corner." On the thirtieth
anniversary of his death, in November 2000, his publisher, Shinchosha, announced a new complete works in forty-two volumes.
So far the first fourteen, the major novels, have been released, and
each volume has sold between five and six thousand copies at a
price of $50. At a time when book sales in Japan are at an all-time
postwar low, these figures are telling. It would appear that the current climate of uncertainty and uneasiness has disposed readers to
find meaning for themselves in Mishima's work and final act, evidence that he understood their plight and might even serve as a
beacon to guide them out of confusion and disheartenment to a
rediscovery of self.

In the 1970s and 1980s, uncertainty about identity and purpose was forgotten in the euphoria of spectacular economic success. Between 1970 and 1985, Japan's GNP increased 450 percent.
In 1986 the value of Tokyo real estate doubled, and doubled again
in 1987; in September of that year, one hundred square feet on the
downtown Ginza was selling for $1 million. (By mid-1988, the
value of Japanese real estate would be worth five times that of the
United States.) With bank vaults stuffed with money, and interest
being held by the government below 2 percent, loans were easy —
far too easy — to obtain. Fortunes were amassed overnight by
purchasing land with borrowed money and turning it over at a
colossal profit.

In 1986, Japan began deploying its yen reserves outside the
country, adding financial services to its long list of exports, and
quickly became the world's largest creditor nation: by 1987, 30
percent of U.S. debt was financed by Japan through the purchase

of U.S. Treasury bonds; the world's ten largest banks and four largest security companies were all Japanese; and the Tokyo Stock Exchange was larger than New York's.

As capital accumulated and the yen continued to appreciate against the dollar and other currencies, Japan went on a buying spree in the United States that was perceived hysterically in this country as a threat to sovereignty. Japanese investors acquired banks, golf courses, and resorts all over California, including Pebble Beach, and purchased landmark properties on the East Coast one after the other, including Rockefeller Center. In 1989, when Sony acquired Columbia Pictures, *Newsweek's* cover dressed the company's logo, the lady on the pedestal, holding a torch, in Japanese kimono and hairstyle, and proclaimed in a banner, "JAPAN INVADES HOLLYWOOD!"

In truth, a fantasy of occupying the United States was not unfamiliar to the Japanese imagination. In Yasujiro Ozu's 1962 film, *An Autumn Afternoon,* a jovial mechanic wonders aloud to his former commander in the imperial navy, "What if we had won, sir? What if we had occupied New York? I'll tell you what — you'd have all these foreigners with their white skin drinking sake and eating raw fish and playing their rockabilly music in samurai hairdos!" The fantasy is comic, but not without wistfulness. In 1989, the head of Nomura Securities, the world's largest investment broker at the time, with cash on hand of $4 billion, proposed a Japan-U.S. currency and "joint ownership" of California.

Sudden wealth led to a degree of conspicuous consumption that had no precedent in Japan or elsewhere. Farmers who sold rice paddies or a tiny hillock for unearthly prices replaced their fillings with gold and laid out thousands of dollars for a night with the tall, blond, Caucasian girls who had always danced in their dreams. Japanese shoppers monopolized the boutiques on Rodeo Drive, Madison Avenue, and Via Condotti; controlled the world markets in art, diamonds, yachts, and racehorses; spent $500 on a Madonna concert ticket; imported ice cubes from Antarctica; and paid up to $3.5 million for a membership at one of Japan's more than two thousand private golf courses (in 1992, 13 million of the world's estimated 50 million golfers were Japanese).

In 1989, Shintaro Ishihara, a member of parliament at the time, and Sony's founder, Akio Morita, collaborated on a book they titled *The Japan That Can Say No,* a defiant indictment of U.S. trade policies which radiated the confidence and purpose Japan was feeling at the close of the affluent eighties. In September 1990, that apparently robust certainty was undone when the Tokyo Stock Exchange lost 48 percent of its value in four days, a crash that dwarfed "Black Monday" in 1987. In 1993, the land bubble also burst, creating the largest asset deflation in the history of modern capitalism. Japan's banks and brokerage houses were left with $6 trillion in uncollectable property and building loans against collateral that had more than halved in value.

Japan has yet to recover from its plummeting fall, and as the national gloom deepens, familiar, troubling questions have reframed themselves: What does it mean to be Japanese? What are the source and nature of Japan's uniqueness? The continuing absence of satisfactory answers to these pressing questions has brought to the surface once again a national uneasiness that many Japanese experience today as a sense that something fundamental is missing from their lives.

On a recent trip to Tokyo, I was surprised to find an explicit reference to this emptiness in a column on the front page of the *Asahi Shimbun.* The unsigned column, "The Voice of the People," appears daily and is organized around a current event, in this case the World Soccer Cup cosponsored by Korea and Japan which was just ending and had the entire country in a frenzy of excitement:

> Something is missing. That vague feeling is spreading across the country. For a brief moment, our soccer team filled that hollowness. The young man who told me "The World Cup gave us a sense of unity" was expressing himself honestly. I heard a young person in the United States express the same sort

of feeling. He was responding to a speech by the former president Bill Clinton. It was right after an American ship had been attacked by terrorists in the Middle East. The president expressed sadness and called for courage and unity. The American president isn't merely the head of the government. At times he appears before the people in the role of a prophet. He moves people with what he has to say and shores up the American sense of unity. That's one of the roles of American government. At such moments, people confirm with one another that they are Americans.

The United States incorporates a variety of nationalities and races and languages. In our relatively homogeneous society, many people would feel that being Japanese is self-evident and beyond ambiguity. *And yet something is missing from our full sense of being Japanese* [italics mine]. It seems to me we are carrying some kind of emptiness around. What is the current Japanese language boom but an impulse aimed at filling that emptiness? Japanese is our native language but we know so little about beautiful Japanese. The sense of crisis that awakens is appropriate.

I recall a verse by the late poet Shuji Terayama:

> In the brief instant the match flares
> the sea is in fog
> is there a native land I can
> throw myself away for?

These lines are moving to many readers: what appears in the instant of light is not only the loss of a native land but also the longing to be part of one. This "postwar landscape" is still what we return to when the excitement is over. What will be the landscape of our future?

If these words were from the pen of a neonationalist, they would not be so unexpected, or so telling. The *Asahi Shimbun,* re-

viled by the far right, is Japan's leading liberal-leftist paper, an un-
wavering supporter of the constitution as it stands and of détente
with Beijing. It seems reasonable to interpret the column as a
yearning for unambiguous identity that extends far beyond any
political agenda and permeates the culture. Many Japanese of all
ages are aware, consciously or not, that they have lost their hold
on what the novelist Saul Bellow, speaking of his identity as a Jew,
once called "first consciousness." Bellow wrote, "I can continue to
do what I have done all my life; that is, to turn instinctively toward my first consciousness. This first consciousness has always
seemed easily accessible and most real." Few Japanese today have
access to this degree of certainty about themselves. If there is
a central argument in the chronicle of contemporary Japanese
life which is the subject of this book, it is that much of current Japanese thinking and behavior is colored by an urgently felt
need to regain first consciousness and the vitality it enables by
connecting, or reconnecting, to native culture — properly speaking, to native culture as it resides as a memory in the imagination,
before it was alloyed by "foreign" elements in the process of modernization.

While it is clear that many Japanese today are afflicted by a
troubling if often vaguely perceived sense of being lost, it is by no
means true that Japanese society today is paralyzed or static or
even bereft of its fabled vitality. In fact, contemporary Japan is
undergoing convulsive changes in values and behavior in government and politics, business, popular culture, education, and
family life, which are in the process of transforming the society
into a landscape radically different from its traditional, or even recent, past. The chapters that follow will chronicle some of these
changes and, where possible, account for them in the context of
existential uneasiness on one hand and the related longing to re-
discover and reclaim in a certain and tangible way the meaning of
"Japaneseness" on the other.

Some of these changes are ominous. Riotous classrooms in a

country long famous for respectful children, and the recent epidemic of juvenile violence and crime, are disturbing symptoms of the breakdown of the traditional family system. Others, the new breed of politicians whose doors are always open to their constituents, or the recent emergence of young entrepreneurs, may hold within themselves, like puzzles waiting to be unlocked, the promise of new and heretofore unimaginable solutions to wresting a substantial sense of self and purpose, national and individual, from the confluence of "native" sensibilities and values and Western culture.

The book begins with the lawlessness in and out of the classroom which has unseated the adult community and appears to be a reflection of its own confusion. Chapter 2 focuses on the breakdown of the traditional family, until recently the cornerstone of Japanese self-certainty. Chapter 3 examines the unraveling of the familial ties between the business organization and the company man. I have used the fundamental restructuring of Nissan Motors, Japan's first major business organization to be led by a foreigner, as the most dramatic example of a company struggling to achieve global viability while preserving traditional Japanese business practices and social values. Chapter 4 chronicles the growth of entrepreneurship that has occurred in parallel with the breakdown of the corporate family. Chapter 5 profiles the demagogue cartoonist Yoshinori Kobayashi in the context of emerging neonationalism. Chapter 6 considers other manifestations of nationalism as a quest for pride and self-certainty: the history textbook controversy of 2001 and recent trends in national policy. Chapter 7 profiles Japan's most prominent neonationalist and xenophobe, Shintaro Ishihara. Chapter 8 introduces Ishihara's nemesis, Yasuo Tanaka, governor of Nagano Prefecture, the new hero of the grass-roots citizens' movement.

As I write, outside interest in Japan is at a low ebb. Coverage in our national media is a fraction of what it was even five years ago, and is limited to impersonal analyses of the financial crisis and dire predictions for the future. Still mired in its longest recession in postwar history, Japan is perceived by many observers as having permanently lost its footing in the world; some argue that the country is in the process of devolving into a third-world nation. Predicting the future is a fool's game, but such a fall is unlikely. Japan remains the world's largest creditor nation and has reserves of wealth and a level of technology second only to the United States itself. More important, in spite of everything, Japanese society retains its resoluteness and creativity and vitality. I have tried to convey this truth in the pages that follow, and particularly in the profiles of the remarkable individuals who are living examples of the struggle and the national alteration in process. Japan today feels like a bewildered giant. But the country has a long history of discovering in the darkest days of its bewilderment a source of renewal.

1

Monsters in the House: Japan's Bewildered Children

ARRIVING FOR WORK at 6:30 in the morning on May 27, 1997, the janitor at Tomogaoka Middle School in the port city of Kobe discovered the severed head of a sixth-grade schoolboy, Jun Hase, who had been missing for three days. The head was propped in front of the main gate; clamped between its teeth in a plastic bag was a challenge:

> The game begins.
> To all you moronic policemen: let's see you stop me
> Murder is my greatest pleasure
> I love seeing people die
> To the dirty vegetables: the punishment is death!
> For the years of anger, the verdict is running blood!

The note was signed, in English, "SCHOOLL [sic] KILLER."

The police had reasons to suspect a connection between the beheading and two earlier incidents that had terrorized the city. On February 10, two elementary school girls on their way to buy valentine chocolates had been assaulted with a carpenter's mallet by a boy in a middle school uniform. On March 16, a ten-year-old girl playing in the park near her apartment house was beaten to death with a hammer; a few minutes later, a nine-year-old girl was stabbed repeatedly in the stomach and survived.

Handwriting comparisons and interviews with schoolmates, teachers, and parents led police to a fourteen-year-old boy who had dropped out of Tomogaoka Middle School on May 15 after beating his friend unconscious in a nearby park. On June 28, he was arrested; within hours he had confessed to all the attacks and both murders. His only explanation at the time was an urgent desire to experience the feeling of taking a human life. In the diary found in his room at home, he referred to losing his way in the "dark woods" from the opening of Dante's *Inferno,* and he quoted Nietzsche: "The demon in my heart awakens me to the danger of assaults from the outside world and manipulates me just as a skilled puppeteer makes the puppet dance in time to the music."

At the time, juveniles under the age of sixteen were not eligible for criminal prosecution: by order of the Kobe Family Court, the killer was committed to the Kanto Psychiatric Reform and Training School on the outskirts of Tokyo, where he will remain under treatment until he reaches the age of twenty-one, when he becomes eligible for a return to society (he may be legally held until he reaches the age of twenty-six, at which time he must be released). Because he is a minor until he turns eighteen, his name has never been officially released. Shortly after he was arrested in 1997, a photo-magazine called *Focus* published his name and a photograph but was cited for an infraction of the Minor's Act, and the issue was recalled. Subsequently, the same photo and the killer's name appeared on the Internet, where I was able to retrieve them (the picture shows a handsome youngster with wavy hair peering intensely into the camera). But officially he is known to the Japanese public only as "Youth A." In May 2001, the press reported that he talked with his parents for the first time since his arrest and seems eager to return to the world instead of committing suicide.

I was in Tokyo while police were still searching for the demon of Kobe; I remember — and shared — the horror and disbelief that gripped the country as people watched the TV coverage from morning till night and asked themselves how such a thing could happen in Japan. The moment recalled for me another episode in postwar Japanese history which I had also witnessed, in 1970, when members of the Red Army in black stocking masks hijacked a JAL airplane and kept it on the runway for three days and nights, threatening to kill the passengers with their Japanese swords. People had watched these unrelated incidents unfold with a similar sense of foreboding, as though something baleful was just beginning to reveal itself.

It now appears that the atrocity in Kobe was indeed an early symptom — like the mutating cells that signal a moment of emergent evolution — of a shift in the behavior of Japanese youth that continues to rock the country on its heels. In October 1997, a fifteen-year-old bludgeoned a sixty-four-year-old woman to death with a hammer, explaining that he wanted to know how much force it would take to kill someone (like many others, he acknowledged a desire to outdo his hero, the Kobe murderer). Early in 1998, a seventeen-year-old hijacked a city bus and took it on a fifteen-hour trip during which he stabbed a female passenger to death and injured several others. The following year, there were a number of attacks on teachers in middle schools, including the fatal stabbing of a female teacher in front of her class by a thirteen-year-old boy she had scolded. On June 21, 2000, a high school baseball player who had been teased about his hairstyle attacked four teammates with a metal bat, leaving one with a fractured skull, then took the bat home and used it to beat his mother to death. Later he explained that he wanted to spare her the unpleasant consequences of his rampage at school; a second bat killer offered a similar motive later that summer, the desire to spare his mother the embarrassment of his bad grades. The irony of an explanation in which traditional filial piety leads to matricide points toward the disorientation that now seems endemic. On April 8, 2001, an eleven-year-old boy stabbed his mother to death when she reprimanded him for cutting his own wrist in what she took to be a suicide attempt. More recently, on January 25, 2002, three fourteen-year-old boys in the eighth grade dragged a homeless man out of a restroom where he was sleeping and into a vacant lot. They beat him with sticks for ninety minutes, long after he was dead.

Statistics compiled by the National Police Agency confirm a nationwide epidemic of juvenile crime. In 1997, 2,263 youths between the ages of fourteen and nineteen were arrested for violent crimes, a 50 percent increase over the previous year. Since 1998, the same age group, which represents only 7.4 percent of the population, has been involved in 50 percent of all arrests for felony crime, including murder. In the first six months of 2000, juveniles committed a record 532 killings. Most distressingly to Japanese parents, teachers, and lawmakers, it is the youngest segment of the juvenile community, children between the ages of eleven and fifteen, who are increasingly the perpetrators of the most violent and perverted crimes. In the first eleven months of 2001, juvenile crime increased 12.5 percent over the previous year to 920,000 incidents, a postwar high.

Television news and weekly magazines run regular features on how to avoid provoking high school students on subways and trains ("keep your eyes averted and never talk back"). The Japanese public seems largely bewildered by the morbid, immovable determination with which children are denying their authority. Each year the list of bestsellers includes titles like *Who Are My Children?* and *Monsters in the House*.

But violent juvenile crime in the streets is only one extreme aspect of a broader crisis of anger, confusion, and loss of self that is currently afflicting Japanese youth. In the mid-1990s, Japanese elementary school teachers noticed an alarming increase in unmanageable children. Unable to remain at their desks for more than ten minutes at a time, they walked around the classroom or ran into the halls with their teachers in pursuit, talked loudly with their friends or pummeled them with book bags, threw milk bottles and tangerines at lunchtime, and either ignored their teachers sullenly or flew into abusive rages when they were scolded. Their unruliness was infectious: two or three renegades was all it took to render a classroom of forty students unteachable. By 1996, anarchy was epidemic in elementary schools and spreading upward into secondary schools. The first national survey of "classroom breakdown," a well-known term today, was conducted in March 2001 by the National Education Research Institute, an agency of the Education Ministry. Thirty-three percent of the principals and teachers polled said they had firsthand experience of classrooms in which "group education and the teaching process itself have ceased to function over a continuous period of time due to children engaging in arbitrary activity in defiance of instructions by the teacher."

I witnessed this phenomenon myself at elementary and middle schools I visited recently. The superintendent of schools and his assistant were waiting for me when I arrived at the entrance to Kunitachi Middle School No. 2, on the western outskirts of Tokyo. With the principal and the vice principal in tow we made the rounds of classrooms, shuffling down the shiny linoleum corridors in our green school slippers and filing in to stand at the back of the class. I was unhappy about being escorted, assuming that students would be on their best behavior with five adults, including a foreigner, in the room, but I needn't have worried. In an eighth-grade history class, the teacher was explaining Japan's naval strategy during the Russo-Japanese War of 1904 and 1905. The room crackled with restless energy and there was a surprising din; several students were talking with friends across the room. Others sat morosely at their desks with no books in sight, or read comic books openly, or slept, heads down on their desks, or peered at their cell phones as they composed e-mail messages. (For several years, teachers have allowed students to bring their phones to class. "We can't stop them," I was told, "and it sometimes keeps them quiet.") At twenty minutes past the hour, a squat, heavy girl in a full black skirt that reached to her ankles and a black sweater barged into the room with her brows knit defiantly and slumped into an empty seat. The principal exchanged glances with his number two and whispered to me: "Normally she comes only at lunchtime for a hot meal and then leaves again." Abruptly, the girl shrieked: "This stupid map really pisses me off!" (Her choice of verb, *mukatsuku,* properly used to denote the physical sensation of becoming nauseous, is the term in vogue today among the young to express their revulsion at teachers, parents, life in general.) Unnaturally shrill, the girl's voice pierced the hubbub in the room. "Shut up!" yelled a boy across the room. Then he leaped out of his seat, brushed past the teacher to grab an eraser at the blackboard, and hurled it at the girl. In a flash she launched herself out of her seat and charged at him; the boy avoided her nimbly and ran out of the classroom. Now everyone was involved; some shouted for her to sit down and be quiet, others egged her on. "This class makes me sick!" the girl shrieked, then sauntered out of the room. The teacher carried on at the front of the room as if nothing were amiss.

The principal signaled that it was time to move on, and we left the class. "It's a good thing her friend wasn't there today," he offered laconically. The vice principal explained: "She has a friend, and when the two of them are together they can break up any class. Sometimes they team up and wander in and out of classes." I was surprised, and would be surprised many times again, at the resignation I sensed in the adults. "That one you saw just now will attack if she gets scolded." The principal might have been speaking about a dog. The others solemnly concurred. The previous week, a fifteen-year-old in the ninth grade had struck a female teacher in the face when she reprimanded him for smoking in the schoolyard. It was the third time since the school year had begun in April three months ago that the police had been called to take a student into custody.

Kunitachi Middle School is hardly a blackboard jungle in the inner city; it sits on a quiet side street in a residential neighborhood of modest homes. To be sure, the township of Kunitachi has many municipal housing projects, an environment known to be conducive to problem students because it attracts an itinerant population that includes a high percentage of single parents. Even so, episodes more disturbing than the one I had observed are occurring every day in Japan.

Anarchy in the classroom has taken a toll on Japanese teachers: I spoke to many who admitted that they had become physically or mentally ill. Ryoichi Kawakami, a middle school history teacher for thirty years who has written prolifically about "classroom disintegration syndrome" and whose books have titles like *Reports from the Battlefield,* checked himself into the hospital because of dizziness and severe headaches that he thought were symptoms of a brain tumor. The doctors found nothing, but he continues to suffer. "And I'm as tough as they come. Others suffer much more," he told me. "We had a young woman teacher come here recently, her first assignment, and she gave up in three months. She was bright; she had studied hard and passed a difficult battery of tests, and she decided to go into another profession. Each morning I put on my armor and go off to battle. It truly feels that way, and, as we all know, there is the possibility of violence just beneath the surface. When I look at these kids today, it's terrifying to think of them as twenty-year-olds."

Juvenile lawlessness in and outside the classroom is currently the subject of a heated national debate. As with most major issues in Japanese society, the positions tend to polarize around ideology on the left and right. The neoliberal-leftist position, represented by an unlikely coalition that includes the Ministry of Education, the left-wing faction of the Japan Teachers Union, the Federation of Economic Organizations, and the Socialist Party, maintains that Japan is now paying the price for decades of sacrificing trust and intimacy and personal realization to efficiency and economic growth. Recently, the Education Ministry has mandated a series of reforms aimed at shifting educational priorities away from conformity to child-centered education.

In the early 1950s, Japan's school policy was designed to help achieve the accelerated renewal that was the national mission of the early postwar decades. In accordance with the rest of the social infrastructure, the overwhelming priority was rapid achievement: the curriculum was standardized nationally for the sake of efficiency, rote learning was emphasized, and the classroom became an arena of fierce competition for good grades, the sole criterion of success. Moreover, students who aspired to attend the top universities had to distinguish themselves on entrance exams beginning in kindergarten. The competition spawned *juku*, "cram schools," which helped students prepare after regular school hours. By the mid-1970s, 70 percent of schoolchildren were enrolled.

The pressure was intense, but diligence and high achievement paid off: graduation from a preferred college guaranteed a fast-track job in government or industry, and lifetime employment. School was a ticket to a successful life; teachers were trusted and respected.

But by the early 1980s, as the postcollege job market constricted, students began to show signs of stress. Educators were shaken by a wave of violence in middle schools, and there was a rash of suicides by elementary and middle school children who had failed entrance exams. Critics decried "entrance-exam hell" and accused the system of producing automatons incapable of creative thinking. Since the economy collapsed in 1990 and prospects for the future have been further compromised, students have lost their motivation to perform under competitive pressure, and Japan's once vaunted achievement test scores have fallen to just below our own disheartening levels. According to Manabu Sato, a professor of education at Tokyo University, "Throughout the 1980s, educators, economists, and politicians around the world expressed their admiration for the Japanese school system for promoting incredibly high levels of achievement. The negative evaluations that have followed are simply the other side of the same phenomena that gave rise to the positive: a centralized efficient educational system and a standardized curriculum. This system reflects the bureaucratic and industrial nature of Japanese society."

The Education Ministry has responded with reforms aimed at promoting student choice, a so-called shopping mall curriculum, and at relieving stress by creating an "easygoing classroom." The most recent, which were implemented at the beginning of the school year in April 2002, eliminated 30 percent of the content of the core curriculum in elementary and middle schools and introduced group learning in which students choose a subject that interests them and pursue it on their own. In high school, all subjects except physical education become electives. The new emphasis is clear: selective learning, subjectivity, and above all, student autonomy.

Conservatives, including Tokyo governor Shintaro Ishihara and his metropolitan school board and, most vociferously, veteran teachers in the system like Ryoichi Kawakami who have broken from their union, insist that the celebration of student individuality at the heart of the new policy has transformed schools into an extension of the home, where children are encouraged to act on every impulse, and has gradually eroded children's capacity for *gaman,* a key concept in the dynamics of groupism that means the ability to endure difficulty or unpleasantness in the interests of the group. Kawakami characterizes the reforms as "education consumerism" and accuses the Education Ministry of pandering to students: "We are ordered to create an American-style school in which individuality is paramount. But as middle school teachers, we know in our gut from experience that catering exclusively to individuality so that anything goes is a dangerous thing to do."

I spent several days at the middle school where Kawakami has taught for seven years in the agricultural community of Kawagoe, forty-five miles northwest of Tokyo. Classes in academic subjects such as English, mathematics, and Japanese were, in general, rote and stupefying; students were accordingly restless but no more disruptive than their American counterparts in a similarly lifeless classroom. The striking difference was the teachers' restraint: behavior that would have banished an American junior high school student to the hall or to the principal's office — talking to a friend across the class or exchanging notes or wandering around the room — was either ignored or gently reproved with a look or a comment that had no effect.

There were also some heartwarming surprises. In music class, a young, well-trained female teacher coached her girls and then, indefatigably, her hopeless seventh-grade boys in the proper enunciation of the lyrics in a two-part classical Japanese song while an accomplished female musician in the class provided piano accompaniment. As the full chorus broke into song, with the teacher mouthing the words and modeling *le-ga-to* with both hands, the affable principal appeared and joined the boys in a resounding tenor. In industry and technology class, boys and girls dressed in their PE sweats sat together at long tables soldering circuit boards for a product called a "hybrid clock." When one of the devices had been assembled and the radio was switched on, the class applauded. In seventh-grade homemaking, a required subject, students were cutting cloth to patterns and sewing them into Bermuda shorts. Eighth-graders were presenting the menus they had prepared and would cook for the class the following week; team leaders described the dishes they had chosen. Menus included spaghetti pepperoncino (!), udon noodles with kinoko mushrooms, and broiled octopus in teriyaki sauce. When the teacher prompted for "goals," the students recited an identical reply: "To prepare something delicious while observing commonsense rules of safety." It was clear from the atmosphere in these classrooms that the majority of Japanese schoolchildren, despite turmoil in the schools, have retained the earnestness and the innocence that have always distinguished them.

Ryoichi Kawakami had told me that I might not encounter the violence I had heard about because a number of the key disrupters — he used the English term "key men" — had left the school at the close of the previous year. He was mistaken. I was sitting in the teachers' room, where the instructors convene during the ten-minute breaks between their fifty-minute classes to sip green tea and gather their wits. A Bach suite for orchestra was playing over the PA system, undoubtedly a choice designed to quiet jangled nerves. Abruptly, shouts from the hall cut through the music, and I hurried out to see what was going on. The phys ed teacher, in a white judo *gi* and his black belt, was backing a student down the hall as he remonstrated with him, his open hands extended in front of him on either side of the boy's head in what I took to be a protective stance. The student had thrust a sewing needle from the sewing classroom through his earlobe; the instructor insisted that the needle was dangerous to the boy and to others and must be removed. The student continued to back away in silence, a handful of others following gleefully alongside. Suddenly he stood his ground and "broke" or "snapped" — the verb used in Japanese, *kireru,* refers to the snapping of a string on an instrument when it is wound too tightly. I had read about this behavior in books but now experienced it for the first time: the student began screaming abuse into the instructor's face. "Asshole-who-do-you-think-you-are-you-make-me-sick," a hysterical howl of fury that wound higher and still higher. Then he fell silent and glared at the grownup in the judo *gi,* who appeared unfazed and resumed his insistence on removing the needle. In the end, the student agreed to snap off the point of the needle with a pair of pliers and accompanied the teacher back down the hall. "Is he always like that?" I asked a group of girls who lingered. "Always, and so are his friends. But we're not all like that."

When classes end at three, students in Japan's public schools are required to straighten and dust their classrooms and to sweep and mop the halls, a vestigial ritual from an earlier age when school was a training ground for good citizens. I was watching them work on their hands and knees on the second floor when a boy scaled the wall from below and climbed onto a narrow ledge just outside the open window where I was standing. He was naked to the waist, and his dark hair was dyed the rusty orange in vogue among Japanese youth. A group of his friends applauded him from the ground (I had passed this same gang roaming the halls during the day, and later learned that under the new directives they were free to express their individuality in any way they chose). Just then the assistant principal happened along and ordered the boy to come off the ledge at once. Ignoring him, the student called down for a pack of cigarettes, which was promptly tossed up to him. As the principal and I stood watching from a foot away, he lit a cigarette and began to smoke with aplomb. "Listen," the teacher began sternly, "you know that's against the law! Put that out and climb down from there!" With the cigarette between his lips, the boy turned to face the principal and fixed him with a chilling look of utter disregard. The principal caved: "C'mon now," he simpered, "quit fooling around." The boy held him with ice-cold eyes that denied not only his authority but his very existence. The adult shrugged and walked away.

I forced myself to hurry downstairs to talk to his friends, the boy with the needle through his ear among them. He looked at me without curiosity. "Do you like school?" I asked lamely. "Yes." He smiled. "What do you like about it?" "Lunchtime." The others laughed. "What do you do for fun after school?" He gazed at me for a beat, then threw both arms straight up above his head and screamed in my face in English, perhaps the only English he knew: "I am a soldier!" I was stunned. *"I am a soldier!"* he screamed again, and moved off with his friends.

The following Saturday night, I was invited to a meeting of the

Professional Teachers Association, twenty middle and high school teachers in the Kawagoe area who gather two nights a month in the basement of the local community to edit, working all night, their monthly newsletter "We Object!" The designated chef had prepared a pot of the vegetable stew called *o-den,* and as we ate and drank sake from two-liter bottles I asked for an explanation of the passivity I had observed in response to students' disrespect and lawlessness. "That icy look that gave you the chills," a high school teacher began. "Most of the kids in my school have eyes like that. So we all feel the threat of physical danger; often we're acting not as teachers but as individuals who need to protect ourselves."

"Besides," another added, "no one will support us if we try to discipline the students. Teachers in the United States can send kids out of the classroom when they're out of line. If we tried that we'd be in big trouble with the administration. Denying a child his right to be in class is in the same category as physical punishment, striking a student. It's against the law today!

"Under the current policy we're all equals, students and teachers. If a kid asks, 'Why should I listen to you?' and we reply, 'Because I'm a teacher and an adult and you're a seventh-grader and a child,' we would be reprimanded for abuse. We get lectured about it twice a year."

American educators who hear this explanation are incredulous. According to Michael Furlong, a professor in the School of Education at the University of California, Santa Barbara, "No one in the system here would suggest that teachers and children should have equal rights. An effective classroom requires purpose and structure and rules that can be enforced. To achieve that sort of environment, the adults must be empowered with authority."

There is no question that the recent reforms are lopsided and very different from the American system on which they are said to be modeled. In the United States, child study teams and school psychologists are available to help teachers with problem students. In Japan, the burden of classroom management falls entirely on the teachers' shoulders, and many are reluctant to acknowledge the situation in their classrooms because they interpret it as a personal failure and are ashamed. Yet again I was struck by teachers' haplessness in the face of the problem: "If you ask another teacher into your classroom," one teacher told me, "the bad ones are apt to get worse after he leaves and take it out on you! For a couple of months our school was asking parents to observe classes, thinking that would quiet things down. They came for a while, but that turned out to be counterproductive in the same way. When the moms left, the kids had their revenge. So we asked them to stop coming."

In the United States, suspension is a legal option; in Japan today, suspension and expulsion are taboo under any circumstances. Promotion is based on attendance only, and holding a student back is very rare: a high school student can graduate with failing grades in all subjects if he has attended classes 50 percent of the time. A shibboleth of the new education policy is "education of the heart." The permissiveness that underlies it is an example of the distortion that is often manifest in Japanese interpretations of the American way of life.

Classroom breakdown is only part of a larger crisis of anger and withdrawal that has bewildered parents and educators. A growing number of children in grades one through nine reject school altogether and refuse to attend. This phenomenon is not a matter of frequent absences; these children drop out of school as early as the second grade and remain away for years at a time or never return. In a minority of cases they are withdrawn by parents who believe that the stress of school, with its emphasis on performance and expectation of conformity, is harmful to their children. The rest simply refuse to go to school one morning without warning or explanation, and continue to refuse on subsequent mornings despite entreaties and threats from parents. Many have been the victims of bullying at school (often denied by teachers and school boards). Others may have transferred to a new school as the result of a family move and feel left out. Some develop physical symptoms such as headaches or nausea, but most are asymptomatic until the day arrives when they turn away for good.

The conservative estimate is that 150,000 children between the ages of six and seventeen are permanently absent from school. Others assert, extrapolating from their own classrooms, that up to 5 percent of the student population, 350,000 children, are chronically truant. In California, where I live, three unexcused absences in a school year triggers a letter from the office of the district attorney, the first in a five-step process that includes mandatory conferences with school counselors and truant officers and ends, after nine days, with the family in court. Japan has no similar infrastructure; in fact, truancy per se is not against the law — the civil code defines school through grade nine as "a right of children but not an obligation" — and prolonged absence is not a police matter. When it becomes apparent that a child has dropped out, the teacher and the principal will try to talk to the child and the parents at their home, but these visits tend to be unavailing. According to Masao Ishii, Kunitachi superintendent of schools, "If there's a drinking problem, which is often the case, the parents don't want to let us in. Others turn us away at the door because they know from experience that if we do come in the child will be furious after we leave and act up." Two years ago, in a national directive to school administrations that accords with current policy, the Education Ministry characterized chronic truancy as a "natural and inevitable expression of certain students' personality which should not be interfered with."

Stigmatized by neighbors, who are often unwilling to allow their own children to play with them out of fear that they will catch the disease, the stay-at-homes are increasingly isolated. A number of them eventually retreat still further from the pressures of the outside world by secluding themselves in their rooms and refusing to come out except for meals. "Self-incarcerators" turn deaf ears to parents and siblings, and later refuse to see the teachers who visit their home in hopes of reasoning with them. Unimaginably, this condition can last for years, extending into adulthood.

I met some of these damaged children. In the small city of Takasaki, two hundred miles north of Tokyo, a gentle carpenter named Minoru Yamaguchi runs a support group for chronic truants called Pass (as in declining to play the game of life). Yamaguchi is available to counsel students and their distraught parents day and night; on Wednesday afternoons, he borrows the second floor of a clinical psychiatrist's office, a large space like a kindergarten room with a small kitchen at one end and video games at the other, and opens it to anyone who chooses to drop in between 3:00 and 8:00 P.M. There are eighty names on his roster, but on a typical Wednesday, ten to fifteen kids show up. They range in age from six to their early twenties, and most have not attended school for years. Some travel from distant villages; for those who have secluded themselves at home, this outing is the only social occasion of their week. Some are accompanied by their mothers, who use the kitchen to bake cookies with their truant daughters or sit together comparing notes. They have in common a worn and worried look. "We moved here when our eldest son was in the fifth grade, and one day he refused to go to school and nothing we said made any difference. Then both his younger brothers stopped going, too. It's been four years now, and the kids are used to being at home, but we wonder what's to become of them. All we can do is hope they'll decide to go back when they're ready."

At Pass, the younger kids gathered in front of the TV set to play video games; they seemed easily distracted and paced around the room with jerky, angry movements. I was unable to engage them in conversation. The teenagers kept to themselves, leafing through comic books at the long table covered with snacks and soda in the center of the room, or sitting silently with their eyes downcast. Each time I visited, two high school girls sat apart at a small table in the corner, sharing the snacks they brought with them and whispering together. In her first year of high school (tenth grade), one of them had been singled out by a boy in a motorcycle gang and had been harassed into dropping out of school; her friend had left with her.

Yamaguchi, the most disarming person I have ever met, sits at the central table watching for opportunities to help the children unburden themselves. "Thirty percent of the kids who show up here were top students who ran out of steam by the time they got into middle school," he told me. "The pressure is on from kindergarten: if you don't excel you'll be a failure in life. So they drop out to get away from the constant comparisons."

As we spoke, a short young man in gym shorts and a T-shirt approached the punching bag just behind me and laid into it. I had observed other, younger kids pause at the bag to punch at it as they passed, but this display was different: it was a savage assault driven by fury. Powerfully built despite his small stature, the boy threw vicious punches into the bag until his knuckles were raw, and still he attacked. His rage was palpable and terrifying; other children observed with tightened faces, halted in their tracks. I had to force myself to keep my back to him, as though I weren't feeling threatened.

Minoru Yamaguchi moved quickly around the table and threw his arms around the boy from behind. "You're trembling," he said softly, and moved him away to a small table in a corner. For a few minutes they spoke quietly together; then Yamaguchi beckoned me to join them. The young man looked up at me suspiciously. "He's an American writing about Japanese youth and he'll be very sympathetic to your story," Yamaguchi explained. Then, to me, he said, "Young Toyama here has suffered unspeakable chagrin and fury from having been taunted and mistreated all his life."

Toyama nodded and resumed his monologue, his chest heaving, sniffling as he spoke to control his tears. He was twenty-four, though he looked much younger, and lived in a house in a small village an hour away by train with his mother and younger brother, who worked at a local dairy. His father had left home when he was five; his memories of school were about being treated as an outsider, abused by teachers and taunted by the other children. "They called me a midget and said I smelled bad. Kids would talk about me on the train, and I knew they were because I always watched. I taunted them back, but they just laughed. I wanted to kill them. I've never studied judo or karate because I'm afraid I might use it to kill someone."

In seventh grade he was placed in a special class for problem children because of his hot temper; for two years he had suffered the shame of being considered a misfit, but had found no one to confide in. "I loved to play badminton. I played for two years, and the coach never even learned my name. One day he teased me about being short, and I stopped. I don't play anymore." At the end of the eighth grade he had dropped out of school and had been secluded at home ever since.

Yamaguchi listened in his gentle, tuned-in way, sighing and conveying sympathy with his whole body. Presently, he invited a girl who had been sitting alone to join us at the table. "This is Neri. She's had lots of trouble, too." Neri was a wisp of a girl who was twenty and looked thirteen. She smiled sweetly at the boy, and her insubstantial presence seemed to calm him.

"Every time I go outside, I end up getting wounded in my mind — psychologically," said Toyama. "What feels best to me is staying alone in my room. I close the rain shutters so it's pitch-dark and then I can be alone by myself."

"Do you have a dream?" Neri breathed.

Toyama looked at her. "My dream . . . is to get hold of some peace of mind."

Neri beamed. "Me too!"

At 8:00 P.M. the kids cleaned up. Toyama worked side by side with Neri, moving tables and chairs around and bagging trash. He didn't speak, but it was clear that he was bursting with the pleasure of feeling that maybe he belonged. As he shouldered his backpack on the way out, I saw that he had brought his badminton racket with him from home, as though he needed something he could be proud of, a trophy from a distant moment when he had participated in the world.

While Toyama's plight may be extreme, the numbing isolation he experiences appears to be endemic in Japan's youth today and cannot be explained away by shifts in education policy. Profound changes in life at home are another factor. Since the economy collapsed in 1990, the divorce rate has soared: many children live with single parents too harried by their own lives to look after them. Layoffs, unheard of in Japan until recently, have put breadwinners in a vise and promoted anger, alcoholism, and domestic violence. Families in straitened circumstances convey disappointment and bitterness about the value of education. Other parents are not only wealthier, more worldly, and better educated than their children's teachers: unquestioning respect is not their mode.

There is also an alarming communication problem. Turmoil at home and pressure at school, which includes rampant bullying, have created reclusive children who are unable to build friendships with peers that will enable them to talk about their lives. The addiction to computer games and cell phones that Japanese sociologists are calling "thumb culture" has further eroded direct communication skills and deepened isolation. Half-pints in second grade leave home for school with Game Boys and a cell phone around their neck and incessantly check for e-mail messages or compose them, thumbs flying over tiny keys. The word processor in the phones includes dozens of icons: a "heart" for love or desire, "tears" for sad or angry, a "cap" or "jacket" for shopping, a "book bag" for school, and so forth. Communication is accordingly minimalized and standardized: "It is *raining* and I am *sad*. I *don't want* to go to *school*. I *want* to go *shopping*. I *hate* Atsuko but I *love* you. Let's *meet* at one." It is not uncommon to see children exchanging messages while standing together in the schoolyard or riding on the subway a few seats apart. Many of the messages are to "virtual friends" whom they have never met.

But at the deepest level, it seems clear that children are manifesting the same uncertainty about themselves that plagues their parents and the rest of the adults in Japanese society today. The new nationalism emerging in Japan is evidence that the country is once again in the grip of what amounts to a national identity crisis, and children are not immune.

A young middle school teacher from Okinawa recently told me a story that seemed to bear this out. The teacher asked her eighth-graders to write down what they wanted to be when they grew up and what they hoped to accomplish in their lives. "The children just sat there," she said, and then a number of them started to cry, not just cry but weep. It was a terrible moment. I had the feeling that my question had brought them face to face with the reality that they had no sense of themselves, that the confusion of the times had robbed them of any idea of who they were, and they were weeping with the misery of that."

2

The Family Crisis

THE HISTORICAL FOUNDATION of Japanese self-certainty was the extended family. If this principle was true for the samurai class, it was equally true for the farmer and, beginning in the mid-seventeenth century, for the urban merchant and artisan. In the samurai family, respect, obedience, fealty, ascended vertically from sons to father, the head of the house, to the *daimyo,* ruler of the *han,* or feudal domain, to the shogun, the head of the samurai family in control of the country. Finally, at the apex of the system, was the *tenno,* a word that translates as "emperor" but was more symbolic of harmony and integration than the august personage institutionalized in the Meiji and postwar constitutions. At each level in the vertical hierarchy there was also a powerful sense of connection to the ancestral founders of the house.

In the Japanese village, the fundamental unit of agrarian society, this principle of integration applied to sons, fathers, grandfathers, and great-uncles, and the ancestors who had planted rice in the same paddies in the distant past. Above the immediate family was the village headman, the *soncho,* whose own ancestors were likely to have been the founders of the village. The agrarian family may not have felt the same fealty-identification with the shogun as did the samurai class, but the village society was certainly conscious of an ultimate connection to the *tenno,* the progenitive village headman. Community, originating in the immediate family and extending back into the ancestral past and upward to the emperor, was the basis for a substantial sense of self.

In the absence of a monotheistic religion such as Christianity, the extended family also functioned as the wellspring of moral and ethical values. The classical literature is filled with stories and plays that illustrate this point. The domestic tragedies written for the puppet theater in the seventeenth century, based on incidents that were a familiar part of life in Osaka, Japan's first commercial city, are animated by the conflict between obligation to the family, *giri,* and passion, *ninjo.* The hapless protagonist of these dramas is the firstborn son of a merchant or artisan family with a wife and children who is obliged to carry on the traditions of the family and to maintain its honor and reputation. He begins a liaison with a courtesan in the pleasure quarter and is unable to subordinate his passion to his duty to the family; invariably these plays end in the lovers' double suicide.

The samurai family lived according to, and continually renewed in itself, the strictest code of honor. Japan's most abiding morality tale, *Chushingura,* or *The Forty-seven Ronin,* a true story, has been transformed into puppet theater and kabuki plays, films, comic-book series and television dramas, and is familiar to every Japanese even today. In 1701, a feudal lord named Asano was provoked by a samurai official, Yoshinaka Kira, to draw his sword while on the grounds of the shogun's castle in Edo, an offense punishable by death. Because Kira was known to be a villain, the government allowed Lord Asano an honorable death by his own hand instead of executing him and impaling his head on a stake to be publicly displayed. Following his death by hara-kiri, the shogunate condemned Asano's domain, reducing his samurai retainers to the status of *ronin* (homeless), samurai with no fealty-connection to a feudal family. Led by Oishi Kuranosuke, forty-seven of these *ronin* hid their grief from the watchful eyes of the shogun's agents for a year while they secretly plotted revenge. On December 14, 1702, they attacked Kira at his Edo estate and cut off his head, avenging the memory of Asano and his family. *The Forty-seven Ronin* endures as the quintessential Japanese allegory of loyalty, forbearance, and valor within the context of the extended samurai family.

Beneath the structure of the traditional Japanese family lies the concept of *ie,* a word that means literally "house" or "home" or "family" but connotes more. *Ie* represents a unit of kinship that transcends a contemporary configuration of family members whatever that may be, extending backward into the ancestral past and forward into the future.* The title and authority conferred on the head of the *ie* was transferred from one generation to the next through primogeniture; sons other than the firstborn established their own collateral families, which remained subordinate to the main house and subject to its decisions regarding finances and even marriage. Families without a firstborn son frequently adopted the husband of their eldest daughter and conferred on him the title and status of head of the *ie.*

The commitment to preserving the continuity of the *ie* underlies the Japanese system of *miai kekkon,* or arranged marriages. Traditionally, couples were introduced by a *nakodo,* a go-between, who has detailed knowledge of both individuals and their families. The essential considerations were social status and, often, consanguinity. Marriage was a union not of individuals but of two families: it was important to bring together families who not only matched but could respect, complement, and reinforce the continuity of their respective *ie* lineage and pedigree.

---

* See Yoshio Sugimoto, *An Introduction to Japanese Society* (Cambridge: Cambridge University Press, 1997), pp. 136–68.

While the percentage is dropping sharply, <u>arranged marriages</u> <u>still account for 20 to 30 percent of Japanese marriages today.</u> The process begins with parents distributing photographs and a personal history of their marriageable sons or daughters to friends and acquaintances. Someone, often a neighborhood busybody who has served more than once as the required go-between, perceives a feasible match and proposes a meeting to both families. Family members from both sides and the matchmaker customarily attend a lunch or dinner at which the prospective husband and wife are introduced. These occasions often generate an atmosphere of comic awkwardness. The potential bride and groom tend to sit in silence across the table from each other while their relatives, feigning casualness as they chat, seek to uncover dirty linen. If the families are satisfied and the couple feels a spark of interest they may decide to meet alone and this next step may lead to marriage.

Go-betweens search tirelessly for acceptable matches with an eye to discovering similarities or, just as frequently, balancing drawbacks. The woman of the house in the family with whom I lived for several years in the 1960s was head of the neighborhood women's association, the group of wives who took charge of cleaning the open gutters in the neighborhood each morning, and a go-between who spent hours responding to requests for suitable partners. I once heard her say to an anxious parent: "I understand he graduated from a second-rate commercial college. But let's be honest: your daughter limps. I think this match was made in heaven!"

The family tomb has always been an important emblem of the familial continuity that arranged marriages were designed to preserve. The great majority of Japanese families have a tomb in which their ancestors are, or are considered to be, enshrined. Even the most apparently modern, and uprooted, Tokyo families I recently visited, when I asked whether the family was conscious of being Japanese, often cited the family tomb. "I knew I had to stay inside the family," a corporate executive and father of three told me, "because I had been taught to feel obliged as the eldest son to protect and preserve our family tomb. If I left the family or married into another, that tomb might disappear. I know my eldest son feels the same way."

Family tombs are located in the ancestral homeland, or "native place." The cohesiveness of the traditional family and the comfort it provided were always contingent in an important way on staying close to home. Before the mass migration from country to city that began in the mid-1920s, Japan's rural families lived and died where they were born, working the land that had been in their family for generations. The bond between them and their near and distant relatives in the region and their attachment to the land allowed an acute sense of connection to the ancestral past, which fostered a substantial sense of self.

Such families are still to be found. In September 2002, I asked the Nagano Prefectural Government for an introduction and spent a lively morning visiting a family of apple growers at their home. The Dendas have been living in the village of fifty families, Hitotsuya, between the resort town of Karuizawa and Komoro City on the Chikuma River, for sixteen generations. They had never had a foreigner in their house and received me with excitement and hospitality. Four generations lived together in the house: grandfather and grandmother, their son and his wife, their twenty-six-year-old grandson and his wife, and two small children, a girl in second grade and a boy in preschool. We all sat around a low table on the tatami-mat-covered floor while the children were passed around from one lap to another, including my own. We were in the room where the family lived and ate together. Installed in one corner was a Buddhist altar with lit candles, offertory rice cakes, and two photographs of deceased elders. Next to it against the wall was the glass case displaying tsatskes that is to be found in every Japanese farmhouse: family photographs, trinkets, kewpie dolls, and the vermilion papier-mâché heads that look like Humpty Dumpty. Known as Daruma, they have one eye painted out with black sumi ink for good luck. Grandmother sat deferentially apart from the table, her legs folded to the side, near a doorway that led to the kitchen, which was still her domain. She continually left the room as we spoke and returned with trays of small bowls containing food to eat along with our green tea: crisp pickled radishes; mountain chestnuts no larger than a knuckle, which had been cooked black with sugar; and separate dishes of stewed plums and reddish prunes covered in cream. When I smacked my lips after sampling the prunes with a small wooden spoon, she disappeared into the kitchen again and came back with a large serving bowl full of the fruit and cream and placed it in front of me. It was enough for the whole family, but I knew she expected me to empty the bowl myself, which I did with gusto while she watched and nodded approvingly.

Traditionally, the Dendas had grown rice and raised silkworms. Grandfather had planted apple trees for the first time fifty-four years ago, the year his son was born. The family has three thousand trees producing sixteen varieties of apples on three acres of orchards. They also plant three quarters of an acre each of peaches, pears, and plums and have a large vegetable garden in which they grow all the food they need for themselves except for fish and meat. Their farmland is in the foothills of the southern slope of Mount Asama, seven miles from the house. In seasons when the trees require attention and at picking time, the three men "commute" to work — they laughed at this notion — on small motorcycles, a twenty-minute ride, returning home for breakfast at 7:30 A.M. Grandfather, who had just turned eighty-four, still rides his own motorcycle despite the fact that his eyes are no longer "as keen as they used to be." At midday, the two younger women deliver in their truck a hot lunch that Grandmother has prepared. At picking time beginning in late October, the family hires fifteen additional hands.

Making ends meet is tough. The liberalization of trade in the mid-1980s opened the door to U.S. fruit, including the Golden Delicious prized by the Japanese, depressing the price of the domestic product. Juice apples, those that have fallen from the trees before they are harvested, dropped 50 percent to 4 cents a pound when apple juice from China became available in Japan in 2000. Like farmers everywhere, the Dendas are defenseless against the vagaries of weather: twice in the past five years, typhoon winds and hail destroyed their apple crop; the Japanese government does not subsidize rice or fruit growers. "My father taught me always to think about next year," said Ichiro Denda. "This year was no good, but next year will be better."

Many families have sold their land and left the village to work in Nagano's cities. In Masako Denda's elementary school class of thirty-seven, only eight children live on full-time working farms. The Dendas lament the loss of community feeling in the village. But as they spoke about their lives, it was clear that they were proud and happy with their decision to remain on their land despite the economic difficulties. "If the family stays put, there will always be somewhere to come home to no matter what happens," Ichiro Denda told me. "And we'll always be able to eat. Progress and convenience aren't all that's important. Parents who have to raise their kids in a city like Tokyo get neurotic and crazy because they're cut off from their roots. We live with nature; we take care of it and it takes care of us. We all raise the children together. There's nothing better than that."

His twenty-six-year-old son, Hiroshi, didn't seem so certain. After high school, he was one of a very few of his classmates who elected to spend two years on an experimental farm managed by an agricultural college. Now he was raising a family in his ancestral home and devoting himself full-time to improving the quality of the family orchards. Nevertheless, the only slightly awkward moment that morning occurred when I asked what had convinced him to remain on the farm. He hesitated; the elders looked at him sharply. "I've been told I had to take over as the eldest son since I was about three," he said quietly. Did he hope and expect that his own children would follow in his footsteps? Another pause and looks of expectation from his father and grandfather. Hiroshi glanced at his wife, a city girl, and said, "Not especially —"

"Farming is best," Grandfather declared, as if to convince his grandson. "The folks who sold their land for big money in the eighties have no more money left and no land either. They have to worry about making a living, and their lives are woeful. We grow what we eat so we'll always get by. And I don't have to exercise — sometimes I do those radio calisthenics, but I don't need them — I feel good naturally because I work with my body. If this isn't happiness, I'd like to know where it is."

Hiroshi's hesitation notwithstanding, I was convinced. I had experienced my time with the Dendas as relaxing; there was something integrated and harmonious about them. Their easiness about themselves and their connection to one another and their way of life were palpable. They were strikingly present, as individuals and as a family. There was no question in my mind that they knew who they were.

The two young bureaucrats from the prefectural office who had accompanied me were eager to leave before lunch, but the family insisted we stay. Grandma served us soup and rice steamed with mountain herbs and bowls of bamboo shoots sautéed with other vegetables. On my way out I had to pose for photographs with my arms around the children. As I got into the car, Grandma hurried over and handed me a shopping bag containing four jars of peach and plum preserves.

As the postwar recovery gained momentum, rural families in large numbers left their traditional homes to seek employment in the cities. The shift in population amounted to an uprooting; isolated from the sense of community they had derived from life in in their native towns and villages, and deprived of the certainty about themselves that their extended families had provided, nuclear families have experienced increasingly the uneasiness of alienation from their own pasts.

The most popular film series in postwar Japan was Yoji Yamada's *Otoko Wa Tsurai Yo!* (*It's Tough to Be a Man!*), the ongoing chronicle of a lovable misfit who wandered the countryside peddling kitchenware that he had acquired by questionable means. In every film, the peddler is smitten by a woman he calls his "madonna" (the role was always reserved for the most popular female star of the year). When the object of his infatuation spurns him, as inevitably she does, he returns disconsolately to stay awhile with his sister and her family in their home in working-class Tokyo, where his shady dealings and impulsive meddling make trouble for everyone.

Since the first installment was released in 1969, an estimated 65 million people have seen one or more of the forty-two films in the series. Part of its appeal has to do with an emphasis on homecoming; in returning to his childhood home when he is in need of renewal, the peddler plays out the fantasy of millions of moviegoers who had left their own homes in regional Japan to work in the cities (each film includes gorgeous Technicolor scenes of some region in the countryside). Moreover, the films' sensibility and the character of the hero are distinctively Japanese in their bittersweet sentimentality. At a time when the industrial imperative and dryly rational American pragmatism hung in the air heavily, Japanese moviegoers took solace in rediscovering themselves in the soulful peddler and his emotional world.

To be sure, there are families whose native place has been Osaka or Tokyo for generations, and who lead their city lives in the security and certainty about themselves which continuity allows. I had dinner with a construction worker and his family who were bona fide "downtowners," born and raised in working-class Tokyo within walking distance of the Tsukiji fish market (three generations and proximity to Tsukiji define the genu-

ine Edokko, child of Edo, in the same way that a certified Cock-
ney must grow up within earshot of the Bow Bells). Rikutaro
Kawatani, fifty, is not an ordinary laborer; he is a *tobi,* a specialist
in scaffolding and installing beams high above the ground. Originally, in seventeenth-century Edo, the *tobi* were neighborhood
firemen. The word means "kite," a species of hawk, and refers to
the hook, similar to a kite's beak, at the end of the long bamboo
pole the *tobi* used in fighting fires. In a city built of wood and paper, *tobi* were local heroes admired for their bravery and rakish
panache. Today they have nothing to do with firefighting. But
they continue to practice the skills of their traditional métier and
display them in performances and competitions, balancing on the
topmost rungs of a teetering ladder as others carry it down the
street, for example, or traversing a narrow beam as though it were
a tightrope, much as American lumberjacks compete at logrolling
or axe throwing.

Rikutaro Kawatani is the third-generation *tobi* in his family;
his wife's family on her mother's side traces its membership in
the *tobi* guild back to the early eighteenth century. (When her
brother introduced her to Rikutaro, her parents opposed their
marriage: dashing figures in the emerging society of artisans and
merchants, the *tobi* were known to be drinkers, gamblers, and
womanizers.) The Kawatanis live with their three teenage children in a sagging two-story wooden house that was built by
Rikutaro's grandfather and survived the firebombing of Tokyo in
1944. Rikutaro's elderly parents live on the first floor. He and his
two brothers were born in an obstetrics clinic, now an apartment
building, two minutes' walk from the house. Down the block, beneath what is now an overpass of the Tokyo beltway, was a small
river where he and his friends fished as children.

The Kawatanis seemed to have a firm hold on their identity as
Japanese. Izumi Kawatani was proud that the family lived with
her husband's parents: "We eat all our meals together. All Granny
thinks about are the kids; every morning she comes upstairs to

wake up my son Kazu in time for work, and she doesn't go to sleep at night until they're all safely home. She sleeps during the day when everyone is out of the house. Sometimes it's a nuisance, especially for the kids; but this is a real Japanese family just as it was in the past. It feels good to know we're living the kind of life Japanese people have always lived."

Rikutaro didn't entirely agree. "When I was growing up, this was a real neighborhood. When we went out in the evening to the public bath, if we were being noisy and clowning around, a neighbor would come out and yell at us or even slap us around if we were really acting up. If my mom found out about it, she'd thank the neighbor for teaching us to mind our manners. It was like everybody cared about everybody else. It's different now. There were two classes of thirty-five kids each in my elementary school and now there're only about four of us who still live here. The girls married and moved away, and the guys are all gone, too. Now it's just strangers, and everybody minds his own business."

I asked the family if they felt uneasy or dissatisfied about where their lives were leading them. "I think people who expect others to help them worry about that kind of thing," Izumi said emphatically. "People with too much time on their hands. I do worry about Japan when I see teenage girls smoking or putting their feet up on the train —"

"My friends eat on the train," her daughter Kanako interjected.

"Eat in public? That's terrible!" Izumi exclaimed.

"You mean just riding back and forth and not on a trip somewhere?" Rikutaro asked.

Kanako nodded. "Rice balls and sandwiches; on their way home from club activities."

"And they're not ashamed to behave that way in the public eye?" Izumi was appalled. "Eating in public while you're walking down the street! I know that foreigners behave that way," she said, glancing across the table at me as if for confirmation.

"There's nobody to scold them," Rikutaro said, shaking his head.

While the Kawatanis seemed troubled by the diminishment of community and other changes they observed, it was clear that they were at home in their environment, much as the Dendas felt deeply connected to their land. By the mid-1970s, however, Japan's rapidly expanding cities were inhabited principally by uprooted nuclear families whose lives were shaped less by continuity and the legacy of their own past than by economic policies that drove the postwar recovery. On July 18, 1960, Hayato Ikeda took office as prime minister, promising to double the national income in ten years — it was achieved in just six! — and launched a national drive to increase Japan's productivity, the beginning of the so-called economic miracle. In 1963, the International Monetary Fund declared Japan a "developed country"; by 1965, the trade deficit hit zero and turned positive. By 1969, Japan was the world's largest shipbuilder — despite the fact that Japanese steel had to be produced from imported iron ore — and Japan had overtaken West Germany to become the world's second largest economy.

Throughout the 1960s and 1970s, the government's strategy was to finance the engines of export by generating a capital surplus through savings, which required constructing a national savings machine that was unparalleled in history. The white-collar "salaryman" was encouraged to bank his bonus — 25 to 50 percent of his salary, received in lump sums twice a year — and in general to defer consumption, including the purchase of housing. In a reversal of the policy in place in the United States, the government restricted the growth of mortgage loans in order to require consumers to save cash for down payments. At the same time, the Ministry of Finance designed measures to ensure that salary levels were suppressed; until the 1980s, Japan's blue- and white-collar salaries were low out of all proportion to the country's high-priced exports.

Transforming itself into a nation of savers was Japan's greatest triumph of social engineering during the period of recovery and accelerated economic growth. By the mid-eighties, the middle class was saving 16 percent of its annual income as compared to 4 percent in the United States. In 1986, the tax-free postal savings accounts known as Maruyu held deposits totaling $1 trillion. Interest was held to a bare minimum, 1.5 to 1.75 percent.

The white-collar middle class was aware that it was making sacrifices in the interest of increasing national productivity. In 1969, Kiichi Miyazawa, then minister of finance, summed up a feeling that was general all over Japan when he lamented: "We have sold everything, including the kitchen sink. Now we have nothing left for ourselves."

Nonetheless, the salaryman more than acquiesced to the national mission to overtake the United States: he devoted himself obsessively to his work, forgoing leisure time for himself and his family. His incentive was partly job security and the guarantee of expense accounts, club memberships, and other perks as he climbed the corporate ladder. In the seventies and eighties, hard work paid off. Beyond that, he found comfort and gratification in feeling identified with other citizens working in community for the benefit of society at large. During the period of recovery, this national consensus, a manifestation of the groupism that has always been at the heart of Japanese social life, functioned as a competitive weapon.

This strategy was dramatically clear at the time of the Arab oil embargo in 1973. Oil was Japan's largest import, and the country's export-driven economy, based on heavy industry such as steel and shipbuilding, was hit hard by the rising cost of energy. The trade balance with the United States slipped back into deficit while the soaring price of oil drove inflation to 30 percent. Consumers panicked. Sakyo Komatsu's science-fiction novel *Japan Sinks* sold 3 million copies. But Japan recovered quickly, and recovered again within a year when the price of oil soared in 1979. The Japanese, in striking contrast to Americans, reduced their energy consumption drastically, accepted lower wages from employers whose fuel bills had tripled, and worked overtime to design new products that could augment exports and compensate for rising energy costs.

A strategy paper on how to reduce Japanese exports to the European Community published in March 1979 ascribed the country's "outlandish growth" to "backbreaking labor, training, and feudal dedication to the organization" and characterized Japan as "a nation of workaholics living in a rabbit hutch." There was some truth in this; certainly the rabbit hutch had an objective correlative in the housing developments that had proliferated in urban areas.

In 1963, Tokyo's population pushed above 10 million people. With salaries suppressed, housing became a critical problem. The government began making living space available by lottery in newly erected concrete housing projects in outlying areas of the major cities. The projects were described in the media as "distant, expensive, and cramped." The typical apartment for a family of four, a "2DK," consisted of two very small bedrooms — ten by six — and a dining and kitchen area (there was no need for an independent living room because the family had no time to sit at leisure together and guests were never invited home). These families were known as the "projects tribe," and by the early 1960s the advertising industry had determined that the exploding home appliance and electronics boom was driven by the housewife of the 2DK apartment.

Unlike the housing projects in American urban centers, which quickly degenerated into breeding grounds for crime and violence, the Japanese equivalent was beautifully managed and maintained by its occupants and exemplifies the "premodern" Japanese view that individual needs are subordinate to the community's well-being. To be sure, living in high-rise buildings was an obstacle to maintaining the sense of community that was natural to neighborhoods. But the longing for community and the corollary sensitivity to others that are inherent to the Japanese way of life have not been uprooted. I recently stepped into the elevator in an upscale housing project and noticed a button that was marked PET (Japanese uses the English word). When the button is pushed, a light goes on outside the elevator at each floor to warn residents that someone inside is accompanied by a pet.

Transplanted urban families suffer the uneasiness of dislocation, but this is not to suggest that city life is unsustained by any connection to the traditional past. The New Year's season is a prime example. The last two weeks of December are given over to end-of-the-year parties — the Japanese term is "forget-the-year" — occasions at which professional colleagues or coworkers or students or friends eat and drink together and toast one another. On New Year's Eve, subways and buses in every Japanese city run all night; millions of people set out with their families to pay their respects at a Shinto shrine, bringing their hands together and bowing their heads in a silent prayer while Buddhist temples across the city ring in the year with 108 peals of their giant iron bells. At major shrines like Meiji Jingu in Tokyo, the long walkway leading to the main building is lined with festival booths selling fried noodles and fish pancakes, talismans, and special New Year's caramel candy.

Many people time their visits so they can be at home in front of their television sets between 10:30 and 11:45 for "The Song-War Game," NHK's (Japan's BBC) annual New Year's Eve tribute to Japan's top recording artists, which continues to attract the largest audience of the year. Two teams, red for the women and white for the men, take turns performing their hit songs for that year in front of a live audience. A celebrity panel selects the winning team, trophies are presented, and everyone sings the Japanese lyrics to "Auld Lang Syne."

Traditionally, Japan was closed for business from January 1 to January 7. After the war, when increasing productivity became the national preoccupation, this period of rest and contemplation was shortened to the first three days of the month. Many city families with relatives nearby gather on the second or third for a New Year's party; some return to their "native place" in the countryside. On January 2 and 3, politicians and business leaders were traditionally at home to receive unannounced visits from subordinates; this custom is still the case in principle but has been largely discontinued.

In city families even today, no less than in rural communities, New Year's Day means family time at home. The last days of the year are devoted to house cleaning and preparing traditional New Year's food in sufficient quantity to last the first three days of January, when shopping is impossible. Breakfast on New Year's morning always includes shrimp, symbolic of longevity; fish soup with *mochi*, glutinous rice dumplings; and black beans, representing a commitment to work industriously in the new year (the Japanese words for *beans* and *earnestness* are homonyms). On this morning only, breakfast is served with sake, a sweetened variety called *toso*, and getting pleasantly drunk is part of the ritual.

The highlight of the morning is the 10:00 A.M. delivery of *nengajo*, New Year's postcards. To this day, Japanese of all ages take inordinate pleasure in sending and receiving New Year's greetings from friends and family and associates. The cards are decorated with the animal sign for the incoming year, one of twelve — dragon, ram, snake, and so on — borrowed from Chinese astrology. Today imprinted cards are available, but many people still create their own designs and ink them on the cards with a woodblock or a carved potato. The postcards may be briefly personalized, but they invariably include a formulaic greeting, such as "Congratulations on the opening of the New Year. Last year I was a beneficiary of your kind counsel and consideration. I hope I shall be as fortunate again this year."* The postal service promises delivery of the cards on New Year's morn-

---

* I still have a postcard I received in 1964 from a fellow student at Tokyo University. It reads, in part, "Let us resolve to continue our eager study of our national literature in the interest of our great nation." When I showed this note to the novelist Yukio Mishima, he smiled thinly, and said, "Romanticism is easy when you're young."

ing if they are postmarked by December 28. Each year, thousands of auxiliary mailmen are employed to make good on this guarantee.

The ritual of New Year's postcards is an expression of the enduring need to sustain and affirm connection. During the affluent seventies and eighties, when uneasiness about identity was not troubling the national consciousness, the number of postcards in circulation each New Year's season sharply dropped. Since the economy failed in the early nineties, volume has climbed year by year: in 2001, it was estimated that each Japanese household on the census rolls received an average of one hundred cards.

In his 1983 film, *The Family Game,* Yoshimitsu Morita dramatizes a sardonic vision of life in the nuclear family as centerless and alienated. The Numatas live in a housing project built on reclaimed land in Tokyo Bay. The only rooms that appear in their Western-style, antiseptically clean apartment are the dining room, where the family appears to spend most of its time together, and two adjoining bedrooms just large enough to hold a bed and desk for study, one for each of the teenage sons (presumably, there is a third bedroom for the parents, but as there is no intimacy in their lives the filmmaker pointedly does not include it). Mr. Numata is a typical company man: each morning he sucks the yolks from two fried eggs before hurrying to work and does not return until after dark. His distracted attempts to model values for his sons are hollow and unheeded. Mrs. Numata devotes her time to coddling her spoiled, insensitive, uncommunicative boys, preparing snacks for them when they return from school, bringing tea and cookies to their bedrooms at night as they study listlessly, and fretting about whether her younger son will pass the entrance exams to a prestigious high that will increase his chances of admission to a good college. When the parents wish to be alone together, which happens only once in the film, they go downstairs to the garage and sit in Mr. Numata's car, recalling briefly the days when they enjoyed "jazz dancing." The family's dinnertime ritual, a scene that recurs throughout the film, is as telling as it is out-landish. The Numatas sit side by side at a long table, serving themselves from bowls and platters atop a trolley that slides the length of the table and obviates the need of turning to face one another in the course of their desultory conversation.

The Numatas' sterile lives are momentarily roiled by the ar-rival of a bizarrely eccentric college student who is hired to tutor the younger boy. Yoshimoto teaches the boys about sex and how to stand up for themselves against bullies, slaps them around when they are out of line, fights with their teachers at school, and insists on talking turkey with their parents about their feckless-ness. Under his stern tutelage, the younger Numata passes his ex-ams, and Mr. Numata invites him to stay for a celebration dinner. Sitting between the parents and the Numata children at the long table, Yoshimoto drains both bottles of Mr. Numata's wine, initi-ates a food fight with the boys, rabbit-punches them out of their seats, attacks both parents, knocking them senseless, and, on his way out for the last time, upends the table and the trolley, leaving the family on the floor, swimming in spilled food and broken glass. The family suffers Yoshimoto's assault in silence, as if insu-lated against a consciousness of what is happening to them even at this intrusively brutal moment.

The Family Game is an exercise in grotesque realism: the details of life in the nuclear family have been selectively magnified and distorted in fashioning a comic yet unstintingly harsh critique. Nevertheless, Mr. Numata's preoccupation with work at the ex-pense of leisure time and his emptiness at home are real. Begin-ning in the early eighties, the company man was literally working himself to death, collapsing in the street. This new pathology was labeled *karo-shi,* "exhaustion death," an apparent shutdown of the body's systems due to stress and overwork and the total absence of recreation. Exhaustion death syndrome was in the news through-out the late eighties; it became again a topic of national concern in 2000 when it developed that Prime Minister Keizo Obuchi had been working fifteen-hour days for months without a single day off when he fell into a coma and died.

Mrs. Numata's obsession with her sons and how they fare at school is also representative. Many women in urban nuclear families live lonely and alienated lives. Their husbands are too absorbed in their work to attend to the family; their parents often live far away; and they have scant opportunity for contact with other families living in the housing developments that have replaced the once social neighborhood. As a result, they become, like Mrs. Numata, *kyoiku-mama*, "education mothers," transferring their expectations for gratification away from their husbands and focusing them fervently on their children and their futures. Japanese psychiatrists have labeled this morbid fixation "mother-child adhesion." The disorder was nourished by the pressure-cooker competition for admission to the right schools that was confronting children with "entrance-exam hell" by the early 1980s. As I discussed in the previous chapter, growing numbers of children have defended themselves against the stress with chronic truancy. A bizarre related disorder that surfaced abruptly in the mid-1980s became known as "family-refusal syndrome." Husbands developed a paranoid certainty that their place at home had been usurped by their children, especially those who were studying for entrance exams and were the focus of their mothers' obsessive attention. Men afflicted began to hallucinate, to commute to work from hospitals, and eventually, renouncing the gesture of homecoming altogether, disappeared into the streets. In 1989, a daytime TV show for women featured a checklist designed to avoid driving husbands to "home-refusal syndrome."

In the fall of 2002, hoping to assess the confusion and uneasiness that seem endemic in today's Japan, I visited a number of Tokyo families. Kazuya and Fumi Yano and their teenage children are a much healthier, warmer, and more communicative nuclear family than the Numatas of *The Family Game*. Nevertheless, I came away from an evening in their home with a strong sense of their disappointment with life today and their uncertainty about the future.

Kazuya Yano, forty-eight, is a *bucho,* or general manager, who oversees managers of the Tokyo branches of one of Japan's largest banks. He has worked for the company for twenty-five years. His wife, Fumi, forty-three, a lively, attractive woman, is from Kyoto. A friend of Kazuya's mother introduced them and they were married in 1983, the year Kazuya joined the bank. They have two children. Masaichi, seventeen, is a junior at a private high school that is ten minutes by bicycle from home. His precocious younger sister, Yumi, thirteen, is an eighth-grader at one of Tokyo's most prestigious middle schools, Shibuya Kyoiku Gakuen. Yumi rides thirty minutes on the subway to school and back; her father drops her at the station in the morning on his way to work and, when he is available, picks her up in the late afternoons when she calls him on her mobile telephone.

Including his biannual bonus — a benefit now in jeopardy at many Japanese organizations — Kazuya Yano earns $150,000 a year. In 1991, the family purchased for $650,000 a comfortable five-room condo (the Japanese use the English word "mansion") in a newly built development in Minami Senju that overlooks the Sumida River. Their apartment is on the seventh floor of a fifteen-story building that is one of seven in the development. The entire property is fenced and there are well-kept gardens around the buildings. I met the family on a Saturday night at 8:00 P.M., after Masaichi had returned from baseball practice. We sat at a dining table just off the living room, and Fumi Yano brought me coffee and a plate of cookies. The scale of the rooms was small by American standards but not cramped, and the apartment was well appointed.

The family routine is representative of the urban upper-middle class. Kazuya is up at 6:00 and leaves for work at 7:00. Officially he is through at 5:30, but he rarely leaves the office before 8:00. On days when he has had to travel to branch banks in outlying districts of the city he returns between 10:00 and 11:00 at night. "I'm often asleep by the time he gets back," Fumi told me. "Is what we see on television true, that American wives call their husbands at the office several times a day?" she inquired. I suggested that would not be unusual. "That's unbelievable. Companies don't like private calls at work. I wouldn't call unless there was an emergency."

As in most Japanese families, the Yanos do not socialize as a couple. They do occasionally go out to eat and rarely to see a movie, but never without the children. Fumi asked me if it was true that Americans thought nothing of calling a baby-sitter so that the husband and wife could go out alone for dinner and a movie. When I acknowledged that this arrangement was common practice, she shook her head wonderingly. "I would never do that, and neither would any of my friends," she said. "I'd feel guilty about leaving them alone. A Japanese mother can't sleep while the children are studying no matter how late they stay up. We feel it's a mother's job to check in on them or bring them a snack. We know they're in there working as hard as they can and we just can't forget about them or leave them alone."

Fumi is a tennis buff and plays three mornings a week with friends at a nearby club. She devotes the rest of her spare time to supporting her son's participation in his high school baseball club. Masaichi's team is one of 4,300 across Japan that compete throughout the year. He has practice for several hours every afternoon, seven days a week, the year round, including spring and summer vacations. Practice is rigorous and exhausting. And Fumi is always there with tea and snacks and hand towels chilled in ice water. She and Kazuya attend every weekend game at home or away. Masaichi's baseball is a principal focus of life in the Yano family. "Baseball here is a little different from what it is in America," Masaichi explained. "The emphasis is on spiritual stuff like building character. Even at practice, when we step onto the field we straighten up and bow, and when we're finished we clean up and bow again, the way they do at a dojo."

I asked the family if they thought of themselves as, were conscious of being, Japanese. "Definitely," Fumi declared. "We love to travel. We've been to Singapore, and Hong Kong, and Guam. And when we're abroad and we see big Sony or Nissan billboards it makes us happy. The children, too. I don't imagine Americans would feel that way. I guess we're pretty provincial."

"It's like the Ichiro phenomenon," Kazuya added, referring to the Japanese baseball star who has excelled as an outfielder for the Seattle Mariners. "He wasn't that popular when he was playing here. We all thought he was a snob and a showoff. But now he's a hero because he's able to more than hold his own against those superior American athletes."

I asked Kazuya what qualities he would identify as "Japanese." "We're introverts. We don't express ourselves well. I feel that about myself all the time. And we are poor negotiators, particularly with foreigners. If we want a hundred of something we try to get eighty. In the United States if you want a hundred, you'll ask for one-fifty. The Chinese ask for two hundred. And if you say okay, they'll take it."

Yumi was unhappy with her father's choices. "Papa, everything you're saying is negative. How about 'modest'? I think that's a beautiful word."

"We are modest," her brother agreed. "In the States, when a football player makes a long run for a touchdown he slams the football down and struts around like he's the greatest thing on earth. And everybody cheers. If an athlete behaved that way in Japan he'd be criticized. A strong man shouldn't have to show you that he's strong."

I wondered if the Yanos were aware of anything distinctively Japanese about the structure of their own family.

"We stay together," Kazuya said, and his wife nodded emphatically. "In the United States, when the children go off to college, they're pretty much on their own. I think Japan is moving in the same direction. But that's not us. We discuss everything with the children now, and we intend always to stay close. My parents are getting old, and the time is coming when they'll move in with us. But I wouldn't decide that without consulting with the children first."

I mentioned the uneasiness that struck me as pervasive in Japan. How were the Yanos feeling as a family about their own prospects for the future? "We had big dreams until the early nineties," Kazuya began. "I was born in 1954 when there wasn't even that much food around. A chocolate bar was a huge treat for me in those days. So we longed for material things. We wanted things, and we worked desperately hard to bring our material life up to the American standard. The family cooperated; it was a team effort. No matter how late we had to stay at the office working, Saturdays and Sundays and no vacations, they understood and supported us. And we created unbelievable wealth. Even middle-class white-collar workers like me could feel our labor paying off. We don't have a second home the way Americans do. We could never afford that. We'd have no time to go there anyway. But we all have cars and all the latest home electronics. But since the bubble burst, it feels as though our hard work is unavailing. And people my age and older have to ask ourselves why are we working so hard. What's the point? You asked about our dream. We've lost our dream and now we must rethink our way of life.

"The young people have the same problem. My son has to work like crazy if he wants to get into a good college next year. But why should he? Sony or Tokyo University were standards and goals when our economy was strong. But now everyone feels confused. There are no more guarantees. People we know are being laid off all around us. We've lost our confidence and so have our children —"

"Masaichi says he wants to be a high school baseball coach," his mother added. "Ten years ago I would have thought, That's not ambitious enough. I would have urged him to enter a competitive world, to get hired by a great company like Sony, or to become a doctor. But now there are no guarantees of success no matter what you do. Now we feel the children should do whatever they need to do to make their dreams come true."

Kazuya Yano continued, "I am forty-eight years old. All my life I've struggled hard to get ahead without any doubts about what I was doing. Now I feel as if I'm waking up. Maybe I should spend more time doing volunteer work. I don't know. Maybe the children should go their own ways and stop worrying about getting into the right schools. Nothing seems clear anymore. It's very unsettling."

The Yanos are aware that life is less promising than it formerly was, and certainly less secure, and they feel correspondingly disappointed and uneasy, but their family remains cohesive and robust.

Yet many other families across Japan are experiencing the pain and even hopelessness of profound upheaval. Atsuko Matsuda is trapped in an unendurable family situation she is helpless to resolve. When she married in 1987, she moved into her husband's family home in the small city of Takasaki, north of Tokyo. It was an arranged marriage; a cousin had been a classmate of her husband's. She has two sons, fourteen and thirteen. When the elder boy was in the fifth grade he refused to go to school one day and has never gone back. Atsuko doesn't know what happened, but suspects her son may have been sexually abused by an older boy in an adjoining junior high school. Before the year was out, her younger son, insisting he wanted to stay at home with his brother, also dropped out of school. When I met Atsuko in the fall of 2002, her sons had been at home for three years; they spent their time watching television and playing video games and reading *manga,* Japanese comic books, and she had given up her efforts to persuade or force them to return to school. Recently the older boy, Keizo, who was associating with a gang of boys his age, was caught shoplifting and had spent a day in detention at the local police station.

By her own account, Atsuko's marriage had never been a happy one; and having his listless, quarrelsome sons at home had vexed and depressed her already troubled husband. He worked in sales at a plumbing fixtures manufacturer and was frequently on the road. At home he would sit sullenly by himself drinking sake, and when drunk he became abusive, screaming at his sons and reviling Atsuko for having failed to keep them in school.

Just before New Year's 2000, Atsuko began to suspect that her husband was having an affair and she hired a private detective, who photographed him in the company of a younger woman, a secretary at his Takasaki branch office. Atsuko confronted her husband with pictures and demanded a meeting with the other woman. Late one night when the children were asleep, her husband brought his mistress home.

Atsuko accused her of having destroyed her family and betrayed what she called "the sisterhood of women." It was then that the woman told her she was carrying her husband's child. "I was so humiliated, I wanted to die," Atsuko told me unemotionally. "But I couldn't die because of the children. I knew my only choice was to endure."

Two weeks later, Atsuko's husband moved into an apartment with his mistress. His parents, in their seventies, chose to continue living in the house, partly because of their attachment to their grandchildren. According to Atsuko, they hold her responsible for the children's problems — the younger boy has become a "self-incarcerator," rarely emerging from his room except at mealtimes — and also make her feel that she drove her husband out of the house.

When I met her, Atsuko was working as a chambermaid in a Takasaki business hotel. She told me that the strain of working all day while dealing with her children and hostile in-laws at home had made her ill: she was suffering from chronic indigestion, headaches, and what she called "spells," during which she heard voices. She had appealed to her own parents to allow her to move back to their home in Sendai with her two boys. They were concerned about her plight and have been sending her money but would not allow her to return home: "My older brother had moved into the house with his wife and their baby girl, and my folks said it wouldn't be fair to them to allow us to bring all our trouble home," Atsuko explained. "I understand how they feel. But I don't know what to do. It seems as if there's nothing I can do but figure out how to survive. I never dreamed my life would turn out this way."

I hesitated to use this story, which I have recounted exactly as it was told to me by Atsuko Matsuda at a coffee shop in Takasaki (her husband and his parents declined to meet me) because it sounds melodramatic. But if this is melodrama, it is distinctively Japanese: the chronically truant children, the confrontation with the mistress, life at home with the husband's parents, and the victim's own parents' refusal to have her back at home are ingredients that are familiar to the Japanese. And while the details are not directly attributable to an economy in crisis or uprooting and dislocation, this single mother's predicament does reflect the breakdown of traditional structure and stability that is traumatizing families across Japan today.

3

The Culture of Arithmetic

❖

UNTIL THE ECONOMY STALLED, the Japanese corporation provided employees with a basis for identity very much in the manner of a feudal samurai family. The CEO was head of the household and lord of his domain. His thousands of retainers around the world owed and accorded him fealty. The Japanese company man belonged to his organization in the sense that one belongs to a family. It was understood that loyalty to the firm would be rewarded by lifetime employment and a predictable career path based on promotion according to seniority. When a new employee signed on with a company upon graduation from college, a personnel manager sat down with him (and, rarely, her) and mapped out a career program designed to optimize success all the way to retirement. The result was stability and peace of mind that the employee repaid with total dedication.

The Japanese use the English words *wet* and *dry* to differentiate emotional human interaction and dispassionate, arm's-length association. The Japanese corporate environment has been decidedly "wet." Employees traditionally have looked to their managers for counsel and support as if they were respected family elders.

Executives often act as go-betweens in arranged marriages and listen sympathetically to all manner of domestic problems, including marital strife, financial crises, and unruly children. Much of this "wet" interaction occurs after business hours; until the bubble burst and expense-account drinking was curtailed, managers frequently invited staff to join them at a round of bars on the way home from work — the custom was known as "climbing the ladder" — a ritual designed to provide an opportunity for giving advice on personal matters. At some point in the evening, the senior manager would excuse himself and leave his staff alone to talk freely among themselves with an invitation to charge their drinks and food to his account.

The degree to which the company man identified with his organization has not been adequately understood in the West. In a sense, because identification with the group is a distinctively Japanese cultural phenomenon, it is not truly knowable to those outside Japanese society. If the history of modern Japan reveals the extreme difficulty in importing culture, American efforts to replicate the environment that enabled Japan's formidable productivity in the postwar era lead to a similar conclusion. In the 1970s and 1980s, when the United States was losing markets to Japan in autos, steel, machine tools, and consumer electronics, American executives devoured books about Japanese management theory, imported Japanese methods of quality control, and, in the Japanese manner, instituted group discussions between management and labor designed to reach decisions by consensus. More ludicrously, sensing that the phenomenon had to do with relationships, U.S. companies began referring to janitors as custodial associates and created new positions like the vice president of celebrations. The fact remained, in a society that valorized individualism, that many people were not content to work for others: alienation, and the consequent loss of productivity, were inchoate in the moment of hiring. The Japanese never resented sacrificing individuality in the interest of the group; on the contrary, discovering one's place in a vertically integrated group, belonging harmoniously, was the basis for gratification and, beyond that, self-certainty.

Layoffs — the Japanese use the euphemism *ristora* from the English word *restructuring* — were, even under the most extreme circumstances, unthinkable. Employment contracts are still rare in Japan except at the highest level of top management. But a guarantee was always in place: except in cases of flagrant negligence or unlawful misconduct, employees were never fired. Those who failed to reach the lowest rung of the middle management ladder, *kacho*, or manager, by age fifty-five, were deprived of title, deemed "specialists," employees without portfolio, and circulated from department to department to pitch in as needed. Others who had not reached the retirement age of sixty-five but had lost the vigor or clarity required to hold responsible positions were superannuated to positions as secretarial assistants or office coordinators — seniors with silvery hair welcoming visitors as they approached the reception desk were a familiar sight in the lobby of every corporate headquarters. Business downturns occurred cyclically, but somehow the organization honored its commitment to retain employees for life, to keep them in the family.

In April 1999, the president of the giant department store chain Mitsukoshi made headlines when he announced at the opening ceremony for new hires that his company was abandoning the commitment to lifetime employment that had been a Mitsukoshi tradition for three hundred years. He was making public and explicit a rejection of tradition that was already on its way to becoming endemic across Japanese business. The Labor Ministry estimates that 2 million jobs have disappeared since 1998, and expects that figure to double by 2005. In a society where identification with the organization has traditionally been as binding and fervent as family ties, this dislocation has produced confusion and grief, and, as with the breakup of the kinship family, a deep-seated uncertainty about identity itself.

In 1998, Japan's suicide rate abruptly jumped 35 percent to more than 30,000 deaths for the first time in postwar history. This number is twice as many suicides per capita as occur annually in the United States. Suicides increased again in 1999 to 35,000, and have remained above 30,000 ever since. The director of the Mental Health Center attached to Yokohama Hospital, Dr. Yoshi Yamamoto, thinks the figures are misleadingly low because they include only those who expire within twenty-four hours of attempting suicide. Yamamoto estimates that 50,000 attempted suicides are admitted to hospitals across the country each year, and that ten times that number are treated outside hospitals at walk-in clinics. Extrapolating from that number, he concludes that some 5 million Japanese are contemplating suicide at any given moment.

Eighty percent of the suicides on record are company men between the ages of forty and fifty-five.* Beginning in 2000, large organizations began installing suicide emergency counseling offices in their health facilities. Employees who seek help communicate confusion and uneasiness about sudden transfers to new assignments, increased working hours and expectations, and anxiety about layoffs. Discord at home is also cited frequently. During the 1970s and 1980s, as Kazuya Yano, the banker, mentioned, wives were willing to cover for their husbands at home. But feminist consciousness has grown, and women today tend to be less acquiescent about their husbands' preoccupation with work, particularly in the current context of disillusionment about the ultimate value of a company career. Many men feel caught between pressure at work and new demands at home: the divorce rate has climbed in tandem with increasing suicide statistics. According to

---

* Since early in 2003, men and women in their early twenties, jobless and in despair about the future, have been using bulletin boards and chat groups on the Internet to find suicide partners.

a national survey conducted by the Ministry of Health and Welfare in 2002, the complaint heard most frequently is that life has lost its purpose and meaning.

In 2001, in an attempt to deter people from throwing themselves in front of trains, the government installed large mirrors at both ends of subway and train platforms. It seemed a telling response to the crisis, as symbolic as it is psychological: as if a reflection in a mirror might ease for just a moment the suicide's despair by providing, or creating the illusion of, the sense of self that had been lost, often as a result of having been abruptly disowned by a corporate family.

While Japanese business is in the process of adopting the American approach to downsizing, the firing process itself is not yet a simple matter of summary dismissal in the American manner. In the United States, employees are notified by the personnel office that they are being let go and instructed to vacate their offices by a given date. In Japan, a boss is obliged to solicit a resignation by persuading his subordinate that it is in his best interest to leave the firm. He might explain that promotions to general manager will be sharply curtailed due to shrinking profits, point out that the employee's record is not overly impressive, and express his concern that continuing his career at the company may not be the most fulfilling option for him. He mentions that the firm is offering a generous severance package, up to two years of salary and a handsome bonus. Frankly speaking, given the current environment, he would be strongly tempted to take the same package if it were offered to him. "Why not talk it over with your wife?" he concludes. "And let's meet again next week."

Both parties are aware that they are acting out a ritual designed to save face. Twenty percent of those who receive this paternalistic counsel dig in their heels and reject the severance offer. If the company should then become aggressive about forcing them to leave, they can plead their case to the Labor Standards Law Regulatory Commission in the Ministry of Labor, and precedent will be on their side — in many cases, the offending company will be required to retain them or to increase the severance offer. The question occurs, Why adopt a bottom-line-driven American policy of downsizing and then constrain its implementation with this roundabout, not entirely disingenuous, process? There is no law on the books that prohibits firing explicitly, particularly when, as in the majority of cases, no contract exists. What does exist is the organization's unstated promise to employees. Even as the social contract is being abrogated, it continues to impede the firing process with the residual power of its traditional authority.

After deliberation at home with their families, eight out of ten employees will decide, as if on their own, to accept the severance package and leave the company. Typically, they find — are allowed to discover in a face-saving way — the impetus to leave in anger or disappointment at new directions the company is taking. I spoke to a fifty-two-year-old man who had worked for thirty years training salesmen at Japan's largest distributor of foreign automobiles, Yanase Motors. Summoned to an interview, the man had been told that the company could no longer afford to maintain a training department. "The new 1992 models were just coming out, and I volunteered to remain at a reduced salary to help our salesmen learn what they needed to know about them," he told me. "My boss said that Yanase was discontinuing all training. That made me see red: I don't want to work at a company that sabotages its own sales force, and that's when I decided to leave."

The group hit hardest are the baby boomers, men born shortly after the war who have been at their companies for thirty years and are just reaching the lower rungs of middle management. Theirs has been a star-crossed generation in a number of respects. They went to college in the late sixties, when competition for admittance to the elite schools that guaranteed a fast-track career in business and government was at its fiercest, and they were looking for their wives at a time when a promising career was essential to attracting well-educated young women from good families.

Ironically, they were also the generation of white- and blue-collar workers who had driven the engine of Japan's economic recovery throughout the 1970s and 1980s by working for salaries that had been suppressed way out of proportion to their contribution and to the high price of Japanese exports. The expectation had always been that they would be rewarded upon reaching the ranks of middle management in their early fifties; what followed was to be a life of better money for shorter hours, increased vacation time, and later, as retirement neared, a car with a driver and even a country club membership. Now, at the gateway to a more leisurely life, they were being advised to leave.

Though they have been persuaded to resign, the men and women who leave their employers (14 percent are women) are in general angry, disoriented, and, above all, ashamed. Every morning in Tokyo and other cities across Japan, thousands of unemployed white-collar workers set out from home in their business suits between 7:00 and 8:00 A.M., as though they were commuting to work as usual. They make their way instead to public libraries, museums, or parks, where they may be seen sitting apart from one another, whiling away the hours reading magazines and want-ad sections in the paper, their lunches of rice and fish or meat neatly arrayed in plastic containers tied up in the square of silk or linen cloth the Japanese call *furoshiki,* until it is time to return home at a plausible hour at the end of the day. Recently, movie theaters in Tokyo have begun to schedule first screenings at an unheard of 9:30 A.M. for those who prefer to sit alone in the dark with their mortification. The masquerade is intended to keep neighbors from realizing that they are out of work. Many spend part or all of the day preparing themselves to look for a new job in workshops and counseling at a reemployment agency. Within the space of a few years, this distinctly un-Japanese service business has grown into a thriving industry.

I recently spent time at Right WayStation, a "career transition service" that was founded in 1994 in response to a building wave of corporate layoffs (the firm uses the American euphemism "right-sizing"). In fiscal 2002, which ended in March 2001, the company processed 1,679 "candidates." In the year ending in March 2002, the number of clients doubled to 3,500. In May 2001, the largest career counseling agency in the United States, Right Management Consultants, Inc., acquired 71 percent of Way-Station, which is now Japan's second largest placement agency after DBM (Drake Beam Morin), an American franchise that specializes in foreign companies operating in Japan.

The company's paying clients are the organizations engaged in downsizing; Right WayStation's counseling services begin with teaching employers techniques for soliciting resignations with a minimum of conflict. Employers pay WayStation for placement services for new candidates for as long as the process may take (in the United States, outplacement is generally provided for three to six months only). During the first two months, candidates attend seminars and individual counseling sessions almost daily. Eighty percent are placed in new jobs within the first six months, but the process may take as long as two years.

WayStation's approach — "managing the human side of transition" — is modeled on techniques developed in the United States twenty years ago which the company has adapted to meet distinctively Japanese needs. The company president, Motohiro Uezumi, one of the three founders, showed me a graph that recalled Kübler-Ross's stages of denial experienced by the terminally ill. "The Japanese go through the same stages, beginning with surprise and disbelief," he explained, "but it takes us much longer to reach acceptance and a proactive attitude about exploring new possibilities." According to Uezumi, the slower, more painful process of transition in Japan is due in part to a reticence about self-promotion so general and deep-seated that it may be considered taboo. "You Americans love to talk about yourselves, wouldn't you agree? At least you have no trouble selling yourselves to someone new. We have enormous difficulty with that, and it's not simply a cultural matter. We get men in their mid-fifties who have worked at the same company their whole lives and have no idea what they like to do or even what they do best. That's because their careers have been designed by their employers to produce generalists instead of specialists. In a way, they're strangers to themselves."

Traditionally, when a new hire enters a Japanese company and meets with personnel managers to outline a career plan, the employee isn't consulted about what he would like to do, not in the beginning and not later in his career. He is told to begin in, say, accounting and then move to purchasing or sales or marketing as the company sees fit. Even senior executives are customarily informed that they are being transferred to new areas of responsibility, a transfer that is often a promotion, without warning or consultation. This kind of redeployment often follows a personnel shift or major reorganization that is perceived as requiring a new mix of personalities or personal relationships at the top. At all levels of the organization, personnel decisions tend to be based on a subjective assessment of capability rather than on performance; employees follow the career path mapped out for them submissively, trusting that they will climb the promotion ladder at predetermined intervals to reach a predicted rung at the end of their career.

In the first month of the program, to help candidates develop focus on what they would like to do in their new jobs, counselors at Right WayStation coach them in a process the company calls "taking inventory": "We ask them to recall a period in their career when they felt particularly happy and gratified about what they were doing," Motohiro Uezumi told me. "When did they feel confident and well prepared? Was there a time when they received frequent compliments from superiors on the quality of their performance? It's like helping an adult to crawl again before he starts walking on his own two feet. It's unreasonable to expect someone in middle age to become self-reliant after having been guided through a career for thirty years. Many people simply cannot come up with anything they are confident about wanting to do, and without that confidence, selling themselves is very hard."

I sat in on the only one of its seminars the company requires all candidates to attend, a day-long workshop called "Attitude and Presentation in the Interview." There were ten students in the room, seven men and three women, all in their fifties. The instructor, Mika Nakamura, impeccably groomed and dressed in a business suit, was a paragon of good bearing and politesse, with a beautifully modulated voice that made me think she had been trained for the stage, and a delivery that was relentlessly upbeat. As with many Japanese trainers, she was also a virtuoso of microdetail. She began by explaining that the content of the candidate's responses determined a mere 7 percent of a prospective employer's impression. The rest was based on "intonation, volume, and tone of voice," 35 percent, and, most critically, "posture, movements and gestures, facial expressions and eye contact," 58 percent. She then gave the class an exercise designed to relax facial muscles and promote expressiveness and a "beaming smile from ear to ear." Elocution practice followed. Explaining that no one enjoyed listening to a mumbler or a monotone, Nakamura asked class members to insert three fingers in their mouth vertically as a gauge to opening wide and then took them through a series of rounded, fully expressed vowels and tongue twisters.

The main business of the day was a drill in how to enter the room and take a seat in front of the prospective employer, a fifteen-second transition that, according to Nakamura, might account for as much as 50 percent of the impression the candidate created. First she demonstrated each minute phase of the process and had the students practice it. Three knocks on the door: four is too insistent, two is what we use to determine whether a toilet stall is occupied. *"Come in."* Open the door wide and step boldly across the threshold, no tentative peeking into the room; close the door without turning your back and cross the room purposefully to the chair facing the interviewer across a table. Stand at the left (deferential) side of the chair. Eye contact. Say clearly, with a smile: "How do you do. My name is Mika Nakamura. Thank you for seeing me this morning." Bow: a sixty-degree angle for the men, body at ten minutes past six; for the ladies, a quarter past. Straighten slowly, with composure despite your pounding heart. *"Please be seated."* "Thank you." A quick bow. Sit forward in the chair, poised to rise without a heave-ho or a rising skirt when you are dismissed. Men sit with legs apart at shoulder width, hands on knees; women's legs together and straight in front of them, hands folded in the lap, the right (aggressive) hand beneath the left in a welcoming posture. This posture must be maintained for the duration of the interview. *"What size family do you have?"* Reply in one short sentence: "There are six of us." Avoid details about the daughter who teaches in kindergarten, the son who lives at home and practices his drums in the evening. When the interview is concluded — *"That will be all for now"* — rise quickly and stand again at the left side of the chair. You may be feeling more comfortable now, even relaxed, but don't show it. Eye contact. "Thank you very much for your time today. Excuse me." A quick bow. Turn and walk to the door; turn back as you open it. "Excuse me." Another full bow. Straighten slowly. Exit and close the door behind you. Be careful not to exclaim "I blew it!" thinking you are out of earshot.

For the rest of the afternoon, the candidates practiced going through the motions of the routine from beginning to end. The sequence was simple enough, but they struggled with it as though they were attempting to put together the phases of a newly learned golf swing. Nakamura offered suggestions at every turn, with a microscopic focus on details, pointing out candidates who stood rooted just inside the door, or forgot their lines, or neglected to make eye contact, mumbling at the floor, or couldn't bring themselves to smile. One man stepped into the room too boldly and was cautioned to take shorter, more modest steps.

When one of the women smoothed her skirt before sitting down, Nakamura cautioned that the gesture should be made with the back of the hand, because the palm moving downward across the buttocks suggested a subway pervert's groping hand. At the end of the exercise the candidates looked crestfallen. Nakamura assured them that the exercises would get easier, and reminded them to practice speaking and smiling into a mirror at home and not to forget to open their mouths three fingers wide.

According to Motohiro Uezumi, the most difficult challenge his clients face is letting go of their pride. In a society where the group has always been more important than the individual, this barrier to success is formidable. An employee who has spent his career at Sony or at NEC (Nippon Electric) is a Sony or an NEC man, completely identified with the organization. Severance from the group, even when it is nominally a resignation, makes one feel as if he is being disowned by a proud family with a proud tradition. To make matters much worse, a fifty-four-year-old manager's chances of being rehired by one of Japan's Fortune 100 companies are close to negligible; except in rare cases when they are in need of a specialist, top companies hire no one older than thirty-five. Fortunately, marquee companies account for only 2 percent of Japan's corporate community as a whole; thousands of small to midsized companies, with fifty to three hundred employees, are in need of managers with experience in administration or in dealing with agencies in the government bureaucracy. But these modest operations are a far cry from corporate giants. Support staff is an unaffordable luxury, and employees are expected to work longer hours for less pay: candidates whom WayStation succeeds in placing receive, on average, 40 percent smaller salaries than they earned at their former jobs.

Expulsion from the ranks of the elite is hard enough to bear; relinquishing resentment and arrogance is often an insurmountable challenge. "We get to work on the pride issue right away," Uezumi told me. "We try to help candidates see that the Sony way isn't the only way; that big isn't necessarily best; and, most important, that the house of Sony isn't the only place they'll find fulfillment and happiness. Of course, telling people that doesn't make it so for them. When candidates learn they've been rejected after interviews they felt went perfectly, we always probe for pride and arrogance in their attitudes. And if they are dismissed within six months of being rehired — and that happens more frequently than we would like — we'll take them back. In our experience, pride is the main culprit in most of these cases. We explain that the small business owner is watching for signs of attitude. He doesn't want to hear about how things were at the major manufacturer; he doesn't want to see you delegating work to others because you're used to more staff; and he certainly doesn't want suggestions about how to improve his business — we tell people they should deliver great results for at least a year before they expect the boss to be open to their suggestions."

Since April 2002, WayStation has offered a workshop called "Pride in Myself," which uses group dynamics to help candidates liberate themselves from paralyzing identification with their former employers. "We begin with an exercise," Uezumi told me, "in which the participants introduce themselves to one another by saying 'My name is Blank. I was formerly employed by Blank. I was proud of performing my job well. I am a proud person. I take pride in myself!'"

Layoffs are only one among a number of American business practices that Japanese corporations are attempting to transplant to a business culture disposed to reject them. A second is a radically restructured board of directors that includes outsiders to the organization with authority to amend or even to countermand corporate policies and decisions. A third is promotions based on performance rather than seniority. Beginning in the early 1990s, and with mounting urgency as the economy sinks deeper into recession, corporate Japan has been scrambling to Americanize its governance and business practices. At a time when book sales are at a postwar low, the slender distillation of American management wisdom, *Who Moved My Cheese?*, was a record-breaking bestseller in Japan in 2002. American business schools such as Stanford, Columbia, Babson, and Northwestern's Kellogg School of Management have been active in Japan for the first time, marketing Internet and videotape packages in Japanese and offering intensive training seminars: the epidemic loss of confidence among Japanese executives has created a new business opportunity.

In a recent letter to me, a businessman friend of mine characterized this phenomenon with a bitterness common to his generation. His words put me in mind of Natsume Soseki lamenting "Westernization" in 1911. My friend wrote, "Japanese business is trying frantically to adopt an American style of management, and the result is turmoil and confusion. . . . As financial performance continues to drop, top management demands a management revolution, that is, a total denial of our traditional ways of conducting business. This attempt at transformation is producing friction and disharmony at a fundamental level. . . ."

The Nissan Motor Company is currently in the throes of precisely such "turmoil and confusion." Since April 1999, when the French automaker Renault SA acquired a 36.8 percent interest in Nissan for $5.4 billion, the company has been struggling to reject its traditional past in favor of "dry" Western business practice: Nissan today is the scene of corporate Japan's most radical and painful experiment in cultural synthesis.

Nissan had been courting an acquisition by DaimlerChrysler, but its crushing $36.5 billion in debt had driven that company away just two weeks before the deal with Renault was signed on April 26, 1999. At the time, Japan's second largest auto manufacturer after Toyota was edging toward bankruptcy. A recovery plan introduced in 1998 by the company's president and CEO, Yoshikazu Hanawa, had failed to bring mounting costs under control, and domestic and U.S. sales had been dropping year by year since the recession began in the early nineties: at the end of the fiscal year in March 1999, Nissan had reported a loss of $232 million on revenues of $55 billion, marking its seventh consecutive year in the red.

Investing heavily in a company in desperately poor health was a bold gamble for Renault, until recently beset by serious financial problems of its own. But the chairman since 1997, Louis Schweitzer, a grandnephew of Albert Schweitzer and distant cousin to Jean Paul Sartre, was committed to building a network of global alliances. In 1996, he spent $1 billion on a factory in Brazil, the first that Renault had built anywhere in twenty years. Earlier in 1999, he purchased entry into Eastern Europe at the cost of $50 million for a controlling interest in the Romanian carmaker Dacia. In 2000, he acquired a controlling interest in Samsung, the bankrupt South Korean automaker and electronics giant. But Nissan was, and continues to be, Renault's biggest gamble. Slightly smaller in sales than Nissan, Renault does not have the cash reserves that have allowed Ford to transfuse Mazda with $685 million over seventeen years in return for ongoing management problems and little profit. If Nissan should go under, Renault's own survival could be threatened. In fact, in the view of many observers in the auto industry, Renault's future is being determined in Tokyo.

Schweitzer's decision to send Carlos Ghosn (rhymes with "loan") to Tokyo was evidence that he viewed Nissan's recovery as Renault's most critical challenge. The child of a Brazilian father and a French mother, Ghosn was born in Brazil and grew up in Lebanon. He was educated in France, receiving a degree in engineering at the elite L'Ecole des Mines and a doctorate in Economics at the University of Paris. His first job was at Michelin Tire, where he established himself as a prodigy, building the tire maker's Latin American business while still in his twenties and, in 1990, engineering Michelin's merger with Uniroyal Goodrich in the United States. In the process he earned two nicknames, "le

cost-killer" and, a reference to his decisiveness in leaving foundering investments behind, "the parachutist."

Schweitzer hired Ghosn as his second in command in 1996,
when Renault reported losses of $1 billion, and placed him in
charge of restructuring the company. Ghosn mapped a plan to cut
$3.5 billion in costs by 2000; in 1997, he created a furor in Bel-
gium by closing Renault's assembly plant in Vilvoorde and cutting three thousand jobs. In 1998, Renault's profit of $1 billion
was attributed to Ghosn's success at streamlining operations and
it was clear that he was being groomed as Schweitzer's successor.

In April 1999, Ghosn arrived in Tokyo with a team of French
executives and assumed his new post as chief operating officer, the
first foreigner to hold the job at Nissan. On paper he reported to
the president and CEO, but according to Hanawa it was understood from the beginning that Ghosn would be running the company. He spent the first six months studying Renault, touring
plants and suppliers and distributorships and interviewing managers in Japan and around the world. His opening question was
simple: "What changes are necessary to restore Nissan to health?"
Those who replied vaguely were removed from the fast track; in-
ventive, confident opinions led to promotions that often have
broken the time-honored principle of seniority. In October 1999,
Ghosn released his blueprint for recovery, the "Nissan Revival
Plan." His announced goals included transforming the company's
inbred and costly supplier system, creating a new line of appeal-
ing automobiles for both Japanese and Western markets, cutting
the massive debt in half by the end of 2002, and becoming profitable during the 2000 fiscal year that ended on March 31, 2001.

Ghosn's plan called for reducing costs by $100 million and
achieving asset sales of $500 million in the first three years. He has
already closed five plants and a large number of Nissan-owned
dealerships in Japan. "The Japanese believe that the more outlets
you have, the more you will sell," he told me. "They tend to focus
on volume and market share rather than profitability and the

strength of market share." He has demanded lower prices from Nissan's suppliers, many of them owned by the company; he has trimmed incentives paid to dealerships in the United States and Europe. And he has overseen what he describes as "massive asset sales," including Nissan's 4 percent interest in Fuji Heavy Industries, the manufacturers of Subaru, of $210 million. Nissan and Fuji belong to the same *keiretsu,* a horizontal linking of organizations that amounts to an extended family. Ghosn is aware that this kind of disengagement could not have happened even a decade ago. "When we are not able to agree that ties from the past are strategically valuable, even though they are perceived that way, we sever them."

Even as he slashed costs, Ghosn has moved aggressively to achieve the simultaneous profitability and growth that he insists are the key to Nissan's recovery and the focus of his plan. Before the results of the first fiscal year were in, he invested $300 million in reestablishing the company's presence in South America, leveraging Renault's position in Brazil and Argentina. In 2001, he increased the capacity of existing U.S. plants in Smyrna and Deckerd by 50 percent, and construction of a $930 million new plant began in 2003. He has also increased investments in technology by $500 million, recruited new engineers from around the world, and focused marketing efforts on increasing brand power. In 1999, only four of the forty models Nissan sold in Japan were profitable. By the end of 2001, eighteen of the thirty-eight cars on the market were profitable, and Ghosn predicted that "the large majority" would be profitable by the end of fiscal 2003. His plan called for launching twenty-two new models worldwide in the first three years.

So far, it appears that Ghosn's strategies are paying off: on May 17, 2001, one fiscal year into the program, Nissan trumpeted the best financial performance in its history, a net income of $2.8 billion, a consolidated operating margin of 4.75 percent, higher than the 4.5 percent targeted for fiscal 2002, and a reduction in debt of close to 50 percent, a year ahead of schedule. Two months before the announcement, a reconfigured board of five Japanese and three French executives from Renault had moved Hanawa upstairs to the chairman's office and promoted Ghosn to president and CEO. He is currently the only foreigner to whom a major Japanese business organization has ceded complete control.

As in the Japanese proverb "Good medicine is bitter," Ghosn's restructuring of Nissan has created ongoing confusion and pain inside the organization on a cultural level. His unemotional approach to renewing the company includes matching people and jobs with no consideration of seniority. This attitude has resulted in leapfrogging that has overturned the long-standing relationship between superiors and subordinates. When Ghosn arrived at Nissan at age forty-six, the company's managers were all older than he, in their fifties and sixties, and he wanted younger, more vital men around him. To his way of thinking, promotion according to aptitude was a logical matter of course: "We're not merely setting targets and hitting them," he told me, "we are trying to reengineer basic processes and basic decision-making approaches, changing the mindset. We promote those who are more capable of working in this mindset."

I hoped to get a feeling for the cultural turmoil beneath the impressive arithmetic from the man who had handed Ghosn the keys to the company, Yoshikazu Hanawa, and I was not disappointed. Hanawa went to work for Nissan in 1957, the year he graduated from Tokyo University with a degree in economics, and, like other businessmen of his generation, has lived his entire professional life there. He spent fifteen years in personnel, climbing the carefully regulated promotion ladder to the top rung of middle management, general manager, in 1982, twenty-five years into his career, when he was placed in charge of the U.S. Project Office responsible for opening Nissan's Smyrna plant in Tennessee. In 1985, he joined the board of directors on schedule; in 1990 he served for one year as chairman of Nissan U.S.A., and from that position ascended to executive vice president in charge of overseas operations. He became president of Nissan in 1996 and, as Ghosn arrived, chairman, president, and CEO.

Tall and handsome with a golfer's tan, impeccably dressed and groomed, Hanawa at sixty-seven is the model of a Japanese gentleman, cordial and attentive as though I were his most important meeting of the day. He had spent a number of years in the United States, but preferred that we speak in Japanese. I began by asking as offhandedly as I could how he and Ghosn had divided responsibility for running the company. "The division is clear: we have asked Ghosn-san to take over the management of Nissan one hundred percent! My responsibility is our interaction with the world outside the company, which requires a Japanese sensibility. I am Ghosn-san's translator; I stand in for him and explain to people outside the organization what he's doing." Hanawa paused, as though considering whether to continue. "The job amounts to acknowledging my own shortcomings: and now Ghosn-san is repairing the damage. Emotionally it's not such a pleasant job, but it has to be done. . . ."

Hanawa spoke about the pain of being caught in a cultural double bind with remarkable forthrightness: "Before Ghosn-san arrived, I appealed to the entire company to put their doubts aside and to learn from him in a spirit of humility. He is very dry, very unemotional, one hundred percent business. But we were stuck in our old habits and we needed a violent shock to set us back on course. Some people couldn't take it and left the company. Others suffered and are still suffering. But I reject their attempts to complain to me because even though I understand what they are feeling I mustn't sympathize. Sometimes I try to explain why they are now required to report to a younger man, for example, but they can't quite get it or they can't believe I am being serious. They bring me memos I wrote them twenty years ago, angry that what I am saying now is different, and they resent me and feel betrayed. But this is a revolution and I must also reject the past."

Ghosn had demonstrated a gift for grasping the intricate dynamics of a Japanese corporation, but what I found even more remarkable was Nissan's readiness and ability to render itself comprehensible to a foreigner. Clearly, Hanawa had led the way in modeling this openness. Had other key executives throughout the organization been able to follow his lead? "They are all still struggling. But I continue to appeal to everyone to put aside any opposition he may feel to what is going on here, and I am grateful that everyone seems to be listening. In Europe and the United States, employees at Nissan are overjoyed because they're feeling that at last things are making sense to them culturally."

This sentiment was confirmed by Emil Hassan, Nissan's senior vice president of North American manufacturing. "I was at Ford for twelve years before I came here in 1981, and I've never seen anyone so focused on issues or so fast to process feedback and take action," he told me. "When Mr. Hanawa was here as president of Nissan North America, he had a terrible time getting Tokyo to listen to him and respond. Everything had to make its way up through the ranks at headquarters, and that could take years. It was three years after he signed off on it to get approval for the Deckerd plant so we could assemble engines here. And he never succeeded in persuading the company that we should go into the full-size pickup truck business even though he knew it was the right move. Ghosn asked us about it, and we had our truck plant in Canton, Mississippi, in less than a year! He puts you through the ringer with hard questions, and then he responds. It's a whole different ball game."

At my first meeting with Ghosn, in the fall of 2001, I asked in what ways Nissan had moved away from its past under his leadership. His fluent English has a French flavor with a touch of the Portuguese that is his mother tongue; he is cordial but focused — not a kidder — and unhesitating: "I have set simple priorities: we must become more profit-driven, customer-focused, and cross-functional, and we must capitalize on alliances and act from a sense of urgency — plain and simple! Because I have observed that the Japanese hate complexity. They like simple things that are very clear. As they are very process-oriented, they like steps that are clear and priorities that are outlined. They like to work in a predictable environment. So they hate complexity. In Japan you cannot miss it: make things simple!

"We have also introduced very important changes in execution: a lot of communication deployed throughout the company from top to bottom, quantifiable measurements, and fast reactions driven by urgency. The basic goal is to reestablish the company, not only profitability but our competitive power. And that requires a change of mindset from the past. We encourage people not to consider tradition as fatalistic. You can change things, as long as you know why you change them. I am never in a frenzy to change things at Nissan, only when I understand the purpose of the change and the commitment behind it. But whenever we think that a change is necessary, we make the change without any feeling, without any mixed emotions. We just do it."

The turnaround Ghosn is engineering gives rise to a difficult question with broad relevance for all of Japanese business in the current moment of crisis: whether the new mindset Ghosn described could have been achieved by the Japanese themselves, or whether the change required the bottom-line focus and rationality of a Westerner. Like much of what he has to say on the rare occasions when he chooses to generalize about Japan, Ghosn's reply was considered and assured and based on a harsh assessment: "I can't say whether Nissan would ever have been able to do something about its decline. I can only say they watched eight or nine years of it and didn't take the steps that we have taken. One reason they saw bad performance and failed to act may have been because they thought that even the remaining performance was sufficient. I would say based on my experience here that tolerance for bad performance is higher in a Japanese environment than in a U.S. or even a European environment."

Ghosn's implication was clear: he did not believe that Nissan could have transformed itself from the inside out. Fair enough, but what would happen to the company when he had left it? (According to rumors in Tokyo, Louis Schweitzer has told Ghosn that the top job at Renault is waiting for him as soon as he is ready to leave Nissan.) Wouldn't the Japanese go back to doing business in their sentimental way?

"That will depend on when I leave," he began with his signature certainty. "At the beginning, individuals are crucial to catalyzing change. But time will work against the company's overdependency on one man or one style. If I left today it would damage the company. Three to four years from now I will feel comfortable. There will be a whole generation of people who have been promoted to positions of responsibility inside the context of these criteria. That will allow Nissan to have its own personality. A changed culture but retaining its Japanese roots. Ten years more here would be too long. Every company must disconnect from a particular individual or style. When you take a medicament, you must first absorb it, then it delivers its full benefit to your body, and then you must reject it!"

Hanawa's response to the same sort of question — Might Nissan have renewed itself and what would happen to the company after Carlos Ghosn's departure? — was more complex: "If you ask other Japanese companies, they'll tell you, 'We don't need an outsider, we can do it ourselves,' and some of them may be right. We didn't want to take this route either, but our circumstances got so bad — I should say we let them get so bad before we noticed that we were still living the good life even though times had changed — that we had little choice. I tried to change our course, but it was tough for two reasons. First of all, I grew up at Nissan, and there was no way I could have turned the company upside down and retained any credibility with the people who have been with me here for forty years. But the bigger problem was that I grew up in Japanese culture, and I simply couldn't rid myself entirely of our system and be all business in the same way Ghosn-san is. I lived in the United States for a number of years, and I would watch Americans deal and do business and think, Wow! This is fantastic! But I could never do things their way one hundred percent the way Ghosn-san does. There were limits to how far I could go."

Clearly, Ghosn was free to change the company as he saw fit, without cultural constraints, but what would happen to Nissan when Ghosn was gone? Would it remain a "Western" organization?

"We are learning from Ghosn-san how to conduct business logically and dispassionately. We understand the necessity of becoming more logical and unemotional. But we have a culture of our own, and if you ask me I must tell you I don't believe that we will ever be as dry as Ghosn can be because that is not the culture we have grown up in. Right now we are learning Western methods from Carlos. But when the lessons are over we won't be replicas of him. It's at that point that we must figure out how to blend what he has taught us with our ancestral wisdom as Japanese in order to be strong again. I think our challenge now is to devise a way of competing in the world as Japanese with our own Japanese culture as a starting point. That is not something we can learn from a foreigner."

Outside Nissan, business leaders are skeptical about the Carlos Ghosn revolution and what it implies. "It remains to be seen whether what Ghosn is doing is correct," said the chairman of Mitsubishi Trading Company, Minoru Makihara, in his perfect English. "When I was the CEO here, I introduced a merit system, but people are still evaluated more or less according to seniority. My hope is that there will be a gradual change so there will be more competition within the company and more freedom to move elsewhere if people are unhappy. But we reward loyalty and should continue to do so because loyalty is a fundamental virtue in our society. And people still prefer job security to fast-track promotion. I have heard there is a lot of discontent at Nissan. There has to be a happy balance."

Tadahiro Sekimoto, the chairman emeritus of NEC Corporation, was harsher. "The so-called Nissan turnaround is a product of attitudes and ways of behaving that are irreconcilable with our society and culture. It's what I call copycat management. Peter Drucker tells us short-term gains are what matter in postcapitalism, so we cut back on R and D. We take huge write-offs and tell ourselves we're clearing the way for progress. We create an unnatural separation between oversight of the business and execution of the business. We ignore seniority, which means ignoring loyalty, and we lay people off left and right. Copycat management!

"In Japan, we manage from the position that the business is a legacy that must survive forever. That isn't necessarily the governing commitment in the United States. Businesses are bought and sold at a profit. It happens here, too: but generally speaking, we don't build businesses up so that we can harvest them and put money in the shareholders' pockets. We manage a business as a legacy. But Nissan today is all about short-term gains. To achieve that they dumped all their bad assets and many they didn't have to dump, and wrote off a huge loss. But that's something you can't do over and over again, and Ghosn knows that. He doesn't intend to stay around that long."

Sekimoto was emphatic that, once Ghosn was gone, over time, Nissan would revert to the Japanese way of doing things: "We are not inherently dry and rational. When I was sent to the United States for the first time, I was asked to build a new department of modulation technique, the forerunner of digital technology. I was a nobody, Dr. T. Sekimoto, a funny-looking Japanese man who spoke broken English. But in two years I built the largest department in the organization, thirty engineers and twenty consultants, and they were begging me to stay. My secret was *heart-to-heart* communication. When I returned to Japan and became president of NEC, I explained my philosophy of management. The reality we deal with is a weave of chance happenings and fundamental necessities. People encounter one another and take on the responsibilities of their jobs inside that reality. And people have passion that comes from the heart. Japanese management is about igniting that passion. Our fundamental yardstick is whether that passion in each individual ignites or doesn't. We are about nurturing individuals and making their hearts beat passionately. If every Japanese company took the Nissan approach to solving its problems, Japan would fall apart."

At the height of his power, until he resigned as chairman of the organization that he had built into a semiconductor giant, Sekimoto was known as a cunning tactician and a fierce competitor who ruled with an iron hand. Not surprisingly, he was an accomplished player of the strategy game *go* who took pleasure in crushing those he challenged in his inner circle and an avid weekend golfer. His executives disliked playing with him because of his habit of striding down the fairway after his ball with no regard for those playing behind him. As he moved briskly through his crowded business day, in and out of meetings, he was always accompanied by a retinue of assistants who were hard put to keep pace with him, retainers who feared his agile mind and sharp tongue but respected him unquestioningly and, as it seemed to me, would have sacrificed their lives, or certainly their careers, in order to protect him. Observing him in action always made me feel as if I were watching a feudal lord.

I asked Sekimoto to explain his vision of the proper way to compete in the turbulent world of the twenty-first century. He emphasized the importance of regaining what he called "our Japanese mentality." He sounded paternal, as though he were still speaking as the head of the NEC family: "I built a business here with seventy billion dollars in sales and healthy profits, and we did what was needed in order to win. We were tough on ourselves and tough on our suppliers. Up to a point! In the West, you have a hunters' culture, but we are a society of farmers: no matter how severe the times and the circumstances, as an agrarian society, we do everything we can inside the unit of the village to allow everyone to survive and if possible to flourish. More and more, particularly among the younger generation, there are those who will leave the village. But our culture inclines us to remain loyal and dedicated."

I wondered whether increasing job mobility wouldn't erode the loyalty that traditionally has been an engine driving productivity?

"Even if you leave NEC, your NEC number stays on your uniform," Sekimoto explained, invoking a sports analogy. "In the United States, you have no number, so Lee Iacocca can move from General Motors and become the chairman of Chrysler. You won't see that happening here, not in my lifetime. You won't see the chairman of Fujitsu becoming the chairman of NEC. It's true that younger people consider their options in a way that's hard for us to understand. Even our president thinks it's normal for a competent man to change jobs three or four times in the course of his career. That's American thinking. He's a perfect example of a copycat manager."

As of February 2003, Nissan continues to thrive under the leadership of Carlos Ghosn, who is the subject of three bestselling biographies in Japan and has been installed as a hero of Japanese business recovery. The question remains: Is Nissan an anomaly, as many Japanese business leaders insist, or will Japan's reemergence as a global competitor require the radical changes in corporate culture that Ghosn has brought to Nissan? Ghosn's success and similar kinds of change occurring across Japanese business today suggest that some degree of detachment from traditional values and practices will be required if Japanese business is to revitalize. The challenge will be to install American pragmatism uncomplicated by sentimental — familial — considerations while preserving the loyalty and selfless dedication to ensuring the success of the group which has fueled Japan's productivity in the postwar era. Most people in any organization are ordinary. The lesson at the heart of Japan's postwar recovery is that ordinary

Japanese can be inspired by the comfort and deep gratification of feeling identified with the group to overachieve in surprising ways. Can that sense of identification survive in a business environment in which job security is contingent on earnings and individual performance is the sole basis for success? Or will dedication gradually erode to be replaced by the resentment and alienation that are so familiar in the American workplace? Here again, as in other domains of Japanese society, viability in the twenty-first century requires a complex balance between traditional and Western values and practices.

Notwithstanding Ghosn's success, it is unlikely in the long run that a stranger to the culture will be in the best position to engineer the synthesis required. To be sure, Ghosn has been free to mandate change without the constraint of sentimental ties to the organization, which Hanawa encountered. Nobuyuki Idei continues to experience the difficulty of balancing his convictions against the expectations of others who have grown up with him at Sony: the need to handle those of his predecessor Norio Ohga's vassals, who remain in the organization, even when they attempt to enlist Ohga's aid in opposing him. Nevertheless, Idei has succeeded impressively in achieving his vow to "drag Sony out of the shadow of Akio Morita's sentimentalism." And there are other examples of companies that are being transformed without major disruption. Shinsei Bank, for example, has been rebuilt on an American model by a CEO, Masamoto Yashiro, who comes to his job from careers at Exxon, Mobil Oil, and Citibank.

Ultimately, the task of finding a viable, competitive balance between inherent strengths and imported attitudes and practices will fall to the younger generation of Japanese just now embarking on corporate careers. I spoke recently with a group of seniors at Waseda University who were in the stressful process of applying for jobs. One young man was elated at having just received news that he had been accepted at Sony. "My father is a one-company man, and I intend to build a lifelong career at Sony," he told me unhesitatingly. "I hate the idea of downsizing, but I understand it may be necessary to survival. And I'm not afraid to be judged on the basis of what I contribute and not simply on how long I've been around. I think what counts is the commitment to stick it out through good and bad times. You don't walk away from your family when there's trouble."

As I listened to this young man, it was clear to me that he was imbued with respect for the group and well understood the value of belonging and at the same time was open to a rational consideration of economic reality and what was required to cope with it. As I listened, I recalled that the prime movers in the Meiji Restoration were younger samurai with a similar respect for tradition and an eager openness to new and however alien ways of thinking. Nissan's chairman, Yoshikazu Hanawa, had made the connection to me explicitly: "It's as though we had returned to the Meiji period, like businessmen in samurai topknots and Savile Row suits! It's confusing and painful, but it's also exhilarating!"

4

The Entrepreneurs

❖

THERE IS ONE SECTOR of Japanese business that is neither enervated nor despondent: Japan's young entrepreneurs convey vitality, excitement, and hopefulness about the future. They cluster in outlying areas of Tokyo where space is cheaper; the atmosphere in their undecorated, crowded offices crackles with their energy. Some live their lives according to Honolulu or New York or London time, the better to seize new opportunities at the moment they appear. All are characterized by a fearless, unstoppable determination to launch themselves against the force exerted in Japanese society by the group.

Between 1993 and 2002, 990 start-up companies, mostly related to IT and the Internet, went public. Japan seems to be less market-sensitive than the United States. In 2002, fewer than thirty public offerings made their way to the NASDAQ board in the United States, while Japan's three new company exchanges, JASDAQ, Mothers, and Hercules (formerly NASDAQ, Japan) grew by 112 new IPOs. Most of these companies were overvalued, and their inflated stock prices quickly plummeted.

Funding for what the Japanese call "venture business" has

come from angels, bank loans secured with personal guarantees, and large IT companies and trading firms such as Mitsui and Mitsubishi. In response to the surge in entrepreneurial activity, a venture capital infrastructure began to appear in the early nineties. The emerging industry is modeled on Silicon Valley, but Japanese venture capitalists tend to be less aggressive than their American counterparts, who customarily replace founders with seasoned businessmen and become involved in company management. According to Joi Ito, the thirty-six-year-old founder and president of Neoteny, Inc., an IT company incubator, "Japanese VCs have difficulty with the assumption that they have the right to manage a company because they have funded it, and that reticence has created big problems. In my view, if you don't know how to run a business you shouldn't be funding it."

It is tempting to assume that the breakdown of the social contract between the organization and the company man has provided an impetus to individual entrepreneurs. There is no question that a number of capable and ambitious men and women in business have been prompted by the erosion of the traditional guarantee of a lifetime career to leave their organizations and found their own businesses. The former CEO of foundering Intel Japan, for example, Ikuo Nishioka, left the company to found his own venture capital firm.

But Japan's entrepreneurs have not emerged from the ranks of the unemployed. Expulsion from the embrace of a corporate family is a terrible blow to confidence and self-esteem. And beneath the rationalizations about economic circumstances, it is invariably perceived as a personal failure and a cause for deep shame. Besides, even if his energy and confidence were undamaged, a man who has chosen to devote his life to an affiliation with an organization and is accustomed to the security of belonging is unlikely to possess the rebellious mettle he would need to strike out on his own.

In 1984, at age nineteen, Yuichiro Itakura dropped out of

Sophia University to start his first business, Zap, a computer gameware company. In 1991, he founded Hypernet, providing free access to the Internet, and grew its value meteorically. In 1996, he was named "Entrepreneur of the Year" by the Ministry of Commerce and Industry and received a visit from Bill Gates to discuss an alliance. On Christmas Eve 1997, Hypernet went bankrupt, and three months later Itakura filed for personal bankruptcy. Shunned by the business community, ashamed to face his friends, and seeking an outlet for his stymied energy, Itakura wrote a book detailing his debacle, *Disqualified As a CEO*, and a sequel, *How I Destroyed Myself.* Japanese society is cruelly unforgiving of failure. Readers expected self-recrimination from Itakura, and he did not disappoint them, blaming his failure on arrogance and complacency and dissoluteness. In his preface to the second volume, he described his feelings on handing out a new business card bearing only his name and no credentials: "One man stared at my card for a minute and then said awkwardly, 'It's as if you were a politician.' My heart sank in shame."

In the United States, entrepreneurs who succeed and even those who fail heroically are admired for their courage and resourcefulness: Steve Jobs, the founder of Apple, or Fred Smith, who founded Federal Express, both college dropouts, are legendary figures. But the Japanese view loners in general and entrepreneurs in particular with uneasiness and disapproval. In response to the proposition "People you know respect those starting a new business," only 25 percent of the Japanese polled responded positively, versus 85 percent of Americans. Asked whether fear of failure would prevent them from starting a business, 70 percent of Japanese answered "yes" while 80 percent of Americans replied "no!" In Japan, forgoing affiliation with a group and assuming the risk of individual failure and all its social consequences requires an extraordinary resoluteness. Japanese entrepreneurs tend to be not only mavericks but quintessential outsiders who have never fit in or even cherished the hope of belonging.

Masayoshi Son, forty-five, founder and chairman of Softbank, a holding company that was valued at its peak in 1999 at $115 billion, is a prime example. Son is an ethnic Korean, the third generation of a Korean family that had been brought to Japan in chains to work in labor camps between 1910 and 1945 when Korea was a Japanese colony. The nearly 700,000 Koreans now residing in Japan, mostly descendents of conscripted laborers like Son's forebears, live at the periphery of Japanese society, angry and unassimilated. Son's avowed determination to become "Japan's top businessman" certainly includes a measure of defiance. If he appears unburdened by Japanese insularity in his business dealings, it is partly because he grew up a foreigner in what to him was a cultural no man's land.

Son was born and grew up in the city of Fukuoka on the southernmost Japanese island of Kyushu. His father and uncles owned pachinko parlors, a business dominated by ethnic Koreans, and were, by his own account, relatively well-to-do. In the spring of his fifteenth year, he claims to have read a book that changed his life, *The Exploits of Ryoma Sakamoto* (*Ryoma Wa Iku*), Ryotaro Shiba's historical novel based on the exploits of a samurai who lived during the tumultuous mid-nineteenth century when Japan was thrown open to the West and who became a central figure in the downfall of the feudal government that paved the way for the Meiji Restoration. Sakamoto was from the Tosa fief in Kyushu, on the periphery of feudal society, and was driven by a sense of otherness, which may have accounted in part for his appeal to Son's imagination. But Son was moved principally by Ryoma's impact on the course of Japan's history despite the fact that his brief life ended at thirty-two. "Until I read *Ryoma*, I was just a regular kid who enjoyed soccer and baseball and got good grades," he told me in his fluent English. "But that book made me realize that life is limited. I couldn't believe that I was staying in Japan just peacefully, nothing extraordinary, with a nice family environment, without challenging myself. Ryoma wanted to go abroad, but he passed away before he had the chance. I was still alive, so why didn't I continue his life in his footsteps? I decided at that moment that I was going to determine my own destiny."

In the summer of 1973, Son enrolled in a one-month course in English for foreign high school students at the University of California, Berkeley, campus. "Other kids were having fun. For me, seeing shopping malls, and BART [Bay Area Rapid Transit], and highways and skyscrapers was overwhelming. I thought to myself, I have to know all this much deeper." Returning to Japan, Son gave formal notice to his high school that he was dropping out and stunned his family by announcing that he was going to live and study in the United States. His father, who was ill with cirrhosis at the time, heard the news from Son's weeping mother and two brothers in the hospital. "He didn't oppose me because he knew my character, that I would go no matter what. All he said was, 'Why make him wash dishes to support himself!' and then he gave me the money I needed to live abroad."

Son returned to California and was admitted as a sophomore at Serramonte High School in Daly City. Two weeks into the year, he asked to be promoted to junior because the work was too simple. A few weeks later he persuaded the principal to accelerate him a second time, into the senior class. When he appeared again to request a recommendation for college, the principal balked. Son took and passed a high school equivalency exam and was admitted to Holy Names College, where he was on the dean's list for two years, and then he transferred to UC Berkeley and majored in economics. Before he graduated, he had designed and patented a keyboard pocket computer and had sold it to Sharp for $1 million. He used the money to found Softbank in 1981 when he was twenty-three. It was at that point that he dropped the Japanese surname his father had adopted, Yasumoto, and reclaimed the family's Korean name.

Within a few years, Son built Softbank into Japan's leading distributor of PC software and computer magazines. In 1994, he raised $140 million with a public offering. He subsequently bought the Comdex trade-show group for $803 million and paid $3 billion for Ziff Davis's computer magazines and trade shows.

In 1995, Son discovered the Internet. He raised $170 million from investors in the United States and began acquiring Internet services. He paid $100 million for a 33 percent stake in Yahoo! just before it went public and was one of the earliest investors in the online brokerage E-Trade. He went on to acquire 8 percent of the publicly listed value of all Internet properties in the world with a total investment of $1.7 billion that by 1999 was worth an estimated $26 billion. By early 2000, Softbank controlled 80 percent of the Internet portal traffic in Japan, including Yahoo! Japan, and Son had created a venture capital pool of $1.2 billion, which he used to acquire, among other things, a controlling interest in NASDAQ, Japan.

Meeting Son is a surprise: he is a wisp of a man, mild in manner to a degree that is almost feminine and ever so softly spoken. The day we met at Softbank's world headquarters he had just returned from six weeks of traveling back and forth on his Gulfstream between Tokyo and the United States, Argentina and Brazil, Seoul and Beijing. He kept me waiting for thirty minutes of the hour I had been allotted. When he finally appeared he told me apologetically that he had only fifteen or twenty minutes to spare because he was leaving in the morning for Moscow and had meetings backed up all day and into the night. In fact he gave me twenty-seven minutes, and until he stood up and left the room unceremoniously he appeared entirely composed and focused and even relaxed; the unstoppable engine that drives him was nowhere in evidence. I asked what it was that did drive him: Was it money or fame or power, for example? "It's a mixture of many things. I wanted to make my life worthwhile. My father and uncles all made some money. But I never thought they were happy or proud. What excites me is changing people's lifestyle, doing something big! My heroes in Japan are Honda, Matsushita, and

Morita, but did they really change the lifestyle of the world? Did they invent the automobile or electricity? There are not many things that Japanese companies or Asian companies have made that have had such a dramatic impact on mankind — that's not the level that Asians have achieved. And that's the kind of thing that I would like to do!"

I wondered whether this assessment implied that he was identified with Japan as a nation, whether, like Sony's Akio Morita, he was a patriot? "I love Japan very much. And I love the United States. I feel sick when people say something bad about the United States or Americans — you don't know the United States so how can you criticize? But when people say bad things about Japan I feel sick again. Same way with Korea and China. We have six hundred nine companies, and more than half of them are outside Japan. We have many employees and partners and friends all around the world. Any people are great!"

I pointed out that even Japanese businessmen like Morita who appeared to be true cosmopolitans had often found their dealings with foreigners uncomfortable, and I asked whether Son considered himself truly borderless. His answer illuminated his vision of a changing world and how he sees himself inside it: "The twenty-first century will be borderless. The improvement in communication using the Internet will result in a global community. People who are connected to the Internet and those who aren't will have greater differences than those of different nationalities: the digital divide will be a more significant chasm than anything geographical."

The global debacle of the Internet industry hurt Softbank badly. In mid-2001, Son began selling off — or writing off — large portions of his Internet portfolio around the world in a desperate effort to keep the company afloat, including a share of his interest in Yahoo! Japan. He also closed offices in the United States and Europe, and merged unprofitable businesses. Investors were defecting from the company, the stock was trading at $20, down 99 percent from its high in 1999, and Son's accounting practices were being questioned. In November 2001, Softbank announced a loss of $437 million for the preceding six months, its largest deficit to date, and J. P. Morgan lowered its rating to "market under-performer." Pointing to a sharp rise in interest costs and deterio-rating cash flow, analysts questioned the company's ability to ser-vice its debts.

Without breaking stride, declaring that "broadband was the future of the Internet," Son became the leading investor in Yahoo! BB, a joint venture to provide broadband Internet access in Ja-pan. But it is far from clear that he will succeed with the new ven-ture. According to one investment banker in Tokyo, "Softbank's credibility is close to zero at this point. I don't think many people are ready to believe they have a first-mover advantage in broad-band."

Son has been at pains to appear undeterred. At an analysts meeting he dismissed the company's problems as "just accounting stuff" and insisted that Softbank was well positioned to benefit from the Internet as long as it continued to grow. "This is only the first chapter in our scenario," he told analysts. "We have up to six chapters that I am preparing now." Son has often said that his business vision for Softbank extends three hundred years into the future. Such a claim would be laughable coming from someone else, but there is little question that Son is a genuine visionary, notwithstanding his current trouble.

The younger generation of entrepreneurs acknowledges that Son played a pioneering role in developing Japan's venture cap-ital market but seems to be ambivalent about his motives. Said one, "I think he's mercenary for sure, but that doesn't mean he has no humanitarian feelings. I think he's very complex. He has definitely had an impact on our society, but not necessarily in a good way." A second new company founder was more specific: "He has contributed a lot to changing the traditional structure, so I give a lot of credit to him. But at the same time, there is something about the way he runs his business that feels unclean to me."

In the first quarter of 2003, Son launched a frontal attack for broadband market share against NTT-DoCoMo, Japan's AT&T. His sales campaign and pricing were so successful that many modem retailers have become Yahoo! BB dealers exclusively. NTT struck back with a campaign of its own aimed specifically at Yahoo! BB. The price war that resulted has reduced the cost of broadband access to the Internet in Japan to the lowest in the world. Some observers predict that the two companies will destroy each other, but everyone agrees that the consumer will be the beneficiary of Son's determination to win.

Tomoko Namba and her good friend Oki Matsumoto both left brilliant careers at large organizations to launch their own businesses, and they epitomize the courage and determination of Tokyo's younger entrepreneurs. Namba grew up in Niigata Prefecture, a dark, rural area in the snow country far to the north of Tokyo which has always been a conservative bastion of tradition. She went to Niigata High School and then, at her father's insistence, to Tsuda College in Tokyo, a conservative school for young women from good families whose graduates are known to have superior English skills and have traditionally been considered ideal wives for young diplomats embarking on international careers. Namba spent her senior year at Bryn Mawr because she wanted to hone her English, but she had no intention of putting it to use at dinner parties. By her own account, she was tough, ambitious, and very stubborn. "My father was furious when he learned I was going to Bryn Mawr; he flew to Tokyo and nearly choked my Tsuda professor. He said he had already gone too far by allowing me to come to Tokyo alone and that sending me across the Pacific was out of the question. Professor Suzuki talked with him for hours to persuade him to let me go. He even lied, saying that there were no boys on the Bryn Mawr campus."

When she graduated from Tsuda in 1986, Namba went straight to work at McKinsey Japan, which was run by the management guru Ken'ichi Ohmae. For two years she got by on three hours of sleep a night, determined to prove that she was worth the same money as a man. In 1988, exhausted, she asked Ohmae to let her go to the Harvard Business School, and he became angry. "He shouted at me and said I would be betraying the company and him personally if I left now after they had taught me so much. Ohmae hated business schools. I shouted back. I told him I had done as much for the firm as they had done for me and that I was not going to allow him to make me feel guilty. I was very angry, too. The only female senior partner at McKinsey in those days persuaded me that I shouldn't burn my bridges with Ohmae even if it meant lying a little. So I wrote him a long letter; I apologized for having talked back, I expressed my gratitude, and I said I really wanted to come back later. I was lying, but it certainly worked: he invited me to his office and asked whether I would need a car in Cambridge and told me to ask him for anything I needed. He can be rude, but he's actually quite a nice guy."

Namba went to Harvard and earned her M.B.A. (despite, she claims, sleeping through most of her classes). When she graduated in 1990 she received offers from Goldman Sachs and First Boston, but her mother was ill and she wanted to be in Japan. A director from McKinsey flew to Boston and hired her back on the spot. Between 1990 and 1998 she worked with McKinsey's high-profile telecommunications accounts, helping them develop and launch multimedia and Internet businesses. In 1994, at age thirty-four, she became the youngest partner in her group.

The idea for an online auction business had first occurred to her at Harvard, where she was surprised to notice that even wealthy students were interested in buying secondhand furniture for their apartments. "There are no garage sales in Japan," she told me, "because the Japanese find it hard to take money from their neighbors. But we are economically rational people who don't like to throw things away. Still, face-to-face negotiation is always difficult."

By January 1999, working at night and on weekends, she had developed a business plan of her own, and in March she informed the new head of McKinsey Japan, Masao Hirano, that she wanted to leave again, this time for good, to start her own business. Hirano asked her to stay another twelve months to support him in his first year as head of the organization and agreed to let her go in March 2000. Impatient to get started, Namba left the company in August 1999. Her parents and friends tried to stop her from going out on her own, but she was determined. "I had been a consultant for too long," she explained. "I was tired of designing businesses at a desk for someone else without ever having a chance to execute them. And I really believed in my business model; I was very clear that I really wanted to do this. There is nothing stopping a woman in striking out on her own in Japan anymore except her upbringing. We have to force our way past that."

In November 1999, Namba founded a new Internet company, DeNA (pronounced "DNA") and launched Bidders.co.jp., an online auction house that focused its marketing campaign on women, advertising in women's magazines, and differentiated itself by speed, announcing successful bids within twenty-four hours. Her initial paid-in capital was $1.5 million, $500,000 of her own money and $500,000 each from the Sony Communication Network, Sony's Internet provider, and the Recruit Company. "Recruit wanted 67 percent of the company," Namba recalled with a smile, "but I said, 'No way, we're each in for a third, and since it's my idea please give me 34 percent,' and they both agreed." In two subsequent rounds of funding, Namba has raised an additional $24 million from four new investors, including both Mitsubishi and Sumitomo trading companies.

In February 2001, Namba added a new site to DeNA, O-ikura, ("How Much Is That?"), an online recycling shop that connects individual buyers and sellers with three thousand secondhand shops and thrift stores. DeNA takes a transaction fee and charges the stores to register with the service. The company also provides ASPs, application service platforms, to smaller Internet businesses.

As of March 31, 2003, DeNA had 1.65 million registered users, an increase of 170 percent over the previous fiscal year; employed seventy full-time staff; and was in the black, "modestly profitable." Namba's aggressive plan is to double again the company's size by the end of fiscal 2003 in March 2004. Would that mean she would have to lease a space larger than the two floors in a small building where DeNA is currently housed? "I think I can fit more people in. There is a Ping-Pong table that will have to go."

I wondered how her father was feeling about her new career. "We're close again," she said with a smile. "He calls me to ask me to translate letters he receives from a foreign girlfriend. If I'm in a meeting or wherever I am, it doesn't matter — he expects me to translate. I suppose he deserves that. After all, he is my father."

Oki Matsumoto is known to his friends, including Namba, as Don Quixote. In 1998, he left Goldman Sachs at the age of thirty-five to found Monex, an online investment brokerage that has already become the third largest in the country, after Nomura and Daiwa. (Monex, the word *money* with one letter change, is modeled on the perverse computer HAL — or IBM, with each of its letters shifted one place in the alphabet — in Matsumoto's favorite movie, Stanley Kubrick's *2001: A Space Odyssey*.) Matsumoto entered Goldman in 1990 after a year at Salomon Brothers and became a star by taking the company into lucrative derivative swaps based on the fluctuating yen interest rate. In October 1994, he was promoted to partner at the age of thirty-one, the youngest in Goldman's history and, as he told me proudly in English, the only partner except for Marcus Goldman who was never educated in an English-speaking country.

In September 1998, Matsumoto presented a proposal for an

online securities subsidiary, arguing the potential size of the retail market and pointing out that individual investors in Japan had more equity than debt. The response was negative: Goldman was a corporate broker and had no interest in retail. Early in November, as Goldman was planning a public offering that would have put millions of dollars in his pocket, Matsumoto announced his decision to leave the firm. "My American colleagues told me I was fucking crazy," he told me gleefully.

Matsumoto has in common with Namba an affability that conceals fierce rebelliousness in a society that still values conformity, and a restless, indomitable determination to succeed. One of his teachers at the Catholic school he attended through the sixth grade remembers him as the most precocious and unruly student he ever taught. A prodigy in science and math — "it was like having two teachers in the classroom," his instructor recalled — he showed no interest in anything else and was constantly disrupting the lesson by talking or wandering around. Asked whether he intended to continue at the school, he replied, "Only God can read the future," and was asked to leave. In high school he considered becoming a physicist but changed his mind when he learned that Niels Bohr had distinguished himself by the time he was eighteen. He was accepted into the law department at Tokyo University but hated going to classes and considered himself an outsider. In the summer of his junior year he enrolled in a summer session at Tufts in Boston and moved into a dormitory. "I couldn't make myself understood in English, and it drove me crazy," he told me. He left after two weeks, determined to master the language. His English is now fluent.

When he walked out of Goldman Sachs, Matsumoto had no experience with retail business and admits he had no idea where he would find funding to start one. One night in the last week of November, as he was cleaning out his office at Goldman, an older friend whom he declines to name phoned to invite him to a Japanese restaurant on the Ginza where he was having dinner with

Sony's chairman, Nobuyuki Idei. That night, Matsumoto pitched Idei his vision for Monex for two hours. His premise was a shift in the assets of individual investors from indirect investments in banks crippled by bad loans and the postal savings system to direct investments in stocks and bonds. There was plenty of money around: while the Nikkei exchange had dropped 35 percent since the bubble burst in 1990, the economy was much fatter than that suggested; Japan's GDP was, after all, still $5 trillion. Senior citizens alone, who own 50 percent of Japan's individual assets, receive $350 billion annually in social security payments, money that they save in the bank or the post office. There were plenty of resources; the problem was confidence. At that time, only 8 percent of Japan's private money was invested in stocks as compared to 50 percent in the United States. Matsumoto predicted that by 2005, 70 percent of Japan's individual investors, 75 million potential clients, would have their money in the stock market. By then, 87 million people between the ages of fifteen and seventy-five are expected to be using the Internet. Moreover, as Japan's work force continued to shrink, women and seniors would be increasingly mobilized in the absence of an immigrant population (due to a restrictive immigration policy) and there would be less time available for going to the bank. Online investing was bound to increase dramatically, and so was the demand for other banking services on the Internet. Matsumoto's plan included a credit card, the first of its kind in Japan, that would allow investors to deposit or withdraw cash at ATMs against the money in their investment accounts. Ultimately, Monex would replace conventional financial institutions and transform itself into an alternative bank designed to service a new era. Investing in the company, he told Idei, was "like buying a put on Japanese structural changes."

Two weeks later, Matsumoto received an invitation to join Idei for Japanese breakfast at the Hotel Okura. In an impulsive move that recalled the style of his mentor, Akio Morita, Idei invited Matsumoto to bring his idea for Monex to Sony as a full-time employee. Matsumoto declined Idei's offer but said he hoped Sony would see fit to become involved one way or another.

In December 1998, Matsumoto rented an office with three others from the same friend who had introduced him to Idei and set to work on his business plan. At the end of January, Sony called to say it was prepared to do a joint venture if Matsumoto would agree to taking 33 percent to Sony's 67 percent. Matsumoto declined again. That night he was getting himself drunk at a bar when Idei telephoned at 11:00 P.M. from the World Economic Forum in Davos, Switzerland, to say that he had heard what had happened and that Sony was still interested.

Early in April, Matsumoto was invited to present his business plan once again, this time to the management committee that makes Sony's important decisions before they go to the board. Following his fifteen-minute presentation, Idei asked him to remain in the room for the discussion. Ken Kutaragi, the creator of the chip for PlayStation, said the business plan was laughable; Sony should either take full ownership or limit its interest to 20 percent. Tamotsu Iba, the former CFO, was similarly unimpressed and wondered why Sony needed Matsumoto for such a venture. Minoru Morio, Sony's head of technology development, pointed out that Sony had created its own life insurance company by itself. Sensing mounting opposition, Matsumoto looked to Idei for support but got no response. What he may not have known was that the naysayers at the meeting were the old guard from the era of Sony's former CEO Norio Ohga who have continued to oppose Idei in many of the changes he has proposed. In fact, Idei had decided to give Matsumoto what he wanted, but first he had some maneuvering to do lest the opposition go to Ohga, now Sony's honorary chairman. Biding his time, Idei said only, "There may be some things we aren't best at."

Three days later, Sony agreed to a joint venture in which Matsumoto retained a controlling 51 percent interest in Monex. On August 25, 1999, Matsumoto announced the official launch of

Monex at a press conference. Without consulting Idei, he had paid a fee for exterior space directly to the management of the Sony Building at the center of the downtown district known as the Ginza — the site of the original Maxim's that Morita had imported from France and liked to use as his executive dining room, and one of the company's most visited showrooms — and had hung a banner three floors high on which the brand-new Monex logo was inscribed within the embrace of the Sony logo, the most famous trademark in the world. Matsumoto also included the Sony logo in the press kit. Idei was embarrassed but showed up at the press conference nonetheless, the first and only time he has ever appeared at such an occasion. Sitting next to Matsumoto, he held up the press kit photo and declared somewhat grimly, "It appears that we have been taken over by Mr. Matsumoto. We hope he'll grow robustly using Sony as a launching platform."

The media were impressed by Idei's attendance, but what everyone was waiting to hear was the commission that Monex would be charging. One month earlier, a brokerage operation that belonged to Sumitomo Bank, DLJ, had announced a commission of $16.50 per transaction up to $87,000, 20 percent of the previous market rate. ORIX, Inc., had just lowered its rate to $15.60. Monex would charge a commission fee of $8.70 up to $87,000, one tenth of the going rate. Matsumoto explained that it was his intention to create a "financial park with no entry fee."

Monex went public in February 2000; Sony was the leading shareholder with 32 percent, and Matsumoto himself the second with 18 percent. By the end of 2000, the company had 168,000 accounts, 34 percent of the online market.

Matsumoto had just returned from "Davos in New York" when I visited him in February 2002. By this time, Monex had 200,000 accounts; Matsumoto had just moved his headquarters to the eleventh floor of a new high-rise business building in central Tokyo. Seventy young men and women in casual clothing sat at long rows of desks in a single large room; the place looked and felt more like a publishing house for youth magazines than a financial brokerage. Matsumoto's desk was by itself at the front of the room, facing the rank and file. The only decoration in the room was a Shinto shrine installed on the wall behind him, a gift from his friend, Tomoko Namba, on the auspicious occasion of the move to new offices.

We sat down to talk in a small conference room on the other side of a glass wall. When I met him a year earlier, Matsumoto had shown up in jeans and a T-shirt, toting a backpack; this time he was more fashionable in a suit and black T-shirt. I was surprised when he summoned a young woman to take notes on our conversation in English from the far end of the room. In the year since we had met, he had become more corporate.

Matsumoto asked if I had seen Sony's memory-only Walkman and showed me the one he had with him. I knew that he shared Idei's love of gadgetry and liked to spend time browsing in the electronics outlet stores in Akihabara and reading brochures in coffee shops. The new Sony device delivered wonderful fidelity and could hold up to eleven hours of music, two hours at the highest quality. Today he had downloaded Beethoven's Sixth Symphony, Chick Corea, and Pink Floyd. "We're in a killer environment, and it's very stressful going up against Nomura and Daiwa. Music helps me keep my life light. We had a crisis here yesterday that I can't go into, but I went home at around midnight and drank sake and listened to some fusion jazz and I felt back to normal again. I was back in the office at six this morning like a new man."

Notwithstanding Japan's economic crisis, Matsumoto sounded confident that the asset shift at the heart of his business strategy would occur: "The Japanese have yet to develop much confidence in the stock market. They watch the Nikkei average every day as it drops, but it's like — you know the Japanese expression 'observing a fire on the other side of the river.' Capitalism is the basis of our society, but we have no real confidence in the system: it's as if the rule of capitalism is to punch with your bare fists, but we punch with gloves on.

"I'm counting on a growing appreciation of capitalism over time. That's the key variable. Do you know this concept?" Matsumoto chalked a Japanese word on the white board behind him — *fukakuteisei-genri*. I didn't recognize the term, but we found it in a dictionary: "the Heisenberg uncertainty principle. I know this country will move from point A, indirect investment and a distrust of direct investment, to point B, full-bore capitalism as represented by direct investment. I can't predict the path the transition will take or how long it will take to get there. But that doesn't matter. Assume it takes thirty years to close the forty-two percent gap between Japan and the United States. That's one-point-four percent of twelve trillion dollars, two hundred fifty billion dollars a year."

In Matsumoto's view, his principal challenge is to survive while the shift occurs. When I saw him last, Monex was losing roughly $1 million a month and had $70 million cash on hand, enough to stay in business for another six years. "That will be enough," Matsumoto assured me. "I've always had a horrible fear of failure. I wouldn't be doing this if I weren't sure we would succeed."

As of February 2003, Monex was still losing money, and Matsumoto was taking a beating in the business press and, privately, from Idei himself. Even so, his confidence appeared unshaken. I asked him for an update, and received the following e-mail:

> As for Monex, in the middle of historically one of the toughest markets, we are doing fine. We just started offering margin trading to our clients as of last December. We also started a stock-lending service to our retail clients as of this January. We borrow stocks from retail clients and lend them to someone like hedge funds to earn fees and split them with our clients. This is probably the first time such stock-lending has ever occurred on the globe. We keep being innovative!

As I write in the summer of 2003, ambitious men and women with business visions continue to leave corporate careers to strike out on their own. Masayoshi Son single-handedly created a venture capital infrastructure in Japan for the first time, and the success of younger entrepreneurs like Oki and Namba has kept it active and even robust: a determined entrepreneur with a promising business plan is likely to be funded. To be sure, the number of annual start-ups has declined since 2000: the failing economy makes it harder than ever to leave the relative security of employment at a major corporation. But venture capitalists like Joi Ito feel certain that rising unemployment will reinvigorate entrepreneurship. According to Ito, "When the larger companies begin going belly up, young people will be obliged to find ways of creating value with new businesses." Among those who are bold enough to leave their jobs even today, many are focused on China's burgeoning economy. "The Chinese are very upbeat these days," Ito told me, "entrepreneurial by nature and primed to take risks by the incredible growth of their economy. The lack of transparency keeps me wary of investing there, but others bolder than I, venture capitalists and entrepreneurs alike, are drawn to the promise China represents irresistibly. I wouldn't be at all surprised if our next wave of entrepreneurship, and the next wave is certainly building, will be about creating new ventures in China."

5

In Search of a Phantom

DURING THE 1970S AND 1980S, while Japan's economy was flourishing, identity was not an issue. People were secure in their jobs; hard work led to affluence. In general, the Japanese were able to feel that they were participating in and enjoying the benefits of a national effort to achieve the material well-being that the American way of life epitomized for them.

Since 1990, when the highflying economy crashed, confidence and pride and even sense of purpose have been eroded as the recession deepens, security is threatened, and the political leadership continues to demonstrate an inability to respond effectively to the crisis and, what is worse, moral bankruptcy. The illusion of pulling together, of belonging, has been shattered. What remains is a deeply unsettling emptiness that has produced, yet again, an urgent need to feel identified. Japan's new nationalism is a manifestation of that need and a response to it.

Japan's neonationalists hold out the promise of renewed pride and purpose through a reconnection with the unalloyed (and unpolluted) Japanese spirit as it existed in the traditional past, where it still waits to be rediscovered, before the country was pried open and turned away from itself and toward the West. When they speak of reidentification with *kokka,* the "state," they are referring to a notion that had its earliest vogue at the time of the Meiji Restoration, *kokutai,* a vague term that is sometimes translated as "national polity" but should probably be rendered as "national essence" or even "mystical body of Japan."

But what is the "Japanese spirit" as manifested by the "national essence," and what is the traditional past at the emotional center of the neonationalists' appeal? Inevitably, their argument focuses on the imperial court, on imperial culture, and on the emperor himself; underlying the rhetoric about the purity and power of the state is an idealization of the emperor as the embodiment and ultimate source of Japaneseness. This thinking amounts to investing the imperial tradition (and the person of the emperor) with a substantiveness that it never possessed. The emperor as conceived and held in the nationalist imagination is a fantasy; the traditional past in which the Japanese spirit resides is in fact a phantom past, a comforting fiction.

In the 1930s and early 1940s, the philosopher Kitaro Nishida, founder of the influential "Kyoto school," defined the opposition between being and nothingness as it applied in particular to Japanese culture and society. His thinking was a blend of Zen Buddhism and Hegel; his key concept was what he called *mu no basho,* "the place of nothingness," which he located in the imperial court. For centuries, the emperor had resided at Japan's center, defining and containing it, while actual power was in the hands of the feudal leaders known as shoguns. Nishida concluded that Japan's center was "a place of nothingness," an empty ground. In a sense, Japanese nationalism is an attempt to fill emptiness with emptiness.

In the mid-thirties, intellectuals and writers who had been imprisoned for subversive activity as communists converted in large numbers, often while they were still in prison, from Marxism to ultranationalism. In an essay written in 1941, Fusao Hayashi articulated the rationale that animated his own apostasy:

Marxism cannot possibly function as an everlasting support of the Japanese spirit. It is merely an arbitrary theory based on Western class society of the nineteenth century. It is an ideology, but it can never be a cause for which the [Japanese] people can joyfully die. . . . The foundation or support of national spirit must be discovered within the people. Tradition, the product of three thousand years of culture, is the only cause for which the people can die.

Hayashi and his comrades had established the basis for a new identity by converting their faith in Marxism to a faith in tradition. Into the nothingness at the center of Japan's past, they had projected purity, valor, and beauty as the quintessence of Japaneseness: in transforming the negative value of emptiness into positive substantiality, they had discovered "a cause worth dying for."

Hayashi and the other writers in his coterie called themselves the Japan Romantic school. Consciously or not, they were acknowledging that the traditional past they had conjured in their collective imagination was a richly embellished and death-ridden fantasy squarely in the romantic tradition. Small wonder that they joyously welcomed Yukio Mishima as a peer when they read his first full-length work of fiction, *The Forest in Full Flower*, published in 1941 when he was only sixteen. The world-weary (sixteen-year-old) narrator is consumed with longing for beauty, which he considers his birthright. He sees himself as the sole heir to a "tradition of beauty" that he is destined to inherit from his "noble ancestors." In him, the tradition will flower fully into a "song of blessing by the gods." At the tender age of sixteen, Mishima was already adept at confabulating a traditional past in which the imperial presence — "noble ancestors," a "song of blessing by the gods" — was the emanating source of beauty, and he had discovered in that beauty both the focus and the (destined) fulfillment of his longing. Already he was projecting positive values on the insubstantiality of nothingness. To the adults in the

Romantic school, it was clear that Mishima was already a romantic in full flower and, whether he realized it or not, a nationalist.

Mishima's oeuvre affords many examples of his struggle to fashion a traditional past from emptiness. In his essay "The Voice of the Hero Spirits" (1966), the ghosts of the young officers of the February Rebellion and the kamikaze pilots of World War II reproach the emperor for having betrayed them by declining to be a god:

> But if we ourselves are living gods, His Majesty above all must be a god. High on the ladder of gods His Majesty must shine for us. For in his divinity is the source of our imperishability, of the glory of our death, *the one and only thread connecting us to history. . .* [italics mine].
>
> Brave soldiers died because a god commanded them to go to war, and not six months after so fierce a battle had been halted instantly because a god had declared the fighting at an end, His Majesty announced, "Verily, we are a mortal man." Scarcely a year after we had fired ourselves like bullets at an enemy ship for our emperor who was a god. Why did the emperor become a man?

The martyrs' lament, delivered through a medium at a séance, is unironic: the suicide pilots understand that the emperor's declaration of mortality has rendered their deaths meaningless and pitiful, but they are unaware that the cause for which they died, the imperial presence, is itself a fiction, a projection on a void that has no inherent substance or meaning. A troubling question is whether Mishima himself was aware of this contradiction. In November 1970, when he appealed to a division of the Self-defense Force to rise up with him in the emperor's name and then killed himself by hara-kiri, did he believe he was manifesting the "Japanese spirit" as a substantive legacy from the past? What seems more likely is that he knew that the Japanese tradition he invoked and lived out was a fiction, a "place of nothingness," and that dying for a void was all the more beautiful.

In the domain of popular culture today, the demagogue cartoonist Yoshinori Kobayashi employs a skillful sleight of hand in the conjuring of a traditional past that is strikingly reminiscent of Mishima. I once asked Kobayashi if he had read Mishima and what he thought of him. "I've read a little, but I don't want to get into him. Critics sometimes bring him up when they're attacking me, and I don't want to be confused with him. Besides, he scares me."

To those who observe Japan's emergent nationalism with dismay, Kobayashi is more dangerous than Mishima ever was: the raw energy and vividness of his drawings put flesh on the bones of his inventions about the past, powerfully reinforcing the illusion of substance he works hard to create. Kobayashi's fiction about tradition, the state, and the Japanese spirit strikes his readers with the force of undeniable reality.

In 1991, Kobayashi began drawing a comic book series he called *The Arrogant-ism Proclamations* (Kobayashi appended the English suffix *-ism* to the Japanese word for *arrogance*). Known to his fans as "Arro-Procs," each installment was a seven-to-eight-page cartoon essay designed to shock readers into coming around to his iconoclastic point of view on a wide variety of subjects. Over the years, compiled in hardcover volumes and deluxe paperback editions, the *Arrogant-ism Proclamations* have sold more than 20 million volumes. Initially, Kobayashi's readers were high school and college students and men and women in their twenties and thirties. Since 1996, when his stance veered sharply to the right into ultranationalism, he has attracted a much broader readership, including middle managers and senior citizens.

The series was informed by the notion that arrogance was the only antidote powerful enough to rouse Japan from its subservience to foreign ideologies (communism and American liberalism) and foreign interests (Chinese and American), which Kobayashi savagely depicted as fawning and self-abusive. At the end of each installment, his cartoon avatar, Yoshi-rin, an idealized version of himself, asks readers a rhetorical question, *"Goman kamashite yoka desu ka?"* or "May I be arrogant?" The question is posed in the Hakata dialect of Kobayashi's native Kyushu, an affectation that underlines his position at the periphery of establishment society. In the final panel, Yoshi-rin delivers the moral of the fable. For example, in a November 2001 installment devoted to letters from fans which Kobayashi illustrated, a JAL stewardess recalls in silhouette an incident on a recent flight when she served a child's meal at a passenger's request. Children's meals are decorated with a paper Japanese flag, and the passenger in question happened to be Korean. In the next panel, a Korean woman with a huge mouth is berating the kewpie-doll stewardess: "We lost our appetite when we saw this Japanese flag! Apologize!" In silhouette again, the stewardess explains that she would have fallen over herself apologizing until "arrogant-ism" had set her thinking straight. Kobayashi cuts to the stewardess, a poisonous grin on her face, taunting the terrorized, perspiring Korean passenger: "When a Japanese athlete wins a gold medal at the Olympics, do you feel bad when they salute our rising-sun flag? There's a rising sun on the wings of this airplane, too; if it makes you feel bad why don't you get off here — not that we have any parachutes." *May I be arrogant?* Yoshi-rin inquires: "Tactfully turning around juvenile and malignant expressions of anti-Japanese sentiment is the least we can expect from any Japanese with pride and mettle!"

Kobayashi began his career as a best-selling cartoonist for high school and college students. He made his debut in 1975 at the age of twenty-two, about to graduate from Fukuoka University in Kyushu, with a series called *Todai Ittchokusen,* or "The Attack on Tokyo U," a satire on the "entrance exam hell" that was becoming an issue at the time. The student hero, Toru Todai (a pun on "getting into Tokyo University"), was a mean-spirited numbskull with beady eyes who laughably resolved to make his way in life by getting into Tokyo University, the citadel of Japan's elitism and the gateway to a fast-track career. Enrolling in a cram school to prepare for the impossible entrance exams, he studies like a fiend, undeterred by the contempt of his teachers or his terrible test results. Kobayashi spun his story in weekly installments into a saga that extended for four years. By the end of the first, his protagonist had become a hero to students toiling at cram schools across the country; they laughed at his obnoxious antics, cheered his refusal to acknowledge his own witlessness, and held their breath to see how he would fare. In the final episodes, a collector's item on the *manga* market today, Toru is accepted to Tokyo University and then destroys it with the supernatural power he has acquired in the course of his travail.

The Attack on Tokyo U, an allegory of the weak triumphing over the powerful, was a reflection of the idealism Kobayashi had inherited from his Communist father. A similar humanism also animated his next series, a parody of the materialism that characterized Japan's unprecedented affluence during the 1980s. This time he wrote for a younger audience, elementary and middle school students. His eponymous hero Obottchama-kun ("Little Lord Fauntleroy") was the spoiled ten-year-old scion of Japan's wealthiest business magnate, who provided him with an allowance equal to half the annual budget of the Self-defense Force. The brat delighted children by spending his money on resolving problems that were familiar to them in their own lives, purchasing good grades from his teacher and hiring vassals whose only duties were bringing him a pot to pee in or swatting mosquitoes in the summertime. Kobayashi's purpose was to shock his young readers, even as he made them laugh with clever puns and silly pratfalls and bathroom humor, by showing them a petit bourgeois world in which equality had no part. *Obottchama-kun* was serialized for six years and compiled in twenty-four volumes that sold 6 million copies.

By the time he began drawing *Arrogant-ism,* Kobayashi was

having trouble sustaining the idealism that was his father's legacy. In an early installment, "Pretending Not to See Racial Purification in Tibet," he characterized the tension between his father and mother when he was growing up as "passionate Marxist idealism vs. nihilistic Buddhist realism":

> My mother was the daughter of a Buddhist priest in the Esoteric Shingon sect, which taught that mankind's weaknesses, sexual desire, greed and anger, attachment, were to be celebrated rather than condemned. In my house, Marxism lost to Buddhism, but in the confrontation between Tibet and the Chinese Communist Party, Buddhism is losing, and the reason is clear: in this case, the Chinese Communists are the realists and the Tibetan Buddhists the idealists. And Chinese Communist realism is a far cry from my father's Marxist idealism: it is the realism of rape and murder and torture and thought control.

From the beginning, Kobayashi was fearless in his choice of targets. In 1993, when the crown prince married a commoner, Masaka Owada, a graduate of Harvard who spoke fluent French and German, Kobayashi produced an episode in which he pictured her hurling grenades at crowds from her limousine and shouting "Down with the imperial system!" When his publisher, the weekly newsmagazine *Spa!,* declined to run the episode because it was certain to offend right-wing zealots, Kobayashi took it to a much smaller magazine that was about to go out of business, *Garo* (*Gallery*), and told the editor he could have it for nothing if he would publish it. The *Garo* issue sold out within hours of appearing on newsstands. Kobayashi claims he drew the strip out of sympathy for Owada. "Everyone and his uncle project their own bizarre expectations on the imperial family," he said to me. "I was trying to convey how stressed out she must have been feeling after listening to all those opinions about what she must and mustn't do."

The week the *Garo* issue appeared, Kobayashi received a phone call from a man he claims he had never met, Kunio Suzuki, an ultranationalist with powerful connections in business and government and the founder of a patriotic society called Issui-kai (a reference to the group's meetings on the "first Wednesday" of each month). Although he didn't say so explicitly, Suzuki was worried that other right-wingers might threaten Kobayashi with physical violence and wished to defend him. In the dialogue they published together the following week in the magazine *Shukan Bunshun,* Suzuki went out of his way to say that Japan's ultranationalist movement could accommodate differing views and that, in his view, Kobayashi's cartoon was not disrespectful of the emperor. Kobayashi credits the fact that he was not attacked to Suzuki's preemptive approval.

In 1994 and 1995, Kobayashi joined protracted battles simultaneously with the Ministry of Health and Welfare for approving HIV-infected blood for distribution to hemophiliacs; Aum Shinrikyo, the cult, whom he accused of murdering a lawyer who had defected from their ranks, before the sarin nerve gas attack on a subway revealed the degree of their malevolence; and the Burakumin (Untouchables) antidefamation league, an organization staffed by descendents of Japan's pariah caste. His attack on Aum Shinrikyo was savage: his caricatures of the cult's guru, the malefic Shoko Asahara, deformed his features to create a simian beast who appeared in lurid panels that depicted him ravaging young girls in his thrall. Cult lawyers sued Kobayashi for libel unsuccessfully. Kobayashi alleged that he had been marked for assassination, and he drew scenes of Asahara plotting his death and a stakeout of his home and studio by members of the cult. Later police found Kobayashi's name on a list of public figures whom the cult had allegedly ordered killed with VX gas.

Kobayashi's yearlong dispute with the Burakumin was evidence that no subject was too incendiary for him to address. Burakumin, "people from the settlement," is a euphemism for a caste of pariahs who first appear in fourteenth-century chronicles as *eta*, a word that is now prohibited from print in Japan. They were required to live in miserable conditions in refugee camps and were used to capture and execute criminals or worked as leather tanners, a business considered unclean because of the Buddhist injunction against killing animals with four legs.* In 1872, the fourth year of the Meiji Restoration, the pariah caste, which was hereditary, was abolished by law, but discrimination continued and continues in a covert, insidious way to this day. At the time of the Aum Shinrikyo incident, for example, a rumor circulated in the tabloid press that Shoko Asahara was a pariah. There is nothing physical that distinguishes a descendent of the pariah caste from any other Japanese, and those who choose to remain silent are in general not in danger of detection. Those who would like to identify them, and they certainly exist, focus on regions where pariah settlements tended to be concentrated, such as the area around Kobe, the center of Japan's beef and tanning industries. There are a number of sites on Japan's Internet which match public figures and suspicious regions in the country.

Kobayashi was not advocating discrimination against pariahs; he was attacking the antidefamation league for attempting to limit his freedom of expression in a manner he characterized as "reverse discrimination." His anger was triggered when his editors reported phone calls from the league protesting hands he had drawn on which only four fingers and no thumb were visible. Traditionally, a four-fingered hand invoking the paw of an animal had been used as an antipariah symbol, a fact Kobayashi hadn't known. He asked for a meeting with the league, and was further angered by its refusal to concede his right to draw what he liked.

---

* In the 1970s, a British journalist friend of mine was assigned to Tokyo and was perplexed by the curious reaction people had when he explained that his family had been in the shoe business for generations. He learned quickly enough to omit that detail from his history.

"Deformation is the essence of the cartoonist's art," he said in an interview at the time. "If this kind of argument is allowed to prevail, we won't be able to draw anyone without being accused of discrimination. It's already impossible to draw blacks. By this standard, everything Osamu Tezuka [known popularly as the father of *manga*] ever drew is discriminatory."

Beginning in 1996, Kobayashi veered to the right, focusing his anger on Chinese Communism and the Japanese left. In 1998, he published *A Theory of War*. The 380-page "comic book" in the Arro-Procs format again starred Yoshi-rin but attracted a new segment of readers in their sixties and seventies and became an instant bestseller. Three years later he produced a 500-page sequel that also climbed to the top of the bestseller list. At the same time, having joined the inner circle of the Society for the Creation of a New History (see Chapter 6), he was writing the sections on the Pacific War for the rightest *New History*. In contrast to the rhetoric of the textbook, which was carefully restrained, *The Theory of War* was shrill and frenzied. Kobayashi's villains — Hitler and Stalin and Mao, Roosevelt and Truman and Bush and Clinton, and a rogue's gallery of Japan's prime ministers — appeared to play their respective roles in history as caricatures that depicted them as cunning, evil devils or slavering, obsequious fools: in a recurrent image, Kobayashi drew Japanese government leaders naked on hands and knees, faces pressed against a mirror into which they panted apologies to a foreign power who was violating them from behind. His idealized caricatures of the heroes of the piece, the kamikaze pilots and other "selfless patriots," were drawn against backgrounds of setting suns or snowcapped mountains.

The focus of the book's argument, a compendium of neonationalist assertions, was that Japan's left-wing media and the community of leftist scholars and intellectuals, blinded by their "thin-as-water Marxist idealism" to the fact that they were sleeping with the real enemy, had succeeded in brainwashing the public into feeling ashamed and guilty for fifty years about Japan's heroic war effort. In the chapter "Testimony and False Evidence," Yoshi-

rin thundered, "Before we run on about comfort women and the
so-called Nanking Massacre, what about the real holocaust the
Chinese are perpetrating in Tibet!" The chapter on the U.S.
firebombing of Tokyo and the tragedy of Hiroshima was brilliantly illustrated to devastating effect. It was ironically titled
"The Devil's War," a characterization that is associated in and
outside Japan with Japanese aggression in Asia. In contrast to the
rest of the book, in which text crowds the illustrations, the following sequence was silent:

1. The smiling pilot waves from the cockpit of the *Enola Gay*,
   named for the pilot Paul Tibbett's mother.
2. The nose of the plane is above Hiroshima. *August 6, 1945,
   8:15 A.M.*
3. The A-bomb, "Little Boy," is hurtling downward in close-
   up against a field of white.
4. "Little Boy" approaches the ground from above the plane.
5. A white force field buffets the plane from below. *Detona-
   tion: the* Enola Gay *is hurled upward three hundred feet.*
6. Inside the cockpit, the faces of the crew contort in fright.
7. White light sheets across the terrain far below.
8. A pedestrian bridge in the city: an elderly man in a kimono and a straw hat walks his small dog toward us in the
   foreground. On both sides of the street, children are on
   their way to school in summer shorts and white shirts. A
   schoolboy pedals toward us on a bicycle. A car approaches
   from the far side of the bridge.
9. White light obliterates the scene. The car is in the air; the
   figures of the children are blurred as they explode in flame.
10. The mushroom cloud: *8:16 A.M.*

In the concluding chapter of volume 1, "Courage and Pride
That Transcend the Self," Kobayashi pulled out all the stops in a
rhapsodic summary of his argument:

The truth is: the Great East Asian War was an epic poem that expressed the full range of our Japanese spirit.

> The miracle of our early victories
> The horror and poignant beauty of our retreat,
> This was Japan's war!
> We fought alone against the West;
> We had an obligation to fight;
> And when the war had ended, the map of the world
>   was transformed — the age of imperialism had
>   come to an end.

May I be a little arrogant? The day will come when this war is reappraised for what it truly was, the most beautiful, cruel, and noble battle ever waged by mankind.

Let us express our thanks to those brave heroes who transcended themselves on our behalf.

The final panel depicted Zeros hovering like hornets above American destroyers, and, installed like a scroll in an alcove, a final poem by a kamikaze pilot: "Let me die and die again but let my spirit abide forever to defend my honorable land."

The "Epilogue" to volume 2 was an even more fulsome panegyric. In a respectful white suit and buttoned shirt, Yoshi-rin brings his hands together reverently at Yasukuni Shrine. "'I promise to defend Japan,' I whisper in my heart. 'May you rest in peace.'" He walks contemplatively through the grounds, the sun breaking through clouds in streaks of light behind him. He is a small figure now, as though dwarfed by the immense solemnity of his reverie: "I think of myself as someone with power. After all I am an arrogantist. But what can I do for our dead? I must do everything in my power to requite their sacrifice. *May I be arrogant?* Japan is a country of the gods. And a country of the dead. We must never forget that legacy, where we came from and who we are."

On the way to my first meeting with Kobayashi, in December 2000, I didn't know what to expect. His cartoon stand-in Yoshi-rin was a demagogue-madman with a terrible temper. He declaimed, thrusting an admonitory finger at the reader; he sweated and shook and wept at his countrymen's hypocrisy and cowardice; he hissed and snarled and shrieked in rage at enemies of the nation, mouth wrenched open to disclose his giant uvula at the rear of his throat. Into the bargain, Yoshi-rin was a narcissist with a costume fetish. Sometimes, lost in thought at his desk, brooding, he wore a brocade jacket with shiny buttons and epaulets that made him look like a bell captain; at other times he appeared in army uniform, or wore a silk kimono and carried a flute, or stood athwart the globe in his black turtleneck sweater, arms folded defiantly across his chest, his drawing pen glinting dangerously in the fading light.

The Yoshi-rin Studio was housed in a luxury apartment building in an affluent suburb of Tokyo. I rang the bell and announced myself; the door was opened by Kobayashi's assistant, Yuriko Kanamori, an artist in her own right who draws the covers of his books. Kanamori ushered me to a small room at the end of the hall with a table and two chairs and a glass bookcase filled with volumes of the Arro-Procs. She said that "Kobayashi" — the Japanese refer to their bosses without adding the honorific *san,* in deference to the guest — was on his way and bowed out of the room with a smile, closing the door behind her. On the map that she had faxed to my hotel, she had appended a note asking me not to show it to anyone and to destroy it after my visit. Kobayashi had just published another book-length comic called *The True Story of Taiwan.* He had visited the country as the guest of the former Taiwan president Lee Teng-hui, whom he portrayed as the hero of the Taiwan independence movement, the man "who built the foundation of a totally democratic nation that is opposite to China." (The previous year, Lee had attempted to come to Japan for heart surgery and had been denied a visa by the Foreign Ministry in deference to China.) China had officially protested publication of the book, and Kobayashi had insisted on an all-night TV debate program that he had once again been marked for assassination. Alone in the room, I indulged in a fantasy that the door was about to be thrown open by Chinese agents armed with silenced Sten guns, as in *Three Days of the Condor*. There was a knock on the door, but it was Yoshinori Kobayashi who entered and took the seat across the table from me. His clothes were unremarkable, slacks and a sport jacket over a black collared shirt. His features, their composite effect, recalled Yoshi-rin unmistakably. But there was nothing coarse or brutal about him. In fact what surprised me most was a delicacy that was close to fragile (he told me later that he had suffered from asthma all his life and had been sickly in his youth). He had miniature, perfectly formed hands, which he used expressively as he spoke. He was very cordial, if somewhat stiff in the beginning, as though uncomfortable at being alone in the room with a large foreigner, an American at that.

When I asked what accounted for his shift from crusader in the cause of social justice to nationalist zealot, he invoked the Aum Shinrikyo cult: "Their guru, Shoko Asahawa, taught a false history, which included an apocalypse that was due to arrive in 1999. In doing that, he created a discontinuity with history, and that disconnection allowed his followers to turn into monsters. It occurred to me that the rest of us Japanese are no different — we are all living in a present that is disconnected from history because we've been conditioned and brainwashed into reviling and rejecting our own past."

Kobayashi's explanation struck me as too conceptual. There is no question that the cult's malevolence had a deeply unsettling effect on many Japanese artists and intellectuals because of what it implied about the fragility of a moral social order: five years after the attack on a Tokyo subway, Kenzaburo Oe wrote a novel, *Somersault*, in which he examined the psychological dynamics of an evil cult modeled on Aum Shinrikyo. But it appeared to me that

Kobayashi's conversion had been nascent in him long before 1995. In 1972, fourteen members of the militant student left, the Red Army, murdered twelve of their comrades in a mountain hideout for what was judged to be an insufficient commitment to the battle for the people. By his own account, Kobayashi, nineteen at the time, was horrified and disillusioned. And by the time he began drawing the Arro-Procs in 1991, he was already voicing what he described as "a loss of confidence that the Japanese ship of state was unsinkable." The Aum Shinrikyo attack may have traumatized him into embracing ultranationalism, but it seems clear that he was already suffering existential uneasiness that clamored for a transcendent cause. In that sense, Kobayashi's "abrupt" shift recalls the mass apostasy of the 1930s when Japanese leftist intellectuals lost their faith in Communism and were impelled to seek the comforting certainty of identification with Japan's traditional past instead.

Kobayashi handed me a recent volume of his essays. "Look at this beautiful book, the design, the binding, the printing, and the paper. There are few countries in the world that can create a book as aesthetically satisfying as this, wouldn't you agree? This book is the product of a cultural tradition that extends back to the chapbooks of the seventeenth century. We have a responsibility to be grateful for our cultural inheritance, and beyond that to pass it on to future generations of Japanese. If we reject our inheritance we create the emptiness we live in now."

Fair enough, but why not employ his art as a cartoonist and storyteller to celebrate the human legacy of Japanese culture? Why work so hard to glorify Japan's motives and behavior during the Pacific War?

"Because the rejection of everything about our traditional culture is based entirely on having fought that war. Since the U.S. occupation, we've been taught one lesson only: war guilt. The politicians who run this country today are all the products of that deep brainwashing. And it continues to shape our education policy so that our young people continue to learn it. The Chinese can have an army, and the Koreans, but not us because we are evil."

On July 4, 2001, I attended a "Gomanism party" sponsored by Kobayashi's publisher, Sapio, to celebrate the sale of 2 million hardcover copies of the new Arro-Procs, volumes 1 through 6. Fans across the country had entered a lottery; five hundred winners had been invited to gather in the convention hall in Godaiba, the sprawling, futuristic business park built on land reclaimed from Tokyo Bay. An exhibit of the color prints that Yuriko Kanamori had designed as covers for Kobayashi's books was hanging in the lobby: Yoshi-rin as a Kabuki actor in an eighteenth-century woodblock print, Yoshi-rin in eye shadow and lipstick and a white Roman toga, a Claymation Yoshi-rin as Noah, Yoshi-rin as Prince Genji serenading noblewomen on his flute.

Inside, the hall was packed. There were relatively few students; the majority were adults who appeared to be in their thirties and forties, but there were also older fans, a number in Japanese kimono. As the lights dimmed, Kobayashi appeared onstage and was greeted by applause. The young television personality who was the mistress of ceremonies invited him to seat himself in an ornate upholstered chair with a high back, "the Gomanist's throne."

"In an editorial yesterday," he began, "the *Asahi Shimbun* wrote that Prime Minister Koizumi shouldn't visit Yasukuni Shrine on August 15 to honor our war heroes. Who disagrees?"

The crowd applauded wildly. For twenty minutes, Kobayashi excoriated the leftist media and the feckless government in a mild, even voice that was an effective counterpoint to the fury in the message. He ended with Japanese investment in China: "We've been pouring money into China for more than twenty years. The thinking has been that it would lead to peace and increased business between our two countries. That's a perfect example of how dangerous our watered-down leftist idealism can be. Because the reality is that the Chinese are using all that money to build pluto-nium-processing plants. We've created a military monster that has its sights on us. May I be arrogant?" Applause and shouting. "It's time we stopped apologizing and got ready to defend ourselves instead!"

As an entr'acte, Kobayashi told the audience that he had pre-pared a special treat for today only, and he summoned Kanamori onstage from the wings. The audience cheered: Kanamori was well loved by Arro-Proc readers in her perky cartoon incarnation as "Assistant Ms. K.," but this public appearance was her first.

The celebration concluded with a trivia contest. The fans had been given fans (the pun works in Japanese too) that were red on one side and green on the other. While Kobayashi looked on sheepishly from his throne, Assistant Ms. K. read a series of true or false — green or red — questions: "In installment 106, when Yoshi-rin lays siege to the fortress of the media thought-control-lers, he brandishes his pen in his left hand," and so forth. Fifteen readers who must have committed the complete oeuvre to mem-ory remained standing after thirty minutes and received a shop-ping bag full of books and trinkets and a Yoshi-rin T-shirt.

In the crowded lobby after the show, I conducted a brief sur-vey with a single, somewhat loaded question: What is it about Kobayashi that appeals to you? His fans characterized him as "shrewd and perceptive," "easy to understand," "scrupulous," "ab-solutely honest," "well balanced and less biased than the mass me-dia." One fashionably dressed young woman took offense: "I don't consider myself a groupie if that's what you're implying. I appreciate his objectivity, his balance — and his serious attitude toward his work. I also like his black humor." A third-year engi-neering student replied: "I like it when he says that we are the ma-jority. The left-wing media like the *Asahi* say they represent the majority, but they've got it backward." "I've been reading him since he attacked the Aum cult," said another. "He says what's on his mind and isn't afraid of anyone."

The crowd was thinning. I approached a man who had been eyeing me; in his forties, he was wearing a business suit, curiously formal for a Saturday afternoon, and he seemed very nervous. "He expresses my thoughts for me. Things that have been building up in me are given expression in his comics. I can't accept the fact that the whole story is that we were bad. Every country has bright spots and dark shadows in its history. I want Koizumi to go to Yasukuni Shrine."

I had seen two young men in Self-defense Force uniforms leave the hall in the direction of the monorail that connected Godaiba Park and Hamamatsu Station across the bay. I caught up with them just as a train was pulling in. My question appeared to embarrass them. One shrugged and stepped onto the train. The other paused to reflect, staring at his combat boots, and said, "What I like is that he gives us confidence in ourselves as Japanese."

I recalled one of Yoshi-rin's refrains: "Pride and confidence are functions of identity."

6

The New Nationalism II:
Institutionalizing Tradition

IN JANUARY 1996, a group of university professors formed the
Society for the Creation of a New History. Their mission was to
create a middle-school textbook designed to restore balance to a
"masochistic version of history" whose effect, they claimed, had
been to inculcate in schoolchildren feelings of horror and shame
about Japan's past. In their view, the self-vilification that informed
the official version of Japan's motives and conduct during World
War II in particular, promulgated in middle-school textbooks
since 1947, was in large measure responsible for the uncertainty
and disheartenment besetting Japanese society: "History textbooks
in current use not only make absolutely no contribution to the
formation of a national identity," their mission statement declared, "but also serve to obstruct the formation of that identity."

Certainly, textbooks approved by the Education Ministry beginning in 1947 for use in eighth-grade Japanese history class emphatically condemn Japan as the aggressor in China, Korea, and
Southeast Asia. The earliest editions reflect the valorization of
pacifism and democracy that was part of U.S. occupation policy.
Beginning in the 1960s, due to pressure applied by Nikkyoso, the

Japan Teachers Union, which was closely affiliated with the Communist Party, accounts of the war in the Pacific became more doctrinaire, emphasizing imperialism and the cruelty of imperial Japan's colonial policies. Following the fragile détente with Peking in 1975 and the development of Southeast Asia into a critical market for Japanese exports, the Education Ministry's dictates to publishers resulted in more detailed and horrifying accounts of Japanese atrocities. This trend received further impetus in 1982, when Chief Cabinet Secretary Kiichi Miyazawa (later, briefly, the prime minister), in response to a debate about whether to replace the word *invasion* with *advance,* announced to the Diet that "international understanding and cooperation should be a consideration as necessary in the treatment of recent history involving interaction with neighboring nations in Asia."

The seven eighth-grade history textbooks that have been in circulation since 1997 convey similar points of view. The *New Japanese History* published by Nihon Shoseki and approved by the Education Ministry in 1996 is representative. Page one of the section on the "War in China" includes the following insert: "The Chinese people's resistance: When Japan reached into China with the hand of the aggressor, the Chinese people joined together in solidarity and offered stubborn resistance in a variety of ways."

Under the headline "Japan's Enslavement of Korea," the imperial army's inhuman treatment of the Korean laborers brought to Japan in chains to work at coal mines and other sites, where they were beaten and starved and allowed to die, is rendered in vivid detail. And all seven of the texts characterize Japan's occupation of Southeast Asia as "the illusion of the Great East Asian co-prosperity sphere":

> The Japanese military advanced south, proclaiming its intention to liberate the colonies under European and American control and to build a Far Eastern co-prosperity sphere to be led by Japan. At first the local populations welcomed the Japanese

and cooperated with them. Eventually an independent government was created in Burma (Myanmar) and the Philippines,
but the government was actually controlled by the Japanese
military. The army requisitioned oil, rubber, and other materials as well as foodstuffs needed to sustain its military campaigns. In Singapore, more than six thousand Singapore Chinese accused of resisting Japanese domination were executed.

Gradually, people under Japanese rule lost their faith in Japan
and, as anti-Japanese feeling mounted in every region, sought
to liberate themselves on their own. In Vietnam, the Philippines, Myanmar, Indonesia, and elsewhere, Japan encountered
fierce guerrilla resistance against its occupation policies.

Late in 2001, the Society for the Creation of a New History
submitted to the Education Ministry for review and approval
its *New History Textbook* for use in eighth-grade social studies.
Yoshinori Kobayashi drafted the critical chapter on Japan at
war in the Pacific. Kobayashi's close friend Susumu Nishibe was
among the founding members of the society; a former Tokyo
University professor and apostate Marxist who has authored
numerous books on conservativism, Nishibe had introduced
Kobayashi to his colleagues and had persuaded them that he was
the perfect author for the chapter they had in mind. Designed to
inspire students with pride in their country, Kobayashi's version
of Japan's motivation and behavior was antithetical to those in circulation:

The Great East Asian War
In the first hundred days of engagement, Japan achieved a major victory over American, Dutch, and British forces. *This was a
victory made possible by the cooperation of the local populations
who had been oppressed for several hundred years by the Cauca-
sians who had colonized them. Japan's victories in the first campaigns inspired many people in Southeast Asia and India with
courage and the dream of independence.*

In the first stage of the war, Japan's defeat of the Allied forces brought hope and courage to the people of Asia who had long been subject to domination as colonies of Europe and the United States. The Indian republican army was formed from Indian soldiers who had been captured by the Japanese while fighting in the British military; in cooperation with the Japanese military, they moved against the Indian government. Indonesia and Burma also built their military with help from Japan [italics mine].

While the *New History* included references to the cruelty of Japanese rule in the Pacific, they were muted:

As the tide of the war turned against Japan, there were many cases when local populations were forced to perform labor under severe and cruel conditions. In the Philippines, Malay, and elsewhere, guerrillas in league with the Allied forces fought against the Japanese army. Harsh measures were taken to crush this activity and increasing numbers of people perished at the hands of the Japanese army.

Consequently after the defeat, Japan paid reparations to these countries. The notion of the co-prosperity sphere was criticized as an excuse for justifying the war and Japan's occupation of Asia.

The society's heterodox interpretations ("revisionist," as detractors argue angrily) catalyzed a national controversy that was focused on two flash points: accounts of the 1937 Nanking Incident (or "Massacre" or "Great Massacre" depending on the perspective) and comfort women attached (or unattached, depending on the viewpoint) to the Japanese military in Southeast Asia. The earliest account of the Kanto army's occupation of Nanking appeared in *Middle School Social Studies* published by Nihon Shoseki in 1968: "[The Nanking Incident]: As there were people outside the combat zone in civilian clothes who fired on Japanese troops, the Japanese killed 42,000 civilians, including women and children. There were numerous other similar incidents on a smaller scale." The revised 1985 edition was harsher: "There were 70,000 to 80,000 deaths of citizens alone, including women and children. If soldiers who had thrown down their weapons are included, the total number of deaths is said to have reached 200,000."

Other editions added more explicit, and more shocking, detail:

The Japanese army *committed atrocities* in every region of China. During the occupation of Nanking, they murdered Chinese nationals *indiscriminately, including soldiers who had thrown down their arms, old people, women, and children.* Including soldiers, the number of dead is estimated at more than 100,000, and the Chinese estimate over 300,000. In foreign countries this Nanking Great Massacre Incident was severely criticized, but the Japanese themselves were not informed of the facts at the time [italics mine].

The *New History* was dramatically at odds with previous accounts. It not only de-emphasized the numbers of victims involved but implied the possibility, by impugning the reliability of sources, that the Chinese had fabricated the incident for use as anti-Japanese propaganda:

Thinking that Chiang Kai-shek would surrender if the capitol of his [Kuomintang] government were taken, the Japanese army occupied Nanking in December 1937 (the attack mounted by the Kanto Army resulted in large numbers of dead and wounded among Chinese civilians — the Nanking Incident).

At the Tokyo War Trials, it was officially concluded that the Japanese army had killed a large number of Chinese civilians during the occupation of Nanking. However, questions have been asked about the reliability of sources pertaining to actual events at the time, and there is a wide range of differing views. The dispute continues even today.

The prostitutes known as "comfort women" were the second focus of contention. In December 1991, thirty-five South Korean women spoke publicly about having been incarcerated in "comfort facilities" in Burma and other fronts during the war. They claimed to have been starved and beaten while being forced to serve as sexual slaves to Japanese soldiers, and they filed a class-action suit in Japanese courts seeking an apology and $200,000 in reparations for each woman. In 1993, a group from the Philippines filed a similar suit; and other women in Korea, Taiwan, and Southeast Asia also began to speak out. Their accounts in turn encouraged former soldiers in the imperial army to unburden themselves of "dark secrets": the forcible transport of Korean nationals and other women to combat zones and the maintenance of comfort facilities, which they described as "little better than concentration camps."

All seven textbooks revised in 1995 mention comfort women in their accounts of inscription of foreign nationals in the military and coerced labor during the war. The subject is not mentioned in the *New History.* Nobukatsu Fujioka, a professor of education at Tokyo University who was among the founders of the society, justified the omission in an essay titled "Why Middle-school Students Should Not Be Taught about Military Comfort Women." He argued that describing the prostitutes at the front as "comfort women attached to the military" was a misnomer and a distortion of history. "The truth is that comfort women were simply prostitutes who were transported to battle zones by private brokers. There are no documents to support the charge that these women were recruited or confined by any Japanese military organization." Inasmuch as camp followers have played a role in wartime reality since the beginning of history, he continued, making Japan's imperial army the exclusive object of outrage was tantamount to applying a double standard: "When American soldiers occupied Sicily in 1943, they inherited the comfort stations that had been operated by the German and Italian military, along with the comfort women who had been working there. If the goal were to present a balanced picture, facts like these would also have to be included. But in the postwar period, intellectuals and educators have made a virtue of deprecating Japan and the Japanese people. This trend can lead only to moral decline and intellectual decadence." Finally, Fujioka questioned the pedagogical merit in describing prostitutes of any kind in textbooks for children. "Nothing is to be gained from delving into the darker aspects of human nature at this early stage in students' lives. As they grow into adulthood, they will acquire knowledge of this sort on their own." Another member of the society, Eita Namikawa, was more pointedly political: "The inclusion of material describing comfort women in textbooks is also evidence of this country's pathology. When we write our history textbooks, we weigh every word of the reaction from neighboring nations. This is the epitome of intellectual and volitional decadence, and of a nation ideologically and spiritually enslaved. Even a trivial error precipitates ranting from our neighbors, which, in turn, has the power to topple our heads of state. Japan is not a sovereign nation."

On April 3, 2001, the textbook review board attached to the Education Ministry officially approved the *New History* for eighth-grade social studies class. The ministry does not have the authority to mandate particular texts; those decisions are made locally by 543 central textbook boards. When the boards convened that summer, they would select an eighth-grade history to be used at the schools under their jurisdiction for the next four years from a field of eight newly revised editions of the seven already in circulation and the *New History* published by Fuso.

Approval of the textbook ignited outrage among liberal-leftist educators and government officials in Japan and provoked official expressions of protest from South Korea and the People's Republic of China. A national media campaign led by the *Asahi Shimbun,* the country's second largest newspaper, and by the National Broadcasting Company (NHK) characterized the book as a "threat to freedom and to truth," and individuals representing feminist organizations, the Teachers Union, and other labor unions mobilized to influence school boards against it. Within months of the ministry announcement, dozens of books were rushed to market which deconstructed the textbook in order to highlight mistakes in historical fact, intentional omissions, and other kinds of distortion. They pointed out, for example, that the *New History* included a full page and a photograph of the "Great East Asian Conference" held in Tokyo in November 1943, to which Japan invited representatives of Southeast Asian countries "whose independence it had inspired or helped to secure," but neglected to mention or explain why delegates from Korea and Taiwan were not invited. Predictably, criticism focused on the society's "glorification of Japan's aggressive war in China and Southeast Asia." For example:

> The Nanking Incident is a question of acknowledging or not acknowledging that the Japanese military conducted a large-scale massacre of innocent civilians on the Chinese mainland, and is not essentially about how many people were massacred in Nanking. Applying what appears to be the orthodox historian's insistence on objective positivism, the Society for the Creation of a New History projects the uncertainty of the numbers onto the incident itself, shrouding it in the mist of illusion. Their deeper purpose is of course to cast a similar cloak of illusion around Japanese "aggression" during the war in China.

Conservative and right-wing members of the ruling Liberal Democratic Party (LDP) lobbied strenuously for adoption of the book, as did ultranationalist societies across the country and the Sankei media group, which publishes the conservative and widely read *Sankei Shimbun* newspaper and owns a mini-network of television stations. An impressive number of influential business leaders also endorsed the society by joining its corporate board of directors, including Takashi Imai, chairman of Nippon Steel and chairman of the Keidanren, the Federation of Economic Organizations, Japan's most powerful corporate entity.

In July, school boards began their deliberations on textbook selection for the school districts under their jurisdiction. On July 11, after a week of heated debate, a majority of the Tochigi Prefecture's twenty-three-member board voted to adopt the *New History*. The announcement resulted in two thousand angry faxes and a protest demonstration; local school boards of the ten townships in the prefecture declared their intention to reject the textbook. On July 23, the central board reversed itself and chose one of the texts already in circulation.

The most heated protests occurred in Tokyo. In Suginami Ward, as the board prepared to convene on July 24, hundreds of people shouting "No to Fuso!" surrounded the ward office in a human chain, and members of the citizens' committee opposed to the *New History* monopolized the twenty seats reserved for spectators and continually interrupted the proceedings with shouted objections. A similar scene occurred in Kunitachi Township (where I had witnessed rampant bad behavior among students at the middle school). An hour before the selection committee meeting, citizens presented the superintendent of schools with a petition signed by 6,200 residents opposed to the *New History*. Demonstrators outside the ward office carried banners and placards that read: "WE DON'T WANT A TEXTBOOK THAT DISTORTS HISTORY AND GLORIFIES WAR!"

In the end, both Suginami and Kunitachi chose other texts; and when the tally was taken on August 16, the day after the national selection deadline, all but 3 of the country's 543 textbook boards had rejected the *New History*. In total, about 10 of Japan's 10,000 middle schools would be using it beginning in April 2002. Board members who gave interviews to journalists avoided mentioning content or editorial bias as grounds for rejection; they cited the length and difficulty of the text and an inadequate number of color photographs. There were exceptions. In beleaguered Kunitachi, the field narrowed to the *New History* and two others; the superintendent of schools, Masaji Ishii, voted for the text that was adopted, the Kyoiku Shuppan edition, and then added an opinion about the *New History* that seemed to imply that he preferred it: "It seems to me that the Fuso Company edition poses a question that is central to all history textbooks; namely, what is the significance of studying history? And I think it provides a powerful answer when it says, at the end of the volume, 'The most important thing is achieving a substantial sense of self.' I have never read a textbook over again so many times as I did this one." Mr. Ishii's remark resonates sympathetically with the society's emphasis on "history" as a basis for identity.

The only member of the Kunitachi board who argued for the *New History* from beginning to end explained his advocacy in the same context: "In its account of the Russo-Japanese War, the Fuso history takes the position that Japan was fighting for its survival and continued existence, while the other texts imply that this was a meaningless war whose only result was hardship and a loss of life. But if Japan had lost we would likely have become a Russian colony. It seems to me that we need to nurture a healthy *nationalism* in our young people. If we don't allow them to appreciate the marvelous culture that they are heir to, Japan is doomed. The *New History* is written with that goal in mind."

In Tokyo, the metropolitan school board, whose jurisdiction is limited to special facilities administered by the city in all twenty-three wards, chose the Fuso edition for use in four special schools for "handicapped children" (the five board members were private citizens appointed by the nationalist governor of Tokyo, Shintaro Ishihara). This decision provoked a cry of outrage led by, among others, the Nobel laureate Kenzaburo Oe, whose severely retarded son is the subject of many of his best-known novels. In an article that appeared on the front page of the *Asahi Shimbun* on August 8, 2002, Oe accused the board of assaulting "mentally retarded children." (In fairness, the facilities in question were for physically handicapped and emotionally disturbed children, including a large number who were chronically truant, and did not include retarded children.)

On the day following the appearance of Oe's article, I met one of the five members of the Tokyo board. Kunio Yonenaga, a renowned player of *shogi,* the Japanese game derived from the same Indian prototype as Western chess, holds the title "eternal champion," equivalent to grand master. I found much of what he said distasteful, the more so because I felt that I was being manipulated by an expert strategist. "First of all, we chose the *New History* for special schools because those were the only schools we control," he opened. "If we had had the authority we would have put it in all of Tokyo's middle schools because it's the best of the eight."

I asked what he meant.

"Are you a Christian?"

I felt in need of some strategy of my own. "I'm agnostic," I replied, choosing not to reveal that I'm Jewish. "Why do you ask?"

"To me, the *New History* is like the Bible. The Bible is a story, a tale, about love for mankind and how life should be led. Its facts aren't important. Some are correct and some are inaccurate. What matters is that it inspires us in a positive way. The new history has the same effect. It's a story that teaches love for our country, and it's written like the Bible. It even has angels in it."

I protested that a biblical tale was no substitute for an objective account of history.

"Perhaps you say that because you are an atheist," Yonenaga smiled, amending what I had told him. "Faith is important. We need faith in our country to have faith in ourselves. Americans love their Stars and Stripes absolutely, as an article of faith. And the British love the Union Jack. Our children have been taught they mustn't love our flag, our rising sun. They are taught to think of themselves as the grandchildren of the devil. What good can that do us? And is that an objective account of history? I don't believe it is."

Critics celebrated the rejection of the *New History* by textbook selection boards as a decisive victory for the advocates of national contrition about the war, but that conclusion is not entirely defensible. To combat the media campaign against adoption of the text, Fuso released a commercial edition available for sale to the public in bookstores in June 2001. Though there is no law preventing such tactics, it was the first time a textbook had been marketed to the public, and critics objected that Fuso was attempting to influence the selection boards. Members of the society and others took what appeared to be the more reasonable position that the competing texts should all be made available to allow the public to compare and judge for itself. In its first two months on the market, the *New History* was among the ten best-selling titles in Japan, and it had sold 720,000 copies as of February 2002, a figure that cannot be explained away as a function of mere curiosity inflamed by the controversy.

More significant, all but one of the seven textbooks in circulation since 1997 had muted their own accounts of the war in the revised editions they submitted to the Education Ministry for approval in advance of the August 2001 school board meetings. Two editions had substituted "comfort facilities" for "comfort women," one had removed the phrase "attached to the military," one had reported that "many Korean women were sent to the front" without explaining for what purpose, and the remaining three had deleted their accounts entirely. Descriptions of Japanese military atrocities were similarly tempered or, in some cases, deleted. Four of the seven texts removed any reference to Japan's use of poison gas in China and to the notorious Unit 731, which was known to have conducted biological experiments on thousands of prisoners in Manchuria. They also deleted mention of the Kanto army's scorched-earth policy in northern China, known in Chinese as *sanguang zuozhan,* "the three-alls" for "kill all, burn all, loot all." Accounts of the Nanking Massacre were retained, but in five of the six editions the estimated number of victims was deleted: "When the Japanese army occupied Nanking, they murdered large numbers of Chinese nationals (the Nanking massacre incident), but the Japanese people were not informed of this. (Note: There is no agreement as to the number of victims involved.)"

Nominally, revisions to the texts already in circulation were made by authors and editors who were "regulating themselves at their own discretion." This pretext was made necessary by a decision handed down by the Tokyo Superior Court in 1970 stating that the review and approval process might be construed as a form of censorship disallowed by the constitution and was, accordingly, "in theory but not necessarily in practice," against the law.

In fact, publishers were responding to pressure applied by the government. The violent reaction against the 1997 texts was by no means limited to members of the Society for the Creation of a New History. The Sankei media group led a media campaign deploring "anti-Japanese," "masochistic" history for schoolchildren. Ultra-right-wing societies such as the Japan Patriots' League parked their propaganda trucks in front of the publishing houses and harangued them day and night through blaring loudspeakers. Business leaders signed petitions. And conservative factions inside the LDP lobbied in the Diet. On June 8, 1998, the education minister, Nobutaka Machimura, in a reversal of the 1982 "neighboring countries provision," observed that "history textbooks were in certain respects lacking in overall balance, tending to overemphasize negative elements," and he promised to look into "a new process that will help publishers restore balance and improve the reliability of their historical accounts." In December 1999, phone calls to textbook publishers alleged to have come from the office of Prime Minister Mori, a decided nationalist, requested "judiciousness" in their accounts of atrocities, including the treatment and use of comfort women.

"The real battle," Yonenaga said to me, "isn't about the Fuso history per se; the real battle is about the other seven textbooks and about which position from left to right will gain the largest share when the tally is in after August 16."

When the figures were released in September, they confirmed the trend that Yonenaga and members of the society had predicted: the "least masochistic text," published by Tokyo Shoseki, had jumped from 40.4 percent to a majority share of 51.2 percent. Appraised as having taken "a neutral position," Tokyo Shoseki had deleted references to comfort women and revised "200,000 Chinese, including women and children" to read "a large number of Chinese, including women and children." On the other hand, the text published by Nihon Shoseki, the only publisher that had sharpened its emphasis on Japan as an aggressor, adding even more vivid accounts of Japanese military atrocities, dropped from 14 percent to 5 percent of the total. The Nippon Bunkyo edition, which retained drawings of Japanese soldiers beating prisoners and torturing Chinese women, dropped to last place from 3.3 percent to 2.3 percent. (Orders for the Fuso edition accounted for only 0.039 percent of the total, or 521 copies.) "These figures are reassuring," Nobukatsu Fujioka told me. "They are evidence that more and more people share our opposition to instilling self-hatred in our children. I am confident it won't be that long until the *New History* sets the standard."

The textbook controversy did not occur in a vacuum any more than Yoshinori Kobayashi preaches to a lunatic fringe. The same tension between contrition about the war and the need to transform the past into a substantive basis, not only for confidence and pride but for a viable sense of self, exists today at the level of national politics and policy.

The recent history of official visits to the Yasukuni Shrine on August 15, the anniversary of the end of the war, opens a window on this emotional conflict. Yasukuni is a Shinto shrine that was built in 1872 near the imperial palace in Tokyo as a resting place for the spirits of Japanese soldiers and sailors killed in action. The shrine is not funded by the government; during the 1970s, conservative LDP-backed legislation to make it a "national establishment" was defeated five years in a row. Nonetheless, it has always had symbolic status as the official repository of Japan's war dead. (There is no interment of physical bodies at Yasukuni or, with few exceptions, at any Japanese "cemetery"; the presence of the deceased is symbolically represented by an *ihai,* a memorial stick inscribed with his name in life and a posthumous Buddhist or Shinto name.) The Meiji emperor visited the shrine for the first time in 1874; Hirohito worshipped there in 1952, 1969, and, for the last time, in 1975. The first postwar visit by a prime minister was made by Kijuro Shidehara in 1951; in 1975, Takeo Miki became the first prime minister to make his pilgrimage on August 15, but, he insisted, as a private citizen.

In 1978, the shrine's head priest ordered installation of memorial sticks for fourteen soldiers and government officials who had been designated Class-A war criminals at the Tokyo War Trials, including Hideki Tojo and seven others who had been executed. He was acting on his own authority — the MacArthur constitution requires the separation of church and state — but what prompted his decision at the time is unclear. Its effect was to heighten the symbolic significance, political and emotional, of any official state visit to the shrine.

In 1985, Yasuhiro Nakasone became the first prime minister to visit the shrine on August 15 in his official capacity. "Self-confidence must begin," he explained, "with appreciation and respect for the past." The Chinese were outraged; and their anger was compounded by the fact that Nakasone had not used the visit as an opportunity to voice an official apology to China for the war. The following year, Nakasone announced his intention to make a second official visit, but canceled it when China lodged a protest.

While Nakasone represented himself as an "internationalist," meaning that he was determined to achieve parity for Japan with the United States, he was also a nationalist with an agenda that was significantly to the right of LDP conservatives. (This stance helps explain his current role as adviser and confidant to Shintaro Ishihara.) He skillfully separated the Socialists from the Communists at the local level, and weakened the unions by dividing them with a series of privatizations of railways and telecommunications that ostensibly broke state monopolies apart but actually left them in place. In his visit to Yasukuni he violated a long-standing taboo against any show of sympathy or identification with the militarism of the past. He also promoted a revision of Article 9 of the constitution which would allow Japan to wage war, but this effort was defeated by his own party and he ended up on the margins of power.

In the fall of 1992, a scandal implicating yakuza bosses, executives at Nomura Securities, and leaders of the LDP Party in illegal campaign fund contributions in excess of $4 million toppled Prime Minister Kiichi Miyazawa's administration and brought LDP hegemony briefly to an end for the first time in thirty-eight years. In August 1993, a coalition of reform parties, including the Socialists, installed in the office of prime minister a former governor of Kumamoto Prefecture in Kyushu, Morihiro Hosokawa, the aristocratic descendent of a feudal family with an illustrious history that dated back to the fourteenth century.* In his inaugural speech on August 25, 1993, Hosokawa expressed "feelings of regret for the unbearable suffering caused to so many by Japan's aggressive behavior and colonial control." In Seoul on his first overseas trip as prime minister, he announced that he was "reflect-

---

* Sansai Hosokawa (1563–1646), founder of his own school of tea ceremony, inventor, scientist, naturalist, painter, and warrior, was a kind of Leonardo da Vinci of feudal Japan.

ing deeply as an aggressor," and he issued a "profound apology," creating consternation if not panic among bureaucrats in his own cabinet, who hastened to issue a statement insisting that no changes in policy were to be expected.

Hosokawa, at fifty-five the youngest premier to be elected since Kakuei Tanaka had taken office at fifty-four (in 1972), was a handsome idealist who spoke fluent English and had glamorous friends outside the political sphere. His victory at the head of the New Japan Party was viewed by many as a triumph for the forces of reform and a fresh start for Japanese politics. But in February 1994, conservatives in the LDP uncovered a suspicious loan that Hosokawa had received from the same postal delivery company that had brought Miyazawa's cabinet down. Grilled about his finances in open sessions of the Diet, Hosokawa was evasive and unconvincing, his disarming openness gone. The Socialists who had joined his coalition deserted him en masse and returned to the LDP. On April 8, 1994, just eight months after taking office, he resigned in disgrace.

The Socialist prime minister Tomiichi Murayama, who lasted eighteen months, visited Yasukuni Shrine on August 15, 1995, and expressed "painful repentance and heartfelt apologies," but did not mention China. The day before Murayama's visit, the director-general of the Environment Agency told a press conference that Japan's motive for going to war had not been aggression but liberation. He was persuaded to resign.

In April 2001, at his first press conference as LDP president, a position that assured his election by the party to prime minister, Junichiro Koizumi announced his intention to honor Japan's war dead with an official visit to Yasukuni that August 15, the sixty-first anniversary of the end of the war. Coming just as the textbook controversy was gaining momentum, Koizumi's announcement triggered opposition inside Japan and official protests from South Korea and China. In Seoul, demonstrators burned Japanese flags and hung the prime minister in effigy. Through the summer, Koizumi reconfirmed his intention to make the visit as announced, despite criticism in the media and attempts to dissuade him by his foreign minister, Makiko Tanaka (Kakuei Tanaka's daughter), and members of his own party. It is unclear whether his recalcitrance was a product of genuine personal conviction or a tactical display of integrity. One thing is certain: he was encouraged, possibly enabled, to maintain his maverick stance by an unprecedented voter approval rating at the time of 91 percent.

On August 13, 2001, two days before the controversial date he had chosen for his visit, with Japan and the rest of Asia holding its breath to see what would happen, Koizumi announced in a statement his decision to pay his respects one day early, on August 14: "Opinions requesting the cancellation of my visit to Yasukuni Shrine have been voiced not only within Japan but also from other countries," he explained. "It would be totally contrary to my wish and to my intentions if, under these circumstances, my visit to Yasukuni Shrine on August 15 should lead people of neighboring countries to cast doubts on the fundamental policy of Japan denying war and desiring peace." Now nationalists were furious: Koizumi's retreat in consideration of Chinese feelings was interpreted as further evidence that Japan was "not a sovereign nation."

The textbook controversy, the polemic and often hysterical debate about Nanking, and the political explosiveness of official visits to Yasukuni are manifestations of an ongoing tension between contrition about the war and abject apology on the one hand and the urgent need to look to the past for a source of pride and self-certainty on the other. In their efforts to align the past with their own romantic vision, the neonationalists have found a rich fuel for their emotional arguments in Washington's continued refusal even to consider the possibility that it is the United States who owes Japan an official apology. Yoshinori Kobayashi's shocking, persuasive rendering of the Tokyo firebombing is a prime example of an effective attempt to neutralize Japan's viciousness in Asia by evoking the cruelty of the enemy. In the words of General Curtis LeMay, commander of the raid, the indiscriminate — the term used was "strategic" — napalm attacks late in 1944 on Tokyo and other cities "scorched, boiled, and baked to death" some 100,000 civilians in Tokyo alone, more than died in Dresden and Hamburg combined.

The opposition, not only the remnants of the Japanese left but more important in the context of real politics the dovish factions of the ruling party, have been rendered powerless to combat this strategy by their allegiance to the United States, and, by implication, to the self-serving and hypocritical American vision of the war. Since 1945, the United States has held staunchly and intractably to the official position that a desirable end was justified by abominable means. The violent protest occasioned by the exhibition at the National Air and Space Museum in Washington to commemorate the fiftieth anniversary of the end of the war in 1995, just as neonationalism was gaining momentum in Japan, was evidence of this defensiveness. The exhibit was to be titled "The Crossroads: The End of World War II, the Atomic Bomb, and the Onset of the Cold War." As it was originally envisioned in the latter half of 1993, the exhibition would use a restored *Enola Gay* and materials borrowed from Hiroshima and Nagasaki to recreate the experience of the victims on the ground in a manner similar to the galleries of the Peace Museum in Hiroshima. Text on panels would lead viewers to consider the moral issue of the bombs and the real motivation for having employed them, strategic and political. But as plans became public, they catalyzed a massive protest sponsored by the National Air Force Association and the American Legion. In September 1994, the Senate unanimously passed Resolution 257, stating that the exhibition, which had already been toned down, was "revisionist, unbalanced, and offensive" because it failed to represent adequately the "viciousness and criminality" of the Japanese war machine and underplayed the loss of life that would have resulted from an Allied landing and battle on Japanese home ground. Gradually the exhibition was further scaled down; photographs of ground zero were cut in half, objects like a melted lunchbox and children's toys were eliminated, and so were all references to radiation sickness and death as a legacy of the nuclear age. Eventually the museum's director, Martin Hewitt, resigned; the exhibition as it was finally mounted displayed only the nose of the *Enola Gay* and a short video that excluded any commentary on the moral issues.

Japanese attitudes toward the United States remain deeply ambivalent. Japan was, after all, liberated from the military regime by defeat, and the New Dealers in power during the first years of the occupation were genuinely committed to creating a democracy in Japan. After 1948, as the cold war deepened, the growing power of the labor unions persuaded Washington that it had created a monster by liberating the left as a weapon against the right, and the Occupation reversed course, reinstalling former militarists to power and purging the unions and the Communist Party. But Shigeru Yoshida, the U.S. advocate and apologist during the 1950s, maintained that the American military presence in Japan was a watchdog guarding against the spread of Socialism so that energy could be focused on high-speed economic growth. This view is still entrenched inside the establishment elite and has contributed to inhibiting an anti-American stance. In turn, the emotional commitment to affirming the justness of the U.S. response to Japanese militarism prevents the effective dismantling of the neonationalist construction of the Pacific War as a valorous, selfless, heroic battle waged by Japan against U.S. imperialism.

In 1998 and 1999, Prime Minister Keizo Obuchi succeeded where Nakasone and others had failed in clearing the way for right-wing revisionism. Nakasone hated Obuchi, describing him as "a walking void." Obuchi was said to have replied, "Yes, I am a void and that's why I arouse no opposition." The remark invokes appropriately and eerily the "place of nothingness" at the center of Japan's traditional past which has accommodated so amiably the projections of the neonationalist fantasy.

During his two years as prime minister, Obuchi engineered the passage of a package of bills that were viewed as dangerous by conservatives and leftists alike. On August 9, 1999, the Diet legally installed the rising-sun flag and the song "Kimi Ga Yo" as Japan's national flag and national anthem respectively. The new Meiji government had required Japanese merchant ships to display the red sun on a white field beginning in 1870. "Kimi Ga Yo" was first performed at ceremonies on celebration days at the imperial court in 1893. The lyrics, set to music in 1880, are from a classical poem eulogizing the emperor's reign. (The poem appears in an official poetry anthology compiled in the mid-eleventh century.) The title, "Kimi Ga Yo," also the first line of the poem, means "Your Majesty's Life" or "Your Majesty's Reign."

> Let Your Majesty's life
> Extend through the ages
> A great rock grown from smaller stones
> Covered with the moss of time.

Neither the flag nor the song received official status in the postwar constitution. The Education Ministry had been recommending display of the flag and singing of the anthem at school graduation ceremonies since the 1950s, but opposition from the Teachers Union had prevented such shows of nationalism. By the early 1990s, the union's membership had decreased by more than half, and its influence was further weakened when members who identified strongly with the Communist Party walked out to form their own, much smaller union. In pushing the bill through, Obuchi and his three-party coalition relied on support from local constituencies across the country who professed remorse over Japan's cruelty during the war but at the same time were angry about living in the only society in the modern world, fifty years after the surrender, that was still denied the right to its own national flag and anthem. Many Japanese who did not consider themselves ultranationalists were nonetheless unhappy about the fact that their children's only opportunity to see the flag or hear the anthem was when Japanese athletes won medals at the Olympics.

Following ratification, the Education Ministry issued a directive instructing public school administrators to display the flag and to lead students in a standing chorus of "Kimi Ga Yo" at graduation ceremonies. At the end of the school year in February 2000, a sixth-grade homeroom teacher sat down in the middle of the anthem and, as he led his class out of the auditorium at the end of the ceremony, raised his right hand in a fist to the audience as a gesture of victory. The teacher had often expressed opposition to the anthem; his anger that day had been enflamed by the principal's refusal to display on stage the copy of Picasso's *Guernica*, which he had assigned his class as an art project. He was charged with "disobedience" and "sacrificing teacher credibility" and issued a "written warning" by his local school board. The warning was more than an admonition: it meant that his schedule of salary raises would be revised downward, diminishing the amount of his retirement pension. Similar cases of insubordination have occurred since the bill was passed — sending children home on the day of graduation ceremony rehearsals is one tactic — and have resulted in the same written warning. Nonetheless, in a national poll conducted by the *Mainichi Shimbun* in October 2001, 63 percent of the respondents approved the flag and national anthem legislation.

In July 1999, Obuchi had violated another taboo when he established committees in both upper and lower houses of the Diet to review the postwar constitution with an eye to its amendment. This was the first time since the end of the war that the central government had embarked on an official reassessment of the constitution. The committees were formalized in January

2000, when the 147th Diet convened. They have been conducting monthly hearings with a diverse group of citizens including students, teachers, and scholars; writers and critics; former bureaucrats during the occupation years and current politicians. Critics have pointed out that many of those who have been called to testify are professed nationalists or ultranationalists or known to be sympathetic to the emerging nationalist vision for Japan's future. The committees' mandate was to focus on an "appropriate constitution" as part of a "premise for Japan in the twenty-first century." Findings are due in the spring of 2005.

The question of sovereignty, which nationalists insist has been given away, is inextricably related to the postwar constitution. The circumstances of its promulgation in April 1946 were substantially different from the German case. In West Germany, because political elites agreed that the goal was to build a democracy that would be invulnerable to erosion by totalitarianism, and because the Allied position itself was far from integrated, the West German Constitutional Conference was allowed considerable autonomy in drafting the Bonn Basic Law, which became the de facto constitution. While the Bonn document did not clearly stipulate the right of self-defense, neither did it include any provision interdicting remilitarization.

Douglas MacArthur's authority in Japan was final and unalloyed by conflicting interests as in the case of Germany. His instructions from Washington, and his messianic mission, was to demilitarize Japan once and forever in spite of a fanatical right wing that had been disempowered but not destroyed. In January 1946, he summoned Prime Minister Kijuro Shidehara to general headquarters and informed him that he wanted "sweeping constitutional reforms" to include suffrage for women and support for labor unions. When the Diet produced a draft he considered too closely modeled on the original Meiji constitution, he listed his changes on a legal pad and instructed General Courtney Whitney to incorporate them in a new constitution to be drafted in six days. Whitney organized a constitutional assembly of twenty-four junior officers and civilians. Colonel Charles L. Kades, Whitney's deputy, was conscious of the momentousness of his responsibility and the irony of the circumstances: "There we were," he recalled, "a group of ordinary people being required to draft a constitution for one of the world's most powerful nations. And we all knew that we were hardly comparable to the Founding Fathers who had drafted our Constitution!"

MacArthur dictated his word-for-word requirements for one article only, Article 9, which reads as follows:

> Aspiring sincerely to an international peace based on justice and order, the Japanese people forever renounce war as a sovereign right of the nation and the threat or use of force as a means of settling international disputes.
>
> In order to accomplish the aim of the preceding paragraph, land, sea, and air forces, as well as other war potential, will never be maintained. The right of belligerency of the state will not be recognized.

The press was instructed to report that the document had been authored by the Japanese government; the day the constitution was ratified in the Diet, May 3, 1947 (a national holiday today), MacArthur went before cameras at a press conference and solemnly commended the Japanese government for having renounced war to the benefit of all mankind.

There are other constitutions in the world that include clauses prohibiting belligerency, those of Hungary and Italy for example, but none that interdicts as unequivocally as Article 9 a nation's right to military action of any kind, including self-defense beyond its own borders. In fact, with the establishment in 1950 of the Special Police Force, later renamed the Self-defense Force, Japan has contrived, with a series of laws that maneuver around Article 9 with semantic acrobatics, to build ground, sea, and air "self-defense forces" that are today among the five most powerful armed forces in the world. Even so, notwithstanding a new anti-terrorism act legislated in the wake of September 11, 2001, deploying the Self-defense Force outside Japan for any reason is still a subject of emotional controversy.

During the postwar decades of rapid growth, while the country was focused on the pursuit of wealth, the constitution was not a subject of national debate. Ultranationalist extremists harangued the public about the humiliation of a "no-war constitution," but theirs was a lone voice, however strident. I have vivid memories of pausing outside Shibuya Station in Tokyo in the mid-1960s to listen to the demagogue Bin Akao, founder of the Greater Japan Patriot's Party. For years, in all kinds of weather, standing atop his parked propaganda truck, his voice blaring hoarsely through the truck's speakers, Akao vituperated against the "communist filth" that was polluting the country and exhorted citizens to abolish Article 9 so that Japan could strike preemptively against China and North Korea before it was too late. The same trucks, and baleful black buses carrying squadrons of zealots in paramilitary uniforms, are still a familiar feature of the urban landscape. And many journalists and social commentators are still reluctant to express themselves openly about sensitive issues — Japanese atrocities during the war, Yasukuni Shrine, the emperor — because they are afraid of reprisals.

A broad-based popular movement to amend the constitution first appeared in the wake of Japan's experience during the Gulf War of 1990. At that time, despite pressure applied by Washington, the Japanese government declined to join President Bush's coalition on the grounds that involving the Self-defense Force in a war outside Japan's borders was prohibited by the constitution. Instead, in accordance with "a wholehearted commitment to participate in maintaining international peace within the limits of the law," the Diet approved a contribution of $17 billion to help fund the coalition's war effort. The result was a firestorm of international opprobrium; the United States and other nations not involved in the coalition accused Japan of hiding behind the constitution as justification for buying its way out of an international commitment. Many Japanese were shocked, angry, and deeply humiliated by the condemnation that greeted a decision to uphold pacifism and the constitution that they had approved. Nobukatsu Fujioka of the Society for the Creation of a New History told me that the Gulf War had been a turning point in his own thinking: "I remember reading an editorial in the *Mainichi Shimbun* in early 1990 that urged the Diet to approve substantial funding but also argued that we should observe the constitution by refusing to involve our Self-defense Force. I read this with approval and with admiration. Until that time I subscribed to the notion of 'one-nation pacifism' that is the only imaginable justification for Article Nine: that Japan's renunciation of war under any circumstances amounts to a guarantee of world peace. But then I read the international verdict, that we had done the dirtiest thing a country can do, avoid shedding its own blood in the name of peace. I was horrified. And I began to see that one-nation pacifism was an illusion, and that our identification with Article Nine had deprived us of any perspective about how the real world works."

The latent nationalism catalyzed by the Gulf War experience was reflected in a *manga* epic called *The Silent Fleet* which began to appear early in 1989, in installments, and was as popular as Kobayashi's "Arro-Procs," which were being read and admired at the same time. The United States and Japan secretly develop Japan's first nuclear submarine, the *Seabat*; on a test run with the U.S. Seventh Fleet, the ship's elite Japanese crew mutinies, declares the ship an independent nation, and rechristens her *Yamato*, the early Japanese word for Japan and still a synonym for "the Japanese spirit." The United States and Russia join in a hunt for *Yamato* but are outmaneuvered; the ship's resolute commander, Shiro Kaieda, demands worldwide nuclear disarmament, and *Yamato* heads for New York to force the UN to adopt a disarmament resolution. The ship sails under the Arctic icecap, sinking U.S. submarines along the way, and destroys the ships that the United States sends to sink it off the coast of New York. The cartoon's author, Kaiji Kawaguchi, spun his saga into thirty-two hardcover volumes, which sold over 7 million copies between 1989 and 1995. Members of the Self-defense Force were among its most avid readers. Young rightists across the country referred to Kawaguchi as "a new Yukio Mishima."

Late in 1994, Japan's largest daily newspaper, the *Yomiuri Shimbun,* broke the unstated taboo on debating constitutional revision in a public forum by publishing a proposed new constitution "in hope of provoking a national debate." The *Yomiuri* draft, which had been compiled by scholars of constitutional law who were not ultranationalists, simplified procedures for future amendments and provided Japan with the constitutional right to maintain armed forces.

Prime Minister Obuchi's decision to include a constitutional review on the Diet's agenda for the first time in postwar history was a reflection of a shift in public opinion. In polls conducted by the national press from the mid-1950s through 1990, support for the constitution consistently outweighed dissatisfaction by a wide margin. In the wake of the Gulf War, a surge in respondents who shared Fujioka's disillusionment with "one-nation pacifism" reversed the trend, and the gap has widened year by year. In polls conducted by the *Yomiuri, Nikkei,* and *Mainichi* newspapers in April, May, and September 2000, the ratio of those in favor of amendment to those opposed was, respectively, 60 percent to 27 percent, 61 percent to 32 percent, and 43 percent to 13 percent. In May 2001, even the *Asahi Shimbun,* whose editorial position on the emperor, China, and Japan-U.S. relations is decidedly left-wing, reported a ratio of 47 percent in favor to 36 percent opposed.

To be sure, the two thousand surveys indicated that amending Article 9 was not the most pressing concern. The majority of respondents wanted "an amendment to allow citizens to vote directly for prime minister in a national election." "Amending the role of the Self-defense Force" or "clarifying the nation's right to self-defense" was near the bottom of the list. *Mainichi's* was the only survey that asked specifically about Article 9. While only 5 percent voted for abolishing it, 36 percent were in favor of an amendment to make the Self-defense Force a legitimate army to be used in defending Japan. Among those who approved of Article 9, 26 percent wanted an even more explicit emphasis on unarmed neutrality as Japan's official policy, indicating that the commitment to pacifism remained strong. It also provided additional evidence that many Japanese were increasingly uncomfortable about accepting limitations to sovereignty which were legacies from the past.

Since the terrorist attacks of September 11, 2001, debate about the constitution has focused narrowly on Article 9 and its implications. In early meetings with Foreign Minister Makiko Tanaka and others, Colin Powell's deputy, Richard Armitage, made it very clear that Japan's "checkbook diplomacy" at the time of the Gulf War would not be deemed acceptable on this occasion. The pressure Washington applied led to a ludicrously specious debate in the lower house of the Diet on the difference between a "battlefield" and a "combat zone." Leaders of the Socialist and Communist Parties argued that a Self-defense Force deployed to Afghanistan would be operating on a foreign battlefield in violation of Article 9; Prime Minister Koizumi insisted that Japanese troops would be engaged in humanitarian activities in a combat zone, which was not specifically interdicted. Broadcast live on national television, these proceedings were perceived by many as tragicomic, a humiliating reminder that Japan's foreign policy was still governed by American interests. The net effect was to tip the balance of public opinion in favor of amendment. In the context of apparently bottomless recession, some argue that reestablishing a powerful overseas military capability would vitalize Japan's steel, shipbuilding, and other heavy industries and could help to fuel an economic recovery. Others focus on the impossible dilemma posed by Article 9. In September 1997, under the Clinton and Murayama administrations, both sides adopted new guidelines for a Japan-U.S. Security Pact that authorizes Japanese logistical support for U.S. military operations in "areas surrounding Japan," a geography that is not defined but could easily be interpreted as including North Korea and China. As opponents point out, the guidelines mean that in the case of a military emergency, Japan's Self-defense Force would almost certainly become involved in what might be a unilateral American military action. On the other hand, rejecting the guidelines would leave Japan unable to defend itself against attack from "neighboring nations."

Opinion surveys conducted in January 2002 asked, "Should Article 9 be reviewed in light of Japan's commitment to contributing actively to making worldwide peace a reality?" The median response to this question, or one similar to it, was 65 percent in the affirmative. Defenders of the constitution have argued that placing revision of Article 9 in the context of contributing to international peace is a ploy designed to pave the way for the eventual abolishment of the war renunciation clause. Perhaps they are right: there is no question that conservative elements in and outside the government are increasingly dissatisfied with their subordinate role in the U.S. alliance, or that an independent military capability is central to their emerging vision of Japan's future.

7

Shintaro Ishihara: The Sun King

❖

SHINTARO ISHIHARA, the charismatic, inflammatory governor of Tokyo and Japan's most powerful nationalist, paid his respects to Japan's war dead in an official visit to Yasukuni Shrine on August 15, 2001. Prime Minister Koizumi had declared his intention to go and once again had changed his mind. In a headline the following day, the *Sankei* newspapers shrilled: "Ishihara does for Tokyo what the nation lacks the courage to do!" In an essay titled "Why Do We Wait So Eagerly for Prime Minister Shintaro Ishihara?" which appeared subsequently in the neoconservative monthly *Seiron* (*Right Thinking*), an assistant professor at the Takasaki Economic Institute, Hidetsugu Yagi, invoked Ishihara's visit to the shrine:

> This August 15, 2002, Prime Minister Koizumi did not appear at Yasukuni Shrine, but Mr. Ishihara once again was welcomed by a cheering crowd of citizens waving their rising-sun flags. What we beheld in him was an existence unmistakably connected to the vast linkage of chain that encompasses our past, our present, and our future. And through the agency of his ac-

tion, it felt to us as if we were also connected to the eternal life of our state and we felt a certainty close to faith that this leader could resolve the crisis we face today.

Speaking to the press following his visit, Ishihara laid into former prime ministers Hosokawa and Murayama for using their visits to Yasukuni in 1993 and 1995 respectively as occasions for delivering an apology:

"Hosokawa was a horrible prime minister who got in on a fluke and only lasted a year. But what I can't forgive is the ignorance of history that allowed him to declare that our war in the Pacific was a war of aggression. As if the imperialism that drove Europe and the United States to colonialize the rest of the world was acceptable and only our war was evil. I believe that the worst offense a government leader can commit is to sell his own country down the river. Hosokawa's remarks, and Murayama's sentimentalism about 'painful repentance and heartfelt apologies,' amounted to a desecration of our nation's history. I can't forgive that."

At a time when confusion is general and national confidence is at low ebb, Ishihara's insistence on patriotism as the key to regaining pride and discovering a viable role in today's world is soothing music to many ears. He reminds his countrymen that theirs is the only non-Caucasian society to have created a modern superpower, and has declared repeatedly that now is the time for Japan to leverage the power of its superior technology and its wealth, still vast despite thirteen years of deepening recession, in asserting its own interests. In Ishihara's sour view, fifty years of what he calls "eager subservience" to the United States has deprived his country of national purpose and robbed the Japanese people of their capacity for self-determination. If he directs his anger at his own government, he also rails against U.S. meddling in Japan's affairs. At the Davos, Switzerland, meeting of the World Economic Forum in January 2001, where he attracted more attention than Prime Minister Mori, he accused the United States of intentionally precipitating the economic crisis of 1997 in order to damage Asian economies and charged that U.S. foreign policy in Asia was designed to frustrate Japan's efforts at augmenting its influence in world affairs. Two weeks later, he took swift advantage of a near collision between two JAL jumbo jets southwest of Tokyo to reheat his demand that the United States return control of Yokota Air Force Base on the western outskirts of the city. "If the traffic control zone over Yokota wasn't like a giant wall," he declared on a TV talk show, "commercial pilots wouldn't have to zigzag around it and the near miss wouldn't have happened." Asked at a press conference on February 16, 2001, to comment on the sinking of the *Ehime Maru* by the U.S. submarine *Greenville,* he criticized U.S. media coverage of the accident, focusing on specific language: "Everywhere I look, in the papers or on CNN, they refer to the *Ehime Maru* as a 'trawler' or just a 'fishing boat.' The truth is, Ehime Prefecture had spent ten million dollars to build that vessel as a practice ship for high school students. In other words, it was more like a school bus than a fishing boat, but the media doesn't want anyone aware of the fact that a submarine had destroyed a school bus so they call it a trawler or whatever!"

While Ishihara wants revised guidelines that would include U.S. recognition of Japan's right to defend itself against North Korea and China with a military of its own, his position on the Japan-U.S. relationship is in fact less extreme than others to the left and right of him. It is in his hatred of China that he merges indistinguishably with the most zealous elements of the far right. He likes to begin his anti-China harangue by paraphrasing former Chinese premier Li Peng's remarks at a meeting with the Australian prime minister in 1996: "He had the audacity to say that Japan will cease to exist in fifteen to twenty years and vanish from the map! And if we don't come up with a strategy of our own and keep kowtowing to Beijing, he may be right. We pour money into

China so they can continue work on developing a hydrogen bomb. It's no wonder they refer to Japan as 'soft earth.'"

Since taking office as governor in 1999, Ishihara has done what he can to inflame Japan's uneasy détente with Beijing. When the Dalai Lama was in Japan that year, Ishihara invited him to city hall (his Holiness declined the invitation) and wrote an article vilifying China for its treatment of Tibet. In November 1999, he discountenanced the Foreign Office again with a trip to Taipei and a dinner meeting with then president Lee Teng-hui at which he referred to Taiwan as "a state" (Yoshinori Kobayashi, preparing to write and draw his incendiary *In Defense of Taiwan,* accepted a similar invitation). The Chinese demanded an explanation; the chief cabinet secretary issued a statement reaffirming the government's commitment to the "One China" policy and suggesting that Ishihara was merely a local governor. In fact, he was the highest-ranking Japanese official to visit the island since Japan had transferred diplomatic relations from Taipei to Beijing in 1972.

Ishihara was born in the port city of Kobe in September 1932, and grew up in harbor towns, where his father worked as an executive at the Yamashita Steamship Company. In 1937, as Japan's war on China began, the family moved to Kotaru on the northern island of Hokkaido, where Ishihara's father had been appointed the first general manager of Hokkaido operations. The Ishiharas lived well in Kotaru. Ishihara and his younger brother, Yujiro, attended the city's most exclusive private elementary school and were sheltered from exposure to the war in any form. In the spring of 1944, his father was transferred to headquarters in Tokyo, and the family moved again, this time to Zushi, thirty-five miles south of Tokyo and just east of Kamakura, the ancient capital. Zushi was, and remains, an affluent seaside resort; the imperial family has a beachside compound in nearby Hayama, and a number of Ishihara's friends at Shonan Middle School were the sons of officers in the

imperial navy who lived in the grander houses on the cliff above
the ocean.

Ishihara was a diffident, inward teenager who spent his time
struggling through Gide and Mallarmé in French, and filling
notebooks with pen and ink drawings he called *esquisses*. In 1999,
his friends arranged a showing of his early work at a fashionable
Tokyo gallery, and 120 of them were bound in a handsome edition titled *Fantasy Dream by Shintaro Ishihara in His Teens*. The
drawings were self-conscious imitations of Arp and Miró and
Paul Klee, but with a certain fantastic humor of their own. Many
were self-portraits — *Le Portrait de M. Ishihara Qui Est un Dadaist*
— in which the artist had represented himself as a figure who had
come apart, a head with one skeletal arm attached by hinges and
the other limbs akimbo and out of reach. It was as if Ishihara were
expressing the disequilibrium he had experienced as a thirteen-
year-old when the war ended in 1945 and the world turned on
its ear.

The defeat left its mark on the imagination of every postwar
Japanese writer. For Mishima, it signified an end to the possibility
of the heroic death in battle that he had fantasized for himself.
The novelist and Nobel laureate Kenzaburo Oe, ten years old at
the time, heard the emperor speaking in a radio broadcast in the
voice of a mortal man and felt betrayed; Oe went on to become a
leading spokesman for the Japanese new left. Ishihara, three years
older, had a similar reaction that would take him in the opposite
political direction. "While we were at war, we were taught the
glory of dying for the emperor; the next thing I knew it was all
about remorse, and democracy, and getting along with America.
Adults seemed shallow and hypocritical."

Ishihara was in high school in 1948 when his father died and
the family was thrown into a financial tailspin; to make ends
meet, his mother was obliged to sell property and heirlooms. The
crisis was aggravated by his younger brother, Yujiro, who was running with a crowd of wealthy Zushi teenagers and getting in trou-

ble with the police. Ishihara hoped to become a painter and had planned to study French literature at Kyoto University; instead, he took a year off after high school and remained at home to manage the family finances and look after his wayward brother.

In 1952, a family friend encouraged him to study business and offered to help pay his tuition. Advised that a C.P.A. could earn as much as twenty times the starting salary of a company man, he entered Hitotsubashi University in April, intending to major in accounting. He says he felt out of place from the first day and stopped going to class after six months. He had been a soccer star in high school, and he joined the soccer club, but the captain yelled at him for kicking the ball for a goal when he should have been assisting and he quit the team.

Ishihara's friend Hiroshi Takahashi has known Ishihara since 1952, when they were both freshmen at Hitotsubashi. Takahashi, from the rural northern prefecture of Niigata, was a fifth-level black belt in judo and top dog at the dormitory where they both lived. "Ishihara was a very tall, naïve, young, handsome guy," he told me in his colorful English. "I was a vulgar country boy, and he was well bred. He even asked, 'May I smoke?' I was amazed. He admired me because I was tough. He wanted to be tough; he adored Ernest Hemingway. But he was a very delicate, sensitive guy."

As evidence, Takahashi offers a story. Hitotsubashi in those days was in the middle of nowhere, on the western outskirts of Tokyo. A wildcat had finished off the dogs that lived in the surrounding woods and was brazenly raiding the campus for food. Takahashi and his underlings bludgeoned it to death with a barbell and cut it up for sukiyaki. Ishihara came back that night to find his friends at table and demanded a plate of food: "We were always hungry in those days," Takahashi recalled, "and he ate some and said, 'This is very greasy. What is it?' We told him and held up the bloody hide. He cried out like a girl and raced out and fell down in the hall and was vomiting. To be honest, he was just a mosquito guy."

In 1954, his junior year, a classmate persuaded him to help re-
vive the college literary magazine, *Hitotsubashi Arts,* which had
lapsed after the graduation of its founder, Sei Ito, later a novelist
and critic and the translator into Japanese of *Ulysses.* When it was
time to publish the first issue and the editors had collected poetry
and essays but no stories, Ishihara produced his first work of
fiction, "The Gray Classroom," a portrait of his brother and his
delinquent friends. Ito praised its punchy style and vivid charac-
terizations. Encouraged, Ishihara dashed off a novella in two days
and nights, *Season of the Sun,* and entered it in a contest for new
writers sponsored by the literary monthly *Bungakkai* (*The World
of Literature*). It won first prize. Early in 1956, as Ishihara was
graduating, it was awarded the thirty-ninth Akutagawa Prize,
then as now the gateway to a career as a serious novelist.

Set in Tokyo nightclubs and summer villas and on private
yachts, *Season of the Sun* was a chronicle of bewildered adolescents
seeking an alternative to postwar respectability in drinking and
brawling and promiscuous sex. On the prowl in Tokyo, Tatsuya, a
high school boxer, meets Eiko, a little rich girl, a sexual predator
in her own right, and they become selfish lovers intent on taking
pleasure for themselves. Fearing that he may be in love with her,
Tatsuya begins tormenting Eiko, sleeping with her friends and
finally "selling" her to his elder brother for five thousand yen.
Eiko becomes pregnant, and Tatsuya agrees that she should have
the baby. Then he sees a photograph in the newspaper of a champion boxer posing with his new child and is disgusted and terrified by the image. "A sloppy smile on his face — that look of
fearlessness he had in the ring was entirely gone." Eiko has an
abortion and dies of peritonitis. Tatsuya shows up at her parents'
home the day of the funeral and hurls an incense burner at the
photograph that has been installed above her coffin:

> He went straight to the high school gym, deserted at this
> early hour. He changed into trunks and began his workout. He
> finished his shadowboxing routine, and as he began punching

the big bag, Eiko's words came back to him: "What's wrong with loving? Why can't you just love someone?" At that instant, behind the careening leather bag, Tatsuya saw a phantom image of Eiko's smiling face. He punched at it with all his might.

Season of the Sun appeared at a time when Japan was earnestly committed to achieving democracy and prosperity: Ishihara's pervasive cynicism was an affront to many readers. Nonetheless, the novel sold 275,000 copies in its first year in print, a postwar record at the time, and established him overnight as the angry young man of his generation.

In May 1956, the Nikkatsu Studios released the film version, in which both Ishihara and his brother appeared in minor roles (Yujiro had dropped out of college after a year and was already a fledgling actor playing bit parts in gangster films). The film's violence and explicit sexuality were thrilling to young audiences. In the most famous scene in the novel and the film, the aroused boxer announces his arrival by thrusting his penis through the paper of a *shoji* room divider. The sequel, *Crazed Fruit,* released three months later, with a script by Ishihara himself, made Yujiro a superstar. Subsequently, the brothers collaborated on a dozen films adapted by Ishihara from his best-selling novels and starring Yujiro as a dangerous antihero in the James Dean mold.

The Ishihara boys were a handsome pair: long and lean, with regular features and perfect teeth and glittering, insolent eyes. By 1958, they had inspired a social phenomenon known in the media as "the sun tribe," teenagers who worshipped them for their cool rebelliousness, dressed in the aloha shirts and baggy pants and two-tone shoes made famous by Yujiro, with hair long on top and clipped close on the sides in a style that was advertised in barbershop windows as the "Shintaro cut."

Recalling his reign as the sun king, Ishihara sounds amused. "Outside Tokyo, Japan was incredibly provincial in those days. Most kids had never seen yachts or water-skiing or motorcycles, and they had certainly never carried on with girls the way we did. We bought fabric for girls' dresses in bright colors and patterns and had one of Yujiro's girlfriends sew them into shirts that knocked everybody out. Yujiro came back from Honolulu wearing a bracelet, and that created another fad. I was amazed that young people could be so blind."

By 1960, angry letters and picketing of theaters by newly formed women's groups and the national association of PTAs had embarrassed the studio into abandoning the film series. Yujiro went on to star in fifty more films and recorded more than a hundred hit singles. When he died of liver cancer in 1987, more than thirty thousand people attended his funeral.

Ishihara wrote prolifically: plays and novels and even a musical version of *Treasure Island.* He tried his hand at directing — "If I had gone on I could have been better than Kurosawa," he assured me — and ran a theater company of his own. He also traversed South America on a motorcycle and turned the journey into a best-selling memoir, traveled to the North Pole, and raced his fifty-foot yacht, *Contessa,* in the first South China Sea regatta from Hong Kong to Manila and, the following year, in the Trans-Pac from Yokohama to Honolulu.

Late in 1955, about to become a celebrity, Ishihara married a woman he had known since his schoolboy days in Zushi, Noriko Ishida, the daughter of a retired army officer. In 1960, he built a house on a hill in Zushi overlooking the harbor. Its scale is extravagant even by today's standards (it dwarfs the house that Sony's Akio Morita built at about the same time). The décor is wealthy, tasteful, macho: marble and leather and mahogany. There are African spears, Japanese relics from burial mounds in glass cases, paintings by Japanese artists whom Ishihara has sponsored. One wall in the sunken living room is hung with framed charts of yacht races signed by Ishihara and his brother and their crew. The eldest of his four sons, Nobuteru, was born in 1961. Nobuteru has had his own career in politics; a member of the lower house, he was appointed in 2001 to the Koizumi cabinet as commissioner of public works. Ishihara's second son, Yoshizumi, is a stage and screen actor; his third, Hirotaka, is an executive at a commercial bank; and the youngest brother, Nobuhiro, is a painter who teaches at the Tokyo branch of New York's School of Visual Art. In February 2001, Yoshizumi published a book of entries from a diary he had kept since childhood in which Ishihara is portrayed as a severe disciplinarian whose word was law. If Yoshizumi's account is to be believed, the brothers walked on eggshells in their father's presence and chafed at his heavy hand in their lives. The most buoyant moments in the book are their visits to the home of Uncle Yujiro and Aunt Mako, where, according to Yoshizumi, they were welcome to swim and play with an exuberance that was not allowed at home. Ishihara was angry about the book, declaring it "rubbish meant for tourists and peeping Toms."

If Ishihara's fiction was against the grain of the times, so were Yukio Mishima's early postwar novels, and the perversity of their characters was distinctly similar. Mishima, seven years older than Ishihara, was his ardent champion from early on. It is easy to imagine that he was drawn to the younger writer irresistibly: Ishihara's reign as the sun king coincided with Mishima's classical period, a brief interlude in his life when he was at pains to demonstrate to the world, and convince himself, that he had left behind the morbid romanticism of his youth and emerged into emotional and mental sunlight. Mishima provided Ishihara with access to writers and playwrights and critics in the literary establishment. Ishihara was Mishima's guide to the sensual world that was his playground. "Mishima-san had grown up in a family of bureaucrats," Ishihara said, "and underneath his pretensions he was conventional and inhibited. I introduced him to jazz singers and strippers and high-society parties, and I took him to nightclubs and boxing matches, which he had never seen. In those days, respectable writers didn't watch boxing. It titillated Mishima, and he took it up himself. I remember going to watch him spar at the gym; he flailed around, throwing jabs that never landed. When I asked him later why he didn't use a hook, he said he hadn't studied hooks yet. He was really something."

I was in Japan in the early sixties and because I was translating one of Mishima's novels, *The Sailor Who Fell from Grace with the Sea,* I saw a lot of Mishima and was a frequent guest at his famous parties, but I never met Ishihara there. "I hated that rococo house of his," Ishihara explained. "It was incredibly bourgeois, and there was something tacky about it, like being on a set. I always felt that Mishima-san had terrible taste."

By the late sixties, when Mishima began formulating his ultranationalism, the friendship had become strained. Ishihara remembers a heated argument about the Shield Society, a paramilitary organization of nearly one hundred young men in Mishima's thrall who had pledged their lives in the defense of the emperor. "He invited me to a dress parade on the roof of the National Theater. I said he should march his army in the streets if he were serious, where ordinary people could see them. And his answer was that people might throw eggs and splatter the uniforms he'd designed for them! I lost my temper. Where are your politics, I asked him? What about the constitution? Nuclear arms? He had no answers. I miss him. Japan's not the same since he's gone, but his politics were a joke."

In 1968, at the height of his fame the first time around, Ishihara resolved to run for election to the Diet. He says he was prompted by his experience in Vietnam the previous year, when the *Yomiuri Shimbun* had sent him there to report on the Christmas Truce. "I spent time with writers and intellectuals in Saigon, and I was flabbergasted by their indifference to the war; I felt certain the country would fall to the Communists. When I got home, I came down with hepatitis. Mishima-san knew how bad it was. He had been infected when he was writing *Sound of Waves* on a fishing island. He wrote me a letter commiserating and advised me to stop working for a while and just think about things.

I looked up to him as an elder brother, so I took his advice. I lay in bed for a month, thinking about Japan, and it began to seem clear to me that we were heading for Communism, too —"

I interrupted to inquire what made him so afraid of Communism?

He shot back a reply: "It takes away individuality and passion and replaces them with uniformity. I consider myself an existentialist. Freedom and passion are the most important things to me. I was horribly disappointed when I learned that Sartre was a Communist!"

Ishihara ran for a seat in the upper house with the campaign slogan "Revolution Inside the System." With backing from the powerful Kakuei Tanaka faction in the LDP, political bosses who saw great promise in his celebrity, and good looks and fluent tongue, he was elected with 3 million votes, the largest number ever received by a single candidate. In 1972, endorsed by former prime minister Eisaku Sato, he was elected to the more powerful lower house, running from Tokyo's affluent Second District, where he lived, and was subsequently reelected for eight successive terms. In 1973, he founded the Seirankai (Spring-Wind Society), an organization of thirty-one ultrahawks from both upper and lower houses who were committed to amending the constitution's antiwar clause and to restoring righteousness and morality to the state. At Ishihara's insistence, the members cut their thumbs with a razor blade and signed an oath in blood, just as Mishima had signed a blood oath with the cadets in his Shield Society in 1969.

Ishihara was minister of transportation in Noboru Takeshita's cabinet in 1988. The following year, when Takeshita resigned in the wake of a scandal involving bribes to top officials from the Recruit Company (a conglomerate of magazine publishers, driving schools, resorts, and other real estate), he ran for president of the Liberal Democratic Party, a position tantamount to being elected prime minister, and was defeated by a man he viewed as a party hack, Toshiki Kaifu. Outwardly philosophical in the face of defeat, Ishihara was inwardly roiled and, according to some, began looking for a way to put politics behind him and return to writing novels.

He drew attention from Washington for the first time the following year when his collection of his political speeches to constituents, *The Japan That Can Say No,* a bestseller in Japan, arrived on Capitol Hill in an unauthorized translation by a bureau in the Pentagon and was held up as an example of Japanese perfidy, "America-bashing of the highest order." The compilation included speeches by Akio Morita, the chairman of Sony, who had accepted Ishihara's invitation to address political rallies more than once during the late eighties. Although Morita's portion of the book was relatively bland — a rehashing of his set pieces on the inequity and bias of U.S. trade policy toward Japan — he was furious that it had surfaced in the United States. Always careful to ensure that he would not be perceived as critical of his American friends, Morita insisted that the most incendiary remarks had come from Ishihara, and orchestrated a public relations campaign to disavow and dissociate himself from the book. When the Japanese edition, which had sold more than a million copies, was reprinted, and again when Simon and Schuster published a complete English translation in 1991, he insisted that his portion of the text be deleted.

The gist of Ishihara's argument was that American attitudes toward Japan, as reflected both in trade policies and mutual security guidelines, were designed to subordinate Japanese interests and were, moreover, animated by racism. In one of his most incendiary flights, a passage that was cited in the press and quoted on Capitol Hill, he suggested that Japan could tip the cold war balance by choosing to sell multimegabit chips for guided missiles to the Soviet Union instead of to the Pentagon.

Ishihara was in the United States that year, and later wrote a column in which he gleefully described a meeting with Senator

Richard Gephardt in Washington. "He walked into the room and said, 'Mr. Ishihara?' I replied, 'No, I'm the devil incarnate in Western dress. That's what they called me in the *Washington Post.*'"

In 1995, after thirty-four years as a politician, Ishihara abruptly resigned from the Diet and the LDP. It was rumored briefly at the time that someone close to him was associated with Aum Shinrikyo, whose sarin nerve gas attack on a Tokyo subway had horrified the country in March of that year. The rumor was never substantiated. Publicly, Ishihara expressed disgust with the bureaucracy and the corruption that continued to surface in the LDP. He stayed away for four years. He painted, wrote a novel, *Angel in the Flesh,* about a motorcycle stunt rider who might have stepped from a Yukio Mishima fantasy, and cruised the Mediterranean on his new yacht, *Crystal Harmony,* with wealthy friends from his college days.

In 1998, he came out of political retirement to run for governor of Tokyo as an independent. The incumbent, Yukio Aoshima, was a former vaudeville comedian famous for his character "Nasty Granny," whom voters had elected in a gesture of disgust with establishment government. (The city of Osaka had also installed the comedian Isamu "Knokku" Yokoyama, a member of the comedy team Knock, Hook, and Punch, as its mayor.)

"Aoshima was a clown," Ishihara told me. "Scapin to the prime minister. And the city was headed for bankruptcy. Someone had to step in, and the job came with real power. It felt presidential." On May 25, 1999, Ishihara defeated the LDP candidate for governor by 1.7 million votes.

Tokyo is the only city in Japan that has a governor, *chiji,* instead of a mayor, or *shicho.* That is because, strictly speaking, Tokyo is a prefecture in its own right, roughly equivalent to the District of Columbia. The largest city in the world, Tokyo has an annual budget of $95 billion, $15 billion more than New York State and more than twice that of New York City. Thirteen mil-

lion people live within the city limits, but if the adjacent prefectures of Chiba, Saitama, and Kanagawa are included in the
greater metropolitan area, the population is 33 million, roughly
one quarter of the population of Japan. The governor of Tokyo
has more power than any American mayor and more influence
over the rest of the country than the governor of any American
state.

Ishihara's first move in office had panache: he declined to live
in the governor's residence and persuaded the city to rent the
property to an Italian food company for $24,000 a month of des-
perately needed revenue (privately, he considered the mansion
"unlivable, a bureaucrat's idea of good taste"). But he was only
warming up. In January 1999, he proposed taxing Japanese and
foreign banks in Tokyo on gross revenue instead of operating income, which had been stuck in the red since the economy had
fallen apart in 1990 (the Socialists had been proposing the same
move for years, but Ishihara took it over as though it were his
own). Notwithstanding a statute in the tax law that allowed local
governments to levy certain kinds of taxes on their own, the Ministry of Finance objected. Ishihara habitually referred to the Ex-
chequer as "Washington's branch office in Tokyo" and was spoil-
ing for a fight. While the country looked on, he powered the
central government out of the way and galvanized the metropolitan assembly into nearly unanimous approval of a 3 percent levy
that has generated revenues of $1 billion a year.*

The victory was perceived as more than financial. The public
was angry at the government for pouring half a trillion dollars
into rescuing the banks from a catastrophe that they had helped

---

* On March 27, 2001, the Tokyo District Court declared the "Ishihara tax" null and
void on the grounds that it violated local tax laws, and ordered the metropolitan government to reimburse eighteen banks a total of $560 million. Ishihara is contesting
the ruling.

create. Ishihara had not only demonstrated that politicians could tell bureaucrats what to do, but he had evoked the possibility that authority could be shifted away from central government to the local level. In May 2000, Osaka legislated its own "Ishihara tax," and other city governments have been inspired to look for ways to claim a larger share of tax revenue for themselves. In 1999, and again in 2000, Ishihara was voted Japan's most effective leader in national opinion polls.

In Tokyo, he is clearly a hero. I once walked with him from his office in city hall to the Century Park Hotel across the street. It was like a procession. An official representative of city hall in a coat with epaulets and a high hat who might have been an usher at Grauman's Chinese Theatre led the way. An agent from the security police was next. The governor and I followed. Behind us came a second plainclothesman, and, last in line, a gaggle of personal assistants who seemed disgruntled at being separated from their boss. It was like being with Tom Cruise: people halted in the street to stare and giggle; the more intrepid approached to bid the governor good day. He smiled and bowed to each one of them. A film crew was working in the street; the director, whom Ishihara seemed to know, left his camera and came over to explain the scene. At the entrance to the hotel, a life-sized cardboard figure of the governor was smiling benevolently, as if to welcome himself. I had seen others like it all over town, in subway stations and underground arcades. The affiche next to the cutout asked: "ARE YOU DOING YOUR PART TO KEEP OUR AIR CLEAN?"

Ishihara had always been adept at using the media to promote himself and his positions, and charmingly at ease in front of a camera; within months of taking office he created a cable TV show called *Tokyo Boy* that has run ever since. The format was wacky variety: banter on a studio set intercut with slapstick sequences in the street. The other regulars were pranksters in funny hats and outlandish costumes. Sitting among them at a table in his double-breasted suit, Ishihara mixed it up as if he were one of the boys. His cohorts called him "Gov" and interrupted him to crack jokes. He rejoined with quick-witted clowning of his own. It was an astonishing performance, unimaginable from a Japanese politician who controls a budget larger than Canada's. Ishihara's friends agree that he is willful and hot-tempered and capable of arrogance. Here, and elsewhere in public, he is affable, unassuming, and irresistibly charming in a boyish way.

The chatter was never random; it always circled around one of the initiatives the governor was promoting. In a manner reminiscent of FDR's fireside chats or Fiorella La Guardia's Saturday-morning radio shows, the program provided Ishihara an opportunity to establish a personal connection with his constituents and to extend his sphere of influence into the surrounding prefectures. He has succeeded magically: to millions of voters in the metropolitan area, he is perceived as the only politician in Japan with their interests at heart.

Episodes have focused on a wide array of issues: his "No! to Diesel Trucks" campaign, high school truancy and teenage violence, reclaiming Yokota Air Base from the United States, even the "crow crisis." Tokyo is infected with fat, brazen crows. They perch in flocks on every ledge, tear garbage bags apart, litter and soil the streets. Ishihara's solution: knock them out of the sky and cook them in crow pies, which can then be fed to the poor. Crow pie, he explains, makes an appearance in Charles Dickens's *Pickwick Papers* as a tasty dish.

A segment called "Tokyo with Heart" begins with a prerecorded sequence. Two schoolboys in uniform shorts and elementary school caps play with Pokemon cards in the middle of a busy downtown street. The crowd hurries by, narrowly avoiding them. A clock in the upper corner of the screen indicates that fifty-seven minutes have elapsed when a businessman stops and yells at the boys for being in the way. At that moment, Ishihara appears from around the corner with his merry band and presents the man with a certificate from the city "for caring." Turning to the camera, he explains: "In a responsible society, children have the right to be scolded by adults."

"Right on, Gov!," cracks Terry Ito, a comic in a bowler hat. "Like getting pounded is a privilege!" Ishihara looks at him with mock disdain.

I hoped to interview Ishihara extensively. In December 2001, as I was considering the best route to approach him, a journalist friend telephoned me on his return from a trip to Tokyo to relate a story he knew I would be interested to hear. In the course of a thirty-minute interview, Ishihara had remarked, speaking through an interpreter, that he was contemplating writing a new novel and hoped to find a translator who could do him justice in English. When the journalist mentioned my name, something remarkable had happened. Flushing with anger, the governor had informed him that he had thrown me off his yacht forty years ago when I had crashed a party he was hosting with his brother. "It was very awkward," my friend told me on the phone. "He seemed apoplectic, as if it had happened yesterday!"

This was disconcerting news, but I was not altogether surprised: I had retained my own vague memory of the incident, a faded picture like the fragment of a bad dream. I could see myself, a student at Tokyo University at the time, standing on a pier with two tall figures dressed all in white. In the dazzling sunlight the faces are obscured, but I know they are the famous Ishihara brothers, the novelist and the movie star, cultural icons at the time. I know as well that we are arguing, but I have no idea what is being said or what I am doing there. That wasn't important now. What mattered was that it had truly happened, and that Ishihara remembered.

I wrote a letter apologizing for what I chose to describe, as vaguely as possible, as my intemperate behavior as a young man, and asked my publisher in Tokyo, who was also Ishihara's, to deliver it into the governor's hands. A day later the publisher called; he had been discussing my predicament with his friends, and they had agreed that a poem by the eighteenth-century poet Ryokan, whose verse was known to have a mellowing effect on the thoughtful reader, should be included in the letter. Notwithstanding my predicament, it pleased me to imagine businessmen in an office building in Tokyo weighing the strategic merits of classical poetry. The poem they recommended was a thirty-one-syllable *waka,* a *haiku* plus two seven-syllable lines, and might be freely translated as follows:

> Let no man revile me
> If the scent of grass is on my clothes,
> For I have labored across the autumn fields.

The amended letter was delivered. A week later I received a phone call from the governor's office in Tokyo informing me that Ishihara was feeling nostalgic about the past and looking forward to seeing me again after such a long time. He proposed dinner together to get reacquainted and an interview the following day at city hall. He would be pleased to know what kind of food I would prefer.

Tucked away on a side street a short walk from the Diet building, the restaurant Hyotei is one of those very private establishments that cater to politicians and business moguls. You don't just wander in; without an introduction you would be waved away at the lanterned gate. Since the bubble burst in 1990, places like this have been obliged to cut their prices in half: today the regulars here can entertain their guests for three hundred dollars a plate. There is no menu, and no money changes hands; on the last day of each month, the tab is hand-delivered.

I had been told to arrive at 6:00 P.M. Before I could introduce myself, the woman in a kimono just inside the entrance bid me welcome and ushered me upstairs to a private room. My Japanese friends had speculated that the governor wouldn't come alone, but the low table was set with just two places. Five minutes later, Ishihara strode into the room and seated himself across the table from me before I could rise to greet him. Sixty-eight at the time and very fit, Ishihara is tall for a Japanese, nearly six feet, and his broad, open face has the yachtsman's weathered look. As he speaks, his eyes shutter open and closed in a tic that furrows his brow as though he were in pain. His English is serviceable, but he preferred that we speak in Japanese: "If I'd known you were going to become a translator, I would never have quarreled with you," he said with a hearty laugh. I mumbled an apology and explained that I had no memory of the details. "You were with a Japanese girl. She probably thought it was a public party, but my brother and I had chartered that yacht club. Yujiro had been drinking, and when he saw a big foreigner standing there with a pretty Japanese girl he went over and told you to get lost. You must have had thoughts of your own, because you two started yelling at each other. I explained that it was a private party and we . . . showed you the way out." He laughed again. "I've often thought since what a dumb thing that was, to pick a fight with a translator!"

The next morning, we met in Ishihara's private office on the seventh floor of city hall, a gargantuan forty-story fortress designed by Japan's best-known architect internationally, Kenzo Tange. The formal chamber where the governor would normally receive visitors was next door: three somber landscapes on the wall and a dozen outsized leather chairs installed at uncomfortable distances, as if to discourage conversation. Beyond the door on the opposite side of the room, his personal staff hovered: civil servants with their faces set in deferential smiles, a complement of unsmiling agents from the special police, and the young women in stylish black dresses who served us coffee and, later, Japanese lunch.

Both doors had been closed, and we were alone in Governor Ishihara's private quarters. On his modest desk were jars of pens and pencils, a mirror and comb and several Japanese fans, and the clunky word processor he uses to write his speeches and his weekly column in the right-wing *Sankei Shimbun,* "Wake Up, Japan!" ("I can't write fiction here," he told me. "I have to do that in longhand at home.") Beneath the desk I could see slippers, barbells, and a baseball bat. The bat is part of an exercise game that includes a specially designed ball and a net. It comes from the United States, "like surfboards and Windsurfers and Hula-Hoops," Ishihara said. "Only you Americans can come up with this kind of dynamic stuff." The Japanese flag was in a stand obliquely behind the desk; when Ishihara took office in April 1999, before the passage of the Diet bill that installed it and the national anthem as official symbols of the state, the left-wing Civil Servants Union had objected to the flag, but he had threatened to resign the office he had won in a landslide if he were prevented from displaying it. There were three pieces of art on the wall: a Robert Rauschenberg print inscribed to Ishihara, a drawing by Christo, and an oil painting by the governor himself, a portrait in a glowing oval against a dark blue background of his younger brother, Yujiro. The painting is titled, in Ishihara's scrawling hand, *Homage à Yujiro.*

The office looks out through a window two stories high at the waffle pattern of smaller windows in the Park Plaza Hotel across the street; the view is framed on either side by vertical marble columns. When he ushered me into the room, Ishihara pointed at the window and remarked, "It's like having your own private Mondrian."

I began by asking how the governor managed to keep his art and politics separate.

"People imagine that artists and politicians are different species, but I've found the opposite to be true. If I had become a musician or a painter I wouldn't be in politics. You know the Japanese expression *kuzetsu no to* (the sword of rhetoric). Writers and politicians both rely on words to express themselves. However" — he paused for emphasis — "the scary thing about this country is that our politicians don't have to say anything to succeed. When Noboru Takeshita was prime minister, his advice to me was 'lucid words, meaning unclear.' In this country it's best to be mysterious. Voters think that means there's something meaningful deeper down."

There is nothing mysterious about Ishihara: he is outspoken about his positions however abrasive they are. I broached the sensitive issue of Nanking: did he truly believe that Japan had not committed atrocities in China? Ishihara looked at me reproachfully, as though I had disappointed him. "I said the Chinese have exaggerated the numbers. You can't kill three hundred thousand people in six weeks. Besides, the entire population of Nanking at the time was two hundred thousand. In the hysteria of war, our army did some terrible things. But the United States destroyed three hundred and fifty thousand people in Hiroshima in a single day."

I was emboldened to ask whether it was true that he hated the United States? "I don't like America particularly," he replied, "but I don't exactly hate it, either." Then he told me a story: "I was in the seventh grade, and we were living in Zushi, on the coast. We were in the flight path of enemy aircraft heading out to sea. The warning bell would ring while we were in class, and we'd take off for home. The Americans could see that we were kids, but they'd strafe us anyway for fun. If you made it to the woods near the beach, you were safe, but one day I got caught short and had to throw myself into a barley field. As I lay there, the Grumman Hellcats and P-51s came roaring over me, flying low, and I could see they had pictures of naked women and Mickey Mouse painted on the fuselage. I couldn't believe my eyes! I was scared to death, and I was angry. But at the same time I was thinking what a place America must be, what a culture, and how much freer than Japan. Then I heard other planes but no machine guns this time; they were Zeros in pursuit, and the Japanese flag was painted on their wings. I'll never forget the sight of that rising sun floating over me. I still love the flag."

A young woman came in with our lunches on lacquer trays, broiled eel on rice for me and a plain bowl of noodles for the governor, whose stomach was bothering him ("too little drinking," he grumbled). Leaning across the conference table, he tore open the packet of spices I was struggling with, sprinkled it on my food, and said, "I'm a patriot. But the Japanese word, *aikokusha,* has fascist overtones. When I meet the foreign press they always ask if I'm a nationalist, and I used to say, 'Of course I am!' Like De Gaulle, or Kennedy or any other government leader. Then an English friend warned me that *nationalist* in English has the same ugly resonance as *aikokusha* in Japanese. Now I use the English word *patriot* even when I'm speaking Japanese. The point is, politics and writing are both about words."

At ten minutes to one, Ishihara crossed the room to the coat rack at his desk, removed his shirt and tie and pinstripe trousers, and stepped into an exercise suit with the Tokyo logo on the jacket; he was expected downstairs to lead union employees in their midday calisthenics, but I was welcome to relax in his office as long as I liked. I was used to Japanese men changing their clothes in front of me, but Ishihara's invitation was surprising: in Japan a man's office is considered an extension of his home, off-limits to visitors. Ishihara punched a button on his phone and told someone that I would be staying. On his way out, he handed me the portfolio volume of his pen and ink drawings as a young man. "There are some poems of mine in here, too, in French, and Mishima-san had something pretty clever to say about them," he said with unconcealed pride. "He called them popular song versions of Rimbaud. Have a look." With a hearty laugh, he left the room.

Ishihara calls himself a patriot, but his critics accuse him of being a fascist. On April 10, 2000, addressing the Tokyo Garrison of the Self-defense Force, he offended the international community, and many of his own countrymen, by asking the troops to be prepared to help Tokyo police maintain law and order in the event of riots by immigrants from China, Taiwan, and Korea in the aftermath of an earthquake. The offensiveness of the remark was amplified by his shocking use of the derogatory term *sangokujin,* which translates as "the people of the three countries," to describe immigrant communities who have always been treated badly — before and during the war, several hundred thousand Taiwanese and Koreans were brought to Japan under coercion and forced to work as conscripted laborers — and are still subjected to discrimination. The remark evoked ugly memories. In the chaos that followed the Tokyo earthquake of 1923, Japanese vigilante roamed the city looking for immigrants who they feared would take the opportunity to loot and riot. People who responded to questioning in a foreign accent were executed on the spot.

The governor's characteristic response to the outcry he had provoked was to demand an apology from the Kyodo News Service for filing a story that omitted his key phrase "illegal aliens." Unrepentant, he declared that illegal aliens from Taiwan and Korea were in fact responsible for the majority of violent crime in Tokyo today, and he charged that the misquote was an intentional effort by the leftist press to discredit him. Eventually, when he threatened to sue, an apology was tendered. Even so, the remark filled immigrant communities across the country with uneasiness about their future.

On September 3, 2000, Ishihara created more general concern when he mobilized seven thousand Self-defense Force troops and eighteen thousand police in an annual earthquake readiness drill, "Big Rescue 2000," in the streets of Tokyo. The maneuver included personnel carriers, hovering helicopters, and infantrymen in camouflage suits armed with saws and other tools to help clear rubble from the subways; it was the most intimidating display of military power in the capital since the early years of the U.S. occupation. The scenario included an evacuation by Prime Minister Mori and his cabinet to a command bunker in the Defense Agency, where they held a teleconference with Ishihara. In his instructions to the troops, the governor told them they should also be prepared to repel "possible foreign invasion" and added, "Unless we have the will to defend ourselves, no one will lend us a helping hand in earnest." It was clear that Ishihara relished the role of commander in chief; television coverage featured him emerging from his helicopter in slow motion, which emphasized his decisiveness. Observers in the streets were left with the troubling impression that the spectacle was less an earthquake drill than a war game.*

In February 2001, Ishihara joined his sidekick, the forty-year-old cultural critic Kazuya Fukuda, in a published dialogue about the government's mishandling of the "mystery ship," an unflagged vessel suspected of being a North Korean spy ship, which the coast guard had finally sunk after twenty-eight hours of cat and mouse in the East China Sea. Fukuda is a fascinating character in his own right. His original ambition was to be a punk rocker, which may explain his affinity for the outrageous, the outré, and the unsavory. A prodigious reader and a prolific author, he has published dozens of books, some tossed off and others carefully considered, on a range of subjects that include punk rock, Henry Miller, the French writers Céline and Robert Brasillach, the historical origins of Japanese identity, and, in 2001, a voluminous biography of Kanji Ishihara (no relation to the governor), a lieutenant-general in the imperial army who played a central role in the Manchurian Incident of 1937. Three of his books have won major literary awards. An assistant professor at Keio University, his alma mater, he lectures to packed classrooms on modern literature, modern thought, and the theory of subcultures. In his popular weekly columns in men's magazines like *Spa!,*

---

* Photos taken that day of Ishihara in his role as commander in chief recall unmistakably photos of Yukio Mishima taken in 1969, when he persuaded the Self-defense Force to admit him and his cadets to ground-force boot camp. Both "soldiers" are in military dress, and their expressions, of solemn satisfaction and indeed repletion, are identical.

he brings readers vivid and jubilant reports of the most scurrilous venues in Tokyo's underbelly. A bon vivant who hosts dinners for his friends several nights a week at an Italian restaurant called La Gola in Roppongi (Ishihara sometimes shows up), Fukuda affects the stylish rake. When he applies his versatile pen to politics, he fancies himself a latter-day version of Yojuro Yasuda, one of the founders of the Japan Romantic school. In 1990, Fukuda's mentor, the late conservative critic Jun Eto, introduced him to Ishihara, whom he had admired from afar. When I met Fukuda for the first time and asked him how he would characterize the governor, he replied without hesitation, *"Masuraoburi,"* a term from the classical Japanese vocabulary which expresses Mishima's ideal, the manly, righteous essence of the samurai warrior.

In recent years, Ishihara and Fukuda have evolved an effective vaudeville routine when they perform together. Fukuda's role, speaking in Ishihara's stead, is to express sentiments he knows Ishihara shares but chooses not to articulate because they are too provocative even for him. Fukuda does so as though apologetically. Ishihara chides him, as though mildly dismayed, but lets the position stand and then plays off of it. The opening exchange in their dialogue about the mystery ship is a prime example:

> *Fukuda:* I hate to begin by sounding intemperate, and I hope Governor Ishihara won't be angry at me for saying this, but I found the sinking of the mystery ship thrilling. It was an action that demonstrated that this country of ours has sovereign rights, but to me the splendid thing was that we "did battle" and killed "an enemy" . . . I'm not suggesting we apply the American standard, that the measure of a country's mettle is how many people it kills, but I would have to say that a country that hasn't killed a single enemy in over fifty years is hardly a country at all . . .
>
> *Ishihara:* [*Laughing*] You're in good form today, as extreme as ever. They describe you on the sash of your new book as "to-

day's wild man of fighting words." "Today's intellectual hoodlum" might be more appropriate.

Fukuda: I feel that an argument has to stir people up or it isn't an argument. So I always end up fighting with someone. The truth is, there are too many things going on that you can't help getting furious about. At heart I'm a warm and generous person.

Ishihara: I wouldn't worry about it. The fact that you can get angry and argue means you have a clear sense of what needs to be defended and preserved. You can't trust people who don't have those standards; besides, they're boring! But you're right about getting angry. I have to wonder if our politicians and bureaucrats really care about this country. I have to wonder about our people. I can't help feeling that there are only a handful of us with our fists clenched.

Fukuda: [*Praises the valor of the guardsmen who were wounded in the battle and snipes at the prime minister*] It would have looked good if Mr. Koizumi had gone straight to visit the wounded soldiers, but apparently he had opera tickets.

Ishihara: In your book *Why Have the Japanese Become So Infantile?* you put your finger on the problem. You define *infantile* as the inability to distinguish what's crucial from what isn't and to focus on the crucial. The total absence of any sense of crisis at the prime minister's residence is a perfect example. These people have no idea of what this incident is really about. Listen to them debating whether the cutter acted in justifiable self-defense! It's sickening: as if they'd never thought about sovereignty. All they can do is fret about what other countries might be thinking.

More recently, in September 2002, North Korea's admission that Japanese nationals had been abducted from Japan and Europe provided Ishihara with a new opportunity to inveigh against North Korea and his own government. Based on ongoing investigations, the Japanese National Police had long asserted that as many as fifty Japanese had been abducted by operatives of the North Korean secret police between 1977 and 1983. The North Korean government had continually denied Japanese allegations of the abductions. On September 17, 2002, Prime Minister Koizumi traveled to Pyongyang for a summit with Premier Kim Jong Il. Koizumi had made clear that resumption of diplomatic relations between the two countries would be contingent on full disclosure by North Korea regarding its nuclear weapons program and the abduction of Japanese citizens.* On the eve of the summit, Koizumi was handed a list of fifteen Japanese the government now admitted to having abducted. Eight were listed as having died while in North Korea under circumstances that were left unclear, several on the same day. Kim Jong Il represented that the abductions had been carried out by a covert operation within the secret police acting without the central government's knowledge. The bizarre explanation for the kidnappings, which had included several middle-aged couples and a thirteen-year-old girl, was that the North Koreans needed native instructors to teach them Japanese, presumably to prepare them for espionage activity in Japan.

Japan's response to the disclosures was a cry of outrage. For weeks following the summit, national television focused on the grieving families of the victims. With one voice they expressed bitterness at their government for failing to pursue the investigations aggressively. Many families and their supporters refused to believe that their children and relatives had perished, as the North Koreans claimed.

On Sunday, November 10, on a live talk show on Asahi Television, Ishihara declared: "We should stop dilly-dallying around and get everyone out of there, even if it means going to war with

---

* In late October 2002, North Korea admitted that it had been developing nuclear weapons in violation of a bilateral accord with the United States signed in 1994.

North Korea. That's what I would do if I were prime minister." Koizumi's administration, in the throes of attempting normalization of relations with North Korea, was horrified by the governor's unilateral threat of war. Pyongyang promptly denounced Ishihara as "a fanatic ultranationalist and a war maniac." The Korean Central News Agency characterized him as "an ultraright reactionary," and "a mentally deranged lout who has no idea what war is like."

A surprising critique, and the most astute, was issued by the North Korean Communist Party paper, *Minju Joson:* "Ishihara's way of thinking and behavior bears close resemblance to the seventeenth-century literary protagonist Don Quixote." There is something droll in a grim way about a humorless Communist Party organ referring to a classic of European literature to convey something fundamental about Ishihara. What it was asserting, of course, was that Ishihara, like the great dreamer of impossible dreams, was in the grips of a romantic fantasy.

In this respect, Ishihara's brand of nationalism is similar to Yoshinori Kobayashi's and issues from the same source as the "politics" evolved by Yukio Mishima, a figure who continues to loom in the governor's imagination thirty-two years after the writer's suicide. At dinner one night, Ishihara recalled for me the moment when he informed Mishima of his decision to put aside his own career as a novelist to run for election to the Diet. "Mishima-san warned me not to mix art and politics. He said that if I were driving along the coast on my way home from a political rally and there was a beautiful sunset, and I had my driver stop the car and got out to admire it, I would never be a real politician. I disagreed. I told him I intended to go on enjoying sunsets even if I became prime minister. Mishima said, "Just wait, you'll see," but he was wrong. I think he was jealous. By that time he was wishing he could get into politics himself."

Coming from a man who had diagnosed himself as "incurably afflicted with the disease known as romanticism," Mishima's distinction between sunsets and the real world of politics was perfectly in character. Ishihara's response is no less telling. He was acknowledging the romantic in himself, which goes a long way toward explaining Mishima's allure to him. At the same time, he was asserting confidence in his ability to inhabit the pragmatic world of politics. Mishima, who had characterized himself as "beauty's kamikaze squad," knew he had no viability in the actual world. His reality was defined by his death-ridden fantasies and extended no further than the pen he wielded from midnight to dawn every day of his life. Ishihara was already a cunning strategist with a gift for manipulating the dynamics of power in his own interests. Unlike Mishima, Ishihara was a pragmatist. But at heart he was, and remains, a romantic as securely in the grip of his own fantasies about the past and his destiny as heir to the legacies of that imagined past as Mishima ever was.

Late in 1944, when he was twelve, Ishihara and his classmates at the Shonan Middle School were sent to nearby Atsugi Air Base to help air force reserve units waiting for Zero fighter pilots returning from air combat with American bombers. In a published dialogue with the cartoonist Yoshinori Kobayashi in August 1999 [*SAPIO*, August 25], Ishihara described what he called a "formative moment" in his "emotional life."

> My classmates and I sat waiting and worrying in the sunset with a group of reserves at the edge of the runway. All of a sudden a Zero came in for an emergency landing, and we all rushed to the plane to help the wounded pilot out. As many times as I have recalled that day, I wasn't feeling sadness or anything of the kind. It was a thrilling moment. Waiting there with those young reserve troops, I felt deep in my heart that I was sitting with the state. . . . Even now, I feel that the state would be extinguished if I died, as if Japan were inside my body and I was perfectly identified.

In one of his weekly "Wake Up, Japan!" columns, Ishihara referred again to this feeling of identification: "If I can liken my thirty years as a politician to a Zen practice, the truth I have come upon, the secret, is that the state lives inside me. I am aware of it as a physical sensation in my body. So I have no fear or hesitation about dying for the state." How to account for the curious jump in Ishihara's train of thought from identification with the state to death? In the final words of Mishima's appeal to the Self-defense Force before he withdrew and committed hara-kiri, he reveals, less elliptically, the connection that certainly exists in Ishihara's own romantic fantasy:

> We shall restore Japan to her true form, and in the restoration, die. Will you abide a world in which the spirit is dead and there is only a reverence for life? In a few minutes, we will show you where to find a greater value. It is not liberalism or democracy. It is Japan. The land of history and tradition we love. Are none of you willing to die by hurling yourselves against the constitution that has torn the bones and heart from that which we love? . . . We know your souls are pure. It is our fierce desire that you revive as true men, as samurai, that had impelled us to this action.

Mishima describes faith as a mystery: the mystery of connection to what is itself a mystery, the state, the mystical body of Japan, a legacy from a phantom past, and, through the agency of that mysterious connection, a sense of self, aliveness, and even imperishability, a physical sensation as Ishihara also described it of Japan living in his body in perfect identification with himself. Herein are all the elements of Ishihara's romantic nationalism and its appeal. Both Ishihara's and Mishima's fantasies usher forth from the same longing for connectedness and a substantial sense of self. Mishima's patriotism was aesthetic, a compound of romantic notions about loyalty, valor, and the beauty of martyrdom, and had little bearing on political reality. Ishihara's politics, his formulations about the past and the current moment, appear to be grounded in actual circumstances, but underlying them is a sensibility and indeed a romantic fantasy very close to Mishima's own. Ishihara's rhetoric, compelling as it is, reflects this. For example, asked to prescribe a cure for Japan's unreasoning reliance on the United States, he recently declared: "Since we respond to pressure from the outside only, let the North Koreans drop a missile on Kyoto and incinerate the Golden Pavilion [a fifteenth-century Zen temple] again. That would open our eyes to the fact that the United States can't really protect us, and we could stop worshipping at that altar." This is more than simple hyperbole: it is a literary conceit that alludes to the Golden Pavilion that resides in a Mishima novel as the symbol of traditional Japanese beauty and has nothing to do with realpolitik.

Nonetheless, in the current season of despondency and skepticism, Ishihara is as close to a national hero as Japan is likely to get. In January 2001, when new scandals implicating LDP officials had lowered Prime Minister Yashiro Mori's public approval rating to less than 10 percent, Ishihara and Makiko Tanaka, a heroine of the women's movement, were running neck and neck as the public's first choice for prime minister. It appeared at the time that the discredited LDP might lose its majority in the upper house in the national elections that were scheduled for August 2001. If a rout should occur, the instability created by the shift in power to the opposition could lead to a renewed call for a new party. Ishihara had been asked before to lead a coalition of conservatives and had declined. But with the LDP no longer in a position to block him, it was hoped that he might accept the invitation, win reelection to the lower house, a requirement for becoming prime minister, and move to the top post from there.

As it happened, Junichiro Koizumi became prime minister in April, and his unprecedented popularity carried the August elections for the LDP, closing the window of opportunity. Beginning in the spring of 2002, following Koizumi's dismissal of Makiko Tanaka as his foreign minister and a related drop in his approval ratings, voices calling for Ishihara's return to the central government began to sound again. For close to a year, Ishihara remained coy about his intentions. "If you're about to attack Pearl Harbor," he told reporters, "you'd have to be pretty stupid to announce it first."

In a published dialogue in the *Shukan Bunshun* in May 2002, he engaged in the following exchange with the social critic Soichiro Tahara:

> *Tahara:* There is mounting hope and expectation that you'll follow Mr. Koizumi as prime minister.
>
> *Ishihara:* I feel honored [*an embarrassed smile*]. There are people who want me to form a new party. But just as with foreign relations, there would be no point in that unless we could take control of the government.
>
> *Tahara:* You're saying you'd go for it if a majority of the electorate really wanted you to?
>
> *Ishihara:* Let me put it this way. Every member of parliament, every town assemblyman for that matter, starts out thinking, In the end I'll be prime minister. I haven't written off the central government. And the truth is, even when I'm focused on Tokyo there are lots of problems that can't be untangled from national issues. It would be a lot more efficient to deal with some of them as prime minister.

When he speaks of "national issues," Ishihara means the stalled economy. Here no less than in foreign affairs, he has articulated a radical view. He accuses the government of dissipating the potential power of Japan's superior manufacturing capabilities and vast wealth (individual holdings in cash, investments, and savings currently total $11.2 trillion) by investing in public works badly managed by bureaucrats and in financial institutions, including banks, that are crippled by irredeemable debt. "The first step to recovery," he wrote recently, "will be to release the taxpayers' hard-earned money from its evil spell and transform it into risk capital that can be used for direct investments in high-growth — and to be sure high-risk — businesses that need it now and can leverage it." To prime this "bold revolution" in monetary policy, Ishihara proposes the creation in the private sector of a "Japan revitalization fund." The goal would be to create a fund of $450 billion in the first year by pooling public money from pension funds and other sources and individual savings. "We are paying the piper today for having failed to convert our assets into high-risk, high-return capital. But if we can resolve to apply the strength we have effectively, there is no question that we will regain our position as an influential presence in the world."

On March 7, 2003, Ishihara came clean, announcing formally his intention to seek a second term as Tokyo governor in the April election. On April 13, he was reelected in a landslide victory. Ishihara received 319 million votes; his closest opponent received only 117,000. "I intend to use Tokyo as a lever to rescue Japan from the national crisis it is in today," he told the prefectural assembly.

Ishihara declines to discuss his decision, but undoubtedly it has partly to do with his desire to write the major novel he has been talking about since he became governor, a *bildungsroman* about a political family whose history spans the war years. Writing while governing Tokyo is difficult enough; sustaining the effort while running the country would be impossible. "The last time I wrote a real novel was eight years ago, after I retired from the LDP," he told me wistfully. "It was a good book. It proved to me that my sword wasn't rusted. I stayed up all night writing more than once. It had been years since I felt exhausted and excited in that special way."

Ishihara's most ardent supporters believe that he can influence national politics from his office in city hall. Shizuka Kamei, former head of the national police and currently the leader of the anti-Koizumi faction in the LDP, suggests that Ishihara might still form a new party and have his followers in the Diet steer the country according to his wishes. Whatever happens, it seems certain that Ishihara will continue to focus and vitalize Japanese nationalism for years to come.

8

Yasuo Tanaka: The Trickster

IF THERE IS AN ANTITHESIS to Shintaro Ishihara's romantic
ultranationalism, it finds expression in the forty-five-year-old
governor of rural Nagano Prefecture, Yasuo Tanaka. Installing
these two men in the same sentence creates a curious imbalance.
Ishihara is a giant figure in the current Japanese imagination. By
comparison, Tanaka is a whippet; he has no national organization, and the quirky, foppish eccentricity he aggressively projects
will almost certainly prevent him from assuming a role in national politics. Yet Tanaka's reforms, his "Nagano revolution,"
continue to attract intense national interest. In three stormy years
in office, he has called a halt to the construction of dams and
ninety other public works projects that have brought huge revenues to Nagano in the past; he has tightened environmental controls on the lumber industry; he has declared a departure from the
time-honored press club system in the name of allowing all journalists equal access to the news; and he has forced increases in
budgets for education and the care of the elderly. Along the way,
he has antagonized the prefectural assembly, local business interests, bureaucrats in the central government based in Tokyo, and the
national press. But at home, his popular support is overwhelm-

ing. And across the country, he is admired by growing numbers of young people in their twenties and thirties who are active in the feminist, environmentalist, and antinuclear peace movements. The youngest governor in Japan, Tanaka has become the hero and champion of the grass-roots citizens movement which is all that remains of the Japanese left as an active political force.

From its inception in 1922, the Japanese Communist Party was driven by a theoretical debate among its Marxist historians about the proper interpretation of the Meiji Restoration. In 1927, and again in 1932, the Comintern intervened, declaring that the task at hand in Japan must be an attack on feudalism. As a result, the JCP was placed in a straitjacket of doctrinaire Stalinism that has prevented it to this day from developing political strategies that have much bearing on the changing reality of either Japanese or international realpolitik.

Japan's new left coalesced around opposition to the U.S.-Japan security treaty. In 1960, the Zengakuren, the national student movement, viewed by the JCP as Trotskyist, mobilized a violent protest against renewal of the treaty. In 1970, it mounted, and lost, a second major protest. By this time the student movement had broken apart into factions at war with one another and internally against their own partisans, not about issues per se but about the purity of their commitment to the battle of the people against the state. This infighting culminated horribly in February 1972, when it was discovered that twelve of the twenty-six members of the militant Red Army had been executed by their comrades, beaten to death or strangled. The victims had been subjected to an inquisition about their personal behavior and values, a "comprehensive" intended to enable the warrior to come to terms with communism; in the confines of their snowbound hideaway, accusations of misconduct and malfeasance had escalated into violence.

The so-called Mount Asama Incident horrified and disillusioned many younger Japanese who had opposed the Vietnam War and were inclined to identify with the social idealism they felt the new left represented. The old left had already been marginalized by its immovable adherence to doctrine. Fossils on the one hand and murderous fanatics on the other. What remained was a void.

The Socialists proved themselves incapable of providing an alternative; since the assassination in 1960 of Inejiro Asanuma, who was a brilliant strategist and a leader of irresistible charisma, the Socialist Party had lost its vitality and its appeal. During the seventies and eighties, the party moved steadily to the right, distancing itself from the Communists while alienating the trade unions and losing seats in the Diet. In 1989, the year Emperor Hirohito died, a scandal involving bribes to top government officials from the Recruit Company compelled LDP prime minister Noboru Takeshita to resign in disgrace. In the upper house elections that fall, the Socialists won decisively, jumping from 10 to 20 million votes. The elderly power brokers in the party crowed that Japan's voters had finally seen through to the perfidy of the LDP. In fact, the Socialists' victory was largely due to the popularity of their leader at the time, Takako Doi, the first woman ever to run a major political party in Japan. Within two years the party bosses, threatened by her presence, conspired with the LDP to oust her from power, an act of political suicide: in the general elections of 1992 the JSP was routed, losing 12 million votes, and has never regained its credibility.

During her brief incumbency, Japanese voters who had defected from the moribund Communist Party in despair looked to Takako Doi as a symbol of social reform. After her fall from power, there was no one to replace her until the unlikely advent of Yasuo Tanaka as governor of Nagano Prefecture.*

Though it is hard to imagine two men more opposed in their

---

* For this perspective on the history of the Japanese left, I am indebted to Akira Asada: see the *New Left Review* 5, September/October 2000, "A Left Within the Place of Nothingness."

values, dispositions, and personal styles than Ishihara and Tanaka, there is an odd similarity to the arc that carried them from private to public life. Born in Tokyo in 1957, Tanaka moved to Nagano with his family in 1963 when his father was appointed professor of economics at Shinshu University. Graduating from high school there, he returned to Tokyo in 1976 to enroll in Ishihara's alma mater, Hitotsubashi University, where he majored in international affairs. In his senior year, 1980, working at night in the university library, he wrote a novel and submitted it for a prize sponsored by the literary monthly magazine *Bungei* (*Arts and Culture*). The selection committee was comprised of three founding members of the so-called postwar school of fiction, Nobuo Kojima, Toshio Shimao, and Hiroshi Noma, and the influential critic Jun Eto. In October, the book was awarded the Bungei Prize for 1980, and appeared in the magazine the following month. It was published in January 1981 and had sold a million copies by the end of that year. Readers in their teens and twenties found Tanaka's novel thrilling: it laid out for them in the minute detail of a blueprint all the components of a stylish life, the ultimate achievement in Japan's newly emerging consumer society.

The title, *Nan to Naku Kurisutaru,* is a challenge to translate. *Nan to naku* means "in a vague way," "somehow," "sort of." *Kurisutaru,* a phonetic rendering of the English word *crystal,* was a term in vogue at the time connoting "wealth," "beauty," "coolness," and the aggregate of those conditions, "happiness." The novel's heroine, Yuri, a twenty-year-old college student who is also a successful fashion model, exemplifies living a somehow or other, in a vague way, crystal life: "Junichi and I are living together without any worries. I buy and wear and eat things that somehow feel nice. I listen to music that sort of makes me feel good. I go to places and do things that are fun in a vague way. That's how I like to live, sort of like crystal. When I'm in my thirties, I'd like to be the kind of woman who looks good in a Chanel suit."

There was nothing remarkable about the story itself, a chronicle of the daily lives and loves of Yuri and two of her fashion model friends. What was original, and drew praise from Jun Eto — the same critic who, more than twenty years earlier, had first admired Ishihara's *Season of the Sun* — were the 440 footnotes, which were at once a Baedeker to Tokyo's fashionable restaurants, discos, and boutiques, and a glossary of European luxury items, brands and designer labels, hot bands and hit albums. Tanaka claims he wrote the book out of his personal experience and had no need for research; if that is so, it suggests that by the age of twenty-four he had expended considerable energy on window-shopping on the Ginza and in Aoyama, Harajuku, and Shibuya, the chic venues of the day, and had had many nights out on the town.* The annotator has an encyclopedic command of all the styles and manners that are the obsessive focus of his characters' — and his readers' — lives and speaks with perfect confidence in his judgments.

> *Cointreau:* The ne plus ultra of after-dinner liqueurs.
> *Virginia Slims:* A British cigarette. Somewhat feminine.
> *Fendi:* Italian brand established in 1918. Famous in the thirties for fox mufflers. Better known in Japan for handbags than furs.
> *Agatha Christie:* About what you'd expect Jun-ichi [one of the characters] to be reading.
> *Bisque D'Or:* It was always so cold in here you needed a sweater even in summer; out of business in late October 1980 due to the cost of air conditioning.
> *Estée Lauder:* Carrying this brand is a measure of a department store's class.

---

* In his critique, Eto asserted that Yukio Mishima would have admired the novel had he been alive. He was undoubtedly talking about the notes. At work on *The Sailor Who Fell from Grace with the Sea* in 1964, when affluence was still a promise beyond the horizon, Mishima had to rely on a guidebook, *500 Luxury Items,* to create the ambiance of the Yokohama boutique that his heroine owned and managed.

Vespa: An Italian scooter that has become a little too familiar.

Jimmy Messina: Of (Kenny) Logins and Messina, whose album *Oasis* conveys the Spanish influence on California's atmosphere.

Guerlain: Founded in 1828 by Pierre-François-Pascal Guerlain. The third-generation Guerlain, Jacques, introduced Mitsuko, a perfume said to reveal a hint of Asia's mystery, in 1921.

On the surface, *Vaguely Crystal* was a paean to the consumerism of the seventies and eighties in which Tanaka grew up. Yet the annotator's voice, now toneless, now arch or admonitory, provides an ironic counterpoint: by magnifying the urgency of his characters' quest for "crystal in a vague way," Tanaka's epicurean commentary reveals the emptiness that lies beneath the pursuit of style. In an essay Tanaka wrote for *Le Figaro* in 1991, he referred explicitly to the self-uncertainty that has afflicted modern Japanese society:

> Japanese sales of Louis Vuitton bags and Chanel chain belts and Hermès scarves are the highest in the world. Europeans may find it difficult to understand why Japanese young women from even middle-class families should spend so much money on high-class brand accessories. In one sense this may be one of the many pastimes that any wealthy society likes to indulge itself in. At a deeper level, however, it is likely that this is a reflection of the psychological desire of the Japanese to affirm their own sense of identity; wearing exclusive accessories helps affirm and reinforce a sense of self that is missing in our society.

Vaguely Crystal launched Tanaka on a career as a writer, but not primarily of fiction. Ishihara was, and remains, a genuine novelist with a novelist's gift; Tanaka realized early on that literature was not his métier. He became a widely read essayist with a reputation for a liberal social conscience and a fluent, lethal pen, and he frequently appeared on television talk shows as a social commentator. Over time he established himself as an arbiter of good taste in all things, a cranky epicure with a sharp eye and a biting tongue, a kind of Gore Vidal with a good measure of Truman Capote added in. In 1993, he began serializing a chronicle of his personal life, his frequent trips to Italy ("I am an Italian inside," he likes to say), the hotels and restaurants he approves of in and outside Japan, and his amorous adventures. He titled the work *The Pero-Guri Diaries.* In interviews with foreign journalists, Tanaka has translated his Japanese coinage *pero-guri* as "grinding and caressing," but this rendering is somewhat bowdlerized: the term refers more specifically to oral sex. Each entry describing a conquest concludes with the English capitals "PG" for *pero-guri:*

> Feb. 3 (Sat.): I cooked at home and ate a lonely dinner by myself. Around midnight, I went to a bar in Shirogane-dai where Mlle. Y and her friends hang out. On our way home, in the car, PG.
>
> May 10 (Fri.): Finished writing for the day and had sushi in Roppongi with Mlle. Y. A middle-aged man who might have been a Mitsui Trading Company executive was dining with a bargirl from the Ginza. She had that "idiot's beauty" that reminded me of Towako Yoshikawa. I asked where she worked, and she replied, "Club Parnassian." I had heard the name but that was all: I know all the clubs where young people go to dance, but have little to do with places where middle-aged men go to drink. Hirata and his wife, of La Cucina Hirata, happened to be with us; we speculated about what the couple might do after we left, and agreed that nothing would happen tonight. PG.
>
> June 27 (Thurs.): Recently, nothing I do with Mlle. S leads to PG except on holidays, O-Bon [the Buddhist festival of the dead in August], Christmas–New Year's, and both our birthdays. This time, we spent three nights together, and even

though it was birthday week, nothing happened. I got home this morning, and this evening I went out for Indian food at the Taj in Akasaka with Mlle. E. Needless to say, PG.

Tanaka has continued to serialize his *Pero-Guri Diaries* in the monthly magazine *The Truth Behind the Rumors,* and his detractors have used the revelations it contains as evidence of his "twisted character." Tanaka is unabashed: "I am doing nothing wrong," he told the Foreign Press Club. "I earn money from my writing. I enjoy good food with friends and sex with women I respect and admire. My life is an open book. I wonder if the Nagano bureaucrats who destroyed the documents relating to spending at the Winter Olympics can say the same?"

Until he announced that he was running for governor of Nagano just weeks before the election, Tanaka had never revealed a desire to enter politics. But he had demonstrated his engagement and his capacity as a civic leader. In January 1995, an earthquake in the region just west of Kyoto severely damaged the port city of Kobe and the surrounding area. The public was outraged at the central government's failure to respond quickly with emergency measures. There were two heroes of the day, the organized crime syndicate based in Osaka and Yasuo Tanaka. Before the smoke had cleared, the yakuza were distributing water and food. Two days later, while the government was still considering appropriate action, Tanaka, in a display of individual volunteerism rarely seen in Japan, was riding from house to house on a moped, handing out blankets, socks, and diapers.

More recently, in June 1998, Tanaka organized voter support in Kobe for a referendum to stop the construction of a new airport to be owned by the city. Kobe already had two airports and was an express stop on a bullet train connecting it to Fukushima in the west and, via Osaka and Kyoto, to Tokyo in the east. The 1995 earthquake had produced an urgent need for new housing, yet city officials were determined to build the airport at an estimated cost of $1 billion (the giant Denver airport, recently completed, had cost only $300 million). Eventually, a referendum signed by 350,000 Kobe residents was submitted, but it was repealed by the mayor and the municipal assembly. In the course of organizing and leading the opposition, Tanaka made more than one hundred trips between Tokyo and Kobe at his own expense.

Late in the summer of 2000, a group of Nagano businessmen approached Tanaka about running for governor as an independent in the October election. They were fed up with the LDP party machine that had governed Nagano behind closed doors for forty years in its own interest, and dismayed by the $12.5 billion debt that was all that remained of the 1998 Winter Olympics. They had watched other prefectures, Kochi, Mie, and Miyagi, unseat party bureaucrats and replace them in the governor's office with independent reformers committed to the interests of the electorate. These victories had in turn been inspired and perhaps enabled by Ishihara's own election as governor of Tokyo in 1999, widely viewed at the time as a major defeat for the entrenched bureaucracy. The leader of the group, Minoru Chino, president of the Hachijuni Bank, the designated financial institution for the Nagano prefectural government, told the *New York Times:* "We had had forty years of the same bureaucratic system, handed down from governor to governor. That system leads to cronyism and works only for the benefit and in the interests of the people inside it, not the people of Nagano." Chino admitted to feeling uneasy about Tanaka's rakish flamboyance, and particularly uncomfortable about his *Pero-Guri Diaries* and what they revealed about his private life. "But he is young and full of passion and energy, and his eyes are focused at the same level as regular people's eyes," he told the *Times.*

Tanaka listened and accepted the invitation to run. On September 7, 2000, just five weeks before the election, he announced his candidacy.

Since 1959, Nagano had had only two governors, both former

lieutenant governors and both LDP party bureaucrats. The out-going governor, Goro Yoshimura, seventy-four, who was stepping down after five terms in office, had chosen his own lieutenant governor, Fumitaka Ikeda, fifty-eight, as his successor. There were two other candidates, Sanae Nakano, fifty-two, endorsed by the Japanese Communist Party, and a fifty-year-old farmer named Shigeo Kusama. Ikeda was the overwhelming favorite to win. He was supported by the political parties that controlled the prefec-tural assembly, the LDP, and the Democratic Party of Japan, and by the mayors of all of Nagano's 120 municipalities. The political machine threw its full power behind Ikeda; following the elec-tion, four officials were arrested for pressuring subordinates to vote for him.

Tanaka campaigned on the promise to bring the process of government out of doors into plain view and to enable and ensure the public's active participation in it. With limited funds and less than a month to campaign, he relied on e-mail to create a coali-tion of citizens' support groups across the prefecture; his advo-cates included community activists, merchants, business leaders, senior citizens, and a large number of housewives.

An adept marketer, Tanaka wanted a visible emblem that would differentiate him from the pack and tie him to Nagano in voters' minds. He chose the goat antelope, or serow, whose princi-pal habitat in Japan is the Nagano mountainside, and asked his friend, the illustrator Hajime Anzai, to create a cartoon version. Anzai produced a lovable creature with limpid eyes and a friendly smile, its hind legs kicking up behind it as though in jubilation that Tanaka was running for governor. Tanaka named his mascot "Yasshi" after his first name, Yasuo, and began using it as his logo on campaign banners and decals and even his business cards. An-other friend made for him a large felt Yasshi pin that he invariably wore on the lapel of his jacket and continues to wear whenever he is in public. Yasshi is unbearably cute and somehow, in a vague sort of way, quintessentially Tanaka.

Tanaka won the election with 589,324 votes to Ikeda's 473,717.

Ikeda carried many rural districts where building dams and new roads was an important source of income. Tanaka had promised to review public works that were in the planning stages or already under way. It seems likely that farm families were also offended and uneasy about his big-city affectations and sophistication. Tanaka won in all but two of Nagano's cities in spite of opposition by the mayors: in choosing him, urban voters were taking a stand against the traditional power structure.

Tanaka followed Daijiro Hashimoto in Kochi, Shiro Asano in Miyagi, and Ishihara in Tokyo as the fourth prefectural governor to be elected without the endorsement of any political party. Ishihara, who is critical of Tanaka in private, publicly hailed his victory, calling on him to "transform prefectural politics with new ideas." The national press reproved the ruling parties for their failure to be responsive to voters at the prefectural level. The *Yomiuri* and the *Sankei Shimbun* reminded readers that the former mayor of Osaka and the governor of Tokyo respectively, two popular comedians, had failed miserably to live up to voter expectations. The *Yomiuri's* editorial on October 17 concluded: "We have already experienced the failure of administrations that ingratiated themselves with the people. We hope that the Tanaka administration in Nagano does not become a latter-day version of the Yokoyama-Aoshima debacle."

The Nagano bureaucracy resented Tanaka's victory. Just days after the election, an incident occurred that made national headlines: Tanaka handed an official his business card, and the bureaucrat folded it in two before placing it in his wallet. To fold a business card is an indication of disrespect equivalent to a slap in the face. Tanaka jokingly glossed over the affront: "I think he was just trying to suggest that it was undignified of me as governor to be handing business cards to bureaucrats." (There may have been some truth in this: I have observed Shintaro Ishihara in public situations many times; he accepts business cards politely but never distributes any of his own.)

Tanaka declared his election "a call for individualism and a triumph for the citizens' movement." He told me, "I am not a patriot. I am not in love with the state — that's Ishihara's game. I care about people. I want a revolution for the people of Nagano. I want people to think for themselves and to take responsibility for transforming their society into the place they want it to be. I stand for individualism in the best sense."

From the moment he took office, Tanaka has introduced himself as "Yasuo Tanaka, in the employ of Nagano's voters." When we spoke, he said, "I am all about service. I don't need flattery and I don't need authority, just the power to help people think for themselves and get what they want. I have no self-interest! I want to serve all those who have no place inside the system where they can express their disappointments and their dreams. Senior citizens who don't know how to use the Internet understand that what I am doing is not for money; that I act out of my calling to be a volunteer, and that's why they support me. My enemies are those who use power and authority to benefit themselves, government bureaucrats, general contractors, leaders of the agricultural union."

Tanaka's first move as governor was identical to Ishihara's: he declined to move into the governor's mansion, saying it was a waste of taxpayers' money to maintain it, and bought a condo with his own money. He then relocated his office in the prefectural headquarters building from the third to the ground floor and enclosed it on one side with a glass wall from floor to ceiling. He had promised to deliver a government that was "crystal clear and without secrets." Now he had placed himself in a fishbowl. On the other side of the glass wall is a large waiting room that is open to the press and to anyone else who wants to observe the governor at work. They can watch him at meetings with visitors or officials on his staff, writing at his computer, or eating lunch with visitors or by himself. All through the day, classes of schoolchildren who are led in by their teachers press their noses against the glass to watch their governor in action.

I was observing from a corner of his office one morning when a class of children arrived. Tanaka was chatting with a group of local businessmen who had come to request a budget allocation to restore Nagano City's main street; they wanted planters with flowers and new streetlamps. Tanaka listened to their earnest pitch, trying hard not to appear bored. As the children took their places in front of the glass wall, the governor, without taking his eyes from the lobbyists, reached for a blue plastic crown on a table next to him and settled it on his head while extending his left hand in the children's direction in a V for "victory" sign. Outside the glass wall, the kids cracked up; the businessmen labored to proceed as though nothing out of the ordinary had occurred.

Tanaka has worked hard to deliver on his promise to bring citizens into the process of government. Twice a month he holds an open house at his office; anyone who wants to speak with him in person is welcome. Twice a month, he travels across the prefecture for "town meetings" with local residents of even the smallest villages. Seated on the edge of a school auditorium stage, or in a chair at the center of a circle of chairs in a local grange, or, in mild weather, in the middle of an apple orchard, he is an outlandish figure in his designer suit and silk tie and lavender socks, his Versace jacket buttoned snugly over his paunch, but no one seems to mind. He is as skilled as Ishihara at disarming a crowd and getting people to talk, and for two hours and sometimes three the locals express their concerns and Tanaka listens while his aides take notes. No Nagano governor has ever gone on the road this way before, not after the election, and Tanaka always attracts a large crowd, senior citizens and farmers and merchants and, invariably, housewives with their children in tow.

Tanaka has an explanation for the support he continues to receive from women voters of all ages. "When a woman goes shopping, she'll do anything she can to save even one yen. Women have that kind of self-interest. But where society is concerned, women are selfless. A man will buy things he doesn't need if he's dealing with a pretty salesgirl, but in society at large or in his company he is out to profit himself. So I believe that in government, in politics, it's the feminine sensibility that is needed. I love women; there's not a gay nerve in my body. But my sensibility is feminine. I am about serving others and I have no self-interest. Women recognize this, and that's why they support me, from young mothers to old grannies."

Notwithstanding his toughness, there is something soft and delicate and vulnerable about Tanaka that does feel womanish. In meetings he constantly examines his hands, and when he feels under pressure his slender fingers flutter at his lips in a manner that recalls the androgynous singer Tiny Tim. At working lunches, while his staff picks through plastic containers of rice and pickles and fish, which is the standard catered fare for public servants, Tanaka unwraps the delicacies he has brought from home from a patterned blue silk cloth.

The décor of his fishbowl office is girlish. The walls are hung with finger paintings and kiddy posters wishing "our dear governor" well. Tanaka's desk and a long table against the interior wall are littered with toy duckies and other stuffed animals, including Yasshi in several sizes. The cover of his laptop is decorated with comic book character decals. On a small table next to the armchair where he sits when receiving guests, near at hand, are a Mad Hatter's hat, a pink stuffed pig, and the plastic crown he dons to amuse the schoolchildren who come to visit. "Writers are all hermaphroditic," he told me once. "On the one hand we're tough and arrogant. On the other we're excruciatingly sensitive and bashful and terrified that we don't really measure up."

Ishihara wouldn't agree. Tanaka's effeminacy is the focus of his disdain; he appears to perceive it as an affront to the machismo at the heart of his image of himself and is unable to see beyond it. "At a press conference live on national television," he has told me more than once, "Tanaka wanted to be sure his mother was in the crowd and called out 'Is Mommy here yet?' No normal man would say that in public." As if that weren't enough, Ishihara recalls a banquet for all of Japan's governors: "He brings in a stuffed animal, that goat or whatever it is that's his mascot, and he sets it down on the table next to his plate. We start eating, and Tanaka says, 'Yasshi must be hungry, too,' and he takes some food in his chopsticks and holds it up to the animal's mouth. Is that creepy or what!"

I asked Tanaka what he disliked about Ishihara. "He's a bully," he said with a sigh. "And he's so coarse."

On February 20, 2001, four months after taking office, Tanaka decreed a halt to the construction of dams in Nagano. In a public document he titled grandiosely "Proclaiming an End to Dams," he announced that he was canceling the Shimosuwa dam on the Asakawa River, a $240 million project that had been in the planning stage for twenty-three years, and implied that he was considering interdictions against other projects. "A concrete dam costing hundreds of millions of dollars places an enormous strain on our global environment," he wrote. "We should not choose to build a dam simply because it will be subsidized in large measure by the central government. . . . I attach greater importance to the value of rivers, lakes, and marshes as assets to be preserved for future generations in the one hundred or two hundred years to come."

The decree was hailed by the environmentalists who had been among his strongest supporters from the beginning. It was also properly perceived as a direct attack on the pork-barreling that has been integral to Japan's financial and political infrastructure since the early postwar period. The central government is obliged to provide 50 percent of the cost of public works approved by the Ministry of Land, Infrastructure, and Transportation. The prefecture is allowed to raise 95 percent of the remainder with bond issues; when the bonds come due for redemption, the government steps in again, financing up to 66 percent of the debt in the form of grants-in-aid: in effect, the central government subsidizes 80 percent of the total cost.

The availability of government funding for public works has

promoted a happy collusion among bureaucrats in ministries and government agencies, local politicians, and private sector business that is so openly acknowledged that it has been given a name, the "iron triangle." Politicians, including the governor and local assemblymen who win authorization from Tokyo for public works projects, receive campaign support from construction companies and related suppliers for bringing home the business. Such support has often been a euphemism for bribes and kickbacks. The money frequently passes through the hands of the politicians themselves, or with guarantees of lucrative directorships on company boards after their retirement.

The master designer and implementer of this mechanism was Japan's most powerful postwar prime minister, Kakuei Tanaka (no relation to Yasuo but the father of Makiko Tanaka, the hapless foreign minister in the first Koizumi cabinet). Between 1948 and 1970, Tanaka secured his power base in Niigata with dozens of pork-barrel projects that brought tunnels, bridges, highways, and high-speed trains to the backcountry. In the process, he made vast sums of money in payoffs from construction companies and from land manipulation based on his insider knowledge of public works projects. In 1971, succeeding his mentor Eisaku Sato, he was elected prime minister. In October 1974, the monthly magazine *Bungei Shunju* published an article suggesting that the prime minister was secretly involved in as many as fifteen dummy companies. The Socialist Party initiated an investigation in the Diet which turned up hidden wealth in the millions of dollars and a raft of shady financial dealings involving key figures in the underworld. On November 26, 1974, Kakuei Tanaka resigned. Ever since, similar scandals have been a commonplace of Japanese politics.

Since 1990, successive prime ministers answerable to vested interests in the LDP have promoted public works as an effective tonic to a stalled economy, a means of channeling revenue into the private sector and invigorating the job market. Currently, there are five hundred major dam projects under way or in planning. Though Japan is less than one twentieth the size of the United States in surface area, it uses more concrete each year.

As part of his campaign promise of a "revolution with no sacred ground untouched," Prime Minister Koizumi has launched his own attack against the iron triangle and the proliferation of public works. But the prime minister is answerable to the party that elected him, and it appears that vested interests in the LDP and the private sector have succeeded in neutralizing his efforts to deconstruct the system.

As governor of Nagano, elected by popular vote, Tanaka was free of similar constraints. He issued his proclamation without consulting the prefectural assembly or even bothering to inform the head of the prefecture's civil engineering division, who resigned in protest the following week. Tanaka's chief political aide also resigned. The assembly was outraged, accusing Tanaka of willfully ignoring his responsibility to build consensus. His only support came from members of the Communist Party. Unfazed, Tanaka pointed out that he had been elected by Nagano's voters and that polls indicated 80 percent popular support for his decision.

When Tanaka took over, Nagano had accumulated a debt of $14 billion, of which close to half was related to expenditures for the 1998 Winter Olympics. The former governor, Goro Yoshimura, a conservative member of the LDP who had ruled for twenty-four years, had engineered approval for Nagano as the site of the 1998 Winter Olympics. While huge sums of money had been channeled into local construction companies, the prefecture had laid out $1 billion for sports facilities and the construction of a bullet train connecting Tokyo and Nagano City which reduced the travel time from seven hours to just under two. The revenues generated during the games were a pittance compared to the debt incurred. Maintaining the Olympic skating rink and bobsled course continues to cost the prefecture $12 million a year. And the bullet train has produced a downturn in the local tourist business since it is now possible to travel from Tokyo to Nagano City, a distance of one hundred miles, and return in a single day. The bullet train has turned out to be a financial disaster in its own right, because the volume of traffic between Tokyo and Nagano cannot support it: most trains are more than half empty; and most passengers use it to commute to the affluent mountain resort of Karuizawa, now accessible from Tokyo in just under one hour.

On May 15, 2001, Tanaka stepped into national headlines again with a second proclamation: "departure from the press club system in Nagano Prefecture." He ordered the three press clubs operating in Nagano to vacate their rent-free offices at prefectural headquarters by the end of June 2001. In their place, he committed the prefecture to establishing a press center "open to all citizens active in media, mainstream or limited circulation, and to free-lance journalists as well." His own weekly press conference — Tanaka and Ishihara are the only governors in Japan today who hold weekly press conferences that are regularly covered by the national media — would be open to everyone active in the media regardless of affiliation.

The significance of Tanaka's action went beyond providing equal access to all journalists: in effect, he was removing the filter between the news and the reading public, a kind of self-imposed censorship, which is the principal purpose and function of the clubs. Japan's approximately eight hundred press clubs are located everywhere that news is made, in government and political offices, police headquarters, courts, sports and entertainment organizations. Run by the journalists who are their members, the clubs are open to newspaper companies, news agencies, and broadcast networks. The clubs sponsor press conferences and in general provide their membership with proprietary access to breaking news and to sources. The hosting organizations are motivated to provide access to the club by the unwritten agreement that member journalists will abide by certain rules and regulations. For example, it is understood that statements made during some kinds of press conferences may be quoted but are not for attribution. If a journalist tries to scoop his fellow members by attributing such a statement, he and his newspaper may be denied the right to attend certain press conferences or even expelled from the club. The clubs have remained closed to most free-lance journalists and to publishing companies not affiliated with the national press: it is no coincidence that most of the major scandals in Japanese government and business have been exposed by weekly or monthly magazines such as *Bungei Shunju*. Since 1993, the foreign press corps has been allowed to join clubs, but a foreign journalist who joins must weigh the benefits of enhanced access against the unthinkable restraints of obeying the rules. It is estimated that 70 percent of the data reported in Japan's national media comes from press clubs — in other words, that 70 percent of the news the Japanese read or see on television may have been censored voluntarily by the journalists reporting it.

Tanaka's rationale was partly financial: he pointed out that providing the press clubs free rent and parking, utilities, and even administrative salaries cost the prefecture in the neighborhood of $1 million per year. But his emphasis was on allowing "the individual journalist to stand at the center of all reporting without constraint." The statement concluded with his hope that the removal of constraints to equal access and reporting would be considered part of the "Nagano model" he was creating for the rest of Japan.

On July 5, 2002, the prefectural assembly handed Tanaka a vote of no confidence, 44 to 5. It was the first time in twenty-three years that a governor had been voted out of office. The precipitating event had been Tanaka's cancellation of a second dam project on the Asakawa River which had been in planning for twenty years. But discontent with other aspects of his Nagano revolution had been building. The statement that accompanied the no-confidence vote did not mention his decision about dams or other specific policies: as Tanaka pointed out, polls and letters and e-mail indicated that somewhere between 70 percent and 80 percent of Nagano's citizens continued to support him. The assembly charged simply that Nagano had been in a state of "stultification and confusion" since Tanaka had taken over.

When a prefectural governor receives a vote of no confidence, he has ten days in which to dissolve the assembly and resign or to call for a new election. On July 15, Tanaka surprised everyone by announcing that he would seek reelection. In repeated interviews, he was clear about his position. He drew a parallel between his predicament and politics on a national level: The prime minister is elected by the Diet and comes from the Diet; if there is a vote of no confidence it is reasonable that he should dissolve the Diet that elected him and resign. Similarly, Tanaka and the assemblymen were elected by the people: neither had the right to dismiss the other. It was the people who must decide.

The second election was watched more closely than the first. Many observers viewed it as a critical confrontation between the party bureaucracy and the local electorate, between vested political interests and grass-roots reform. Observers found symbolic resonance in the fact that voting day had been scheduled for August 15, the anniversary of Japan's defeat in the Pacific War.

Unable to field a candidate of their own, the assembly supported Keiko Hasegawa, a fifty-year-old lawyer and the only woman among the five candidates who entered the race. While Hasegawa ran as an independent, she was supported from the beginning by the ruling LDP. She was also backed by the labor union Rengo, by many local businesses, and by nearly all the mayors of Nagano's 120 municipalities, who resented Tanaka for interfering in local politics with his popular town hall meetings and specifically for his insistence that villages should remain villages and not be incorporated into townships. All the major newspapers and their weekly magazines came out in support of Hasegawa: Tanaka had been a hated figure since he had challenged their preeminence by abolishing the press club system. It was in response to editorials in the *Asahi Weekly* urging her to run against Tanaka that she first announced her candidacy. Tanaka's organized support came from local environmentalist and feminist organizations and from some of the larger business interests that had supported him in his first campaign.

From the outset, the opposition avoided specific issues including public works because it was clear that most voters supported Tanaka's positions. Instead, it launched a venomous attack on Tanaka's methods and character, calling him a dictator and a "green fascist," accusing him of manipulating the media in the manner of Joseph Goebbels, and declaring him "dishonorable" and "psychically disordered and warped." Hasegawa herself, who professed support for Tanaka's anti-dam policy, attacked his style and personality with her own milder brand of innuendo. "If elected," she said in her final campaign speech, "I shall spend my weekends in Nagano trying to improve the prefecture's financial health instead of taking off on the bullet train to Tokyo for a weekend of fancy eating and heaven knows what!"

Tanaka addressed the charges with sardonic humor in an entry in his public diary: "Mr. Akira Shimozaki, chairman of the Nagano governance committee, says the following about me in a public statement: 'The second coming of Hitler. A dictator leading Nagano to destruction while paying lip service to democracy.' Reporters ask for my response. As a chubby fellow who loves Italy, I wish he had at least called me Mussolini. My question to Mr. Shimozaki: 'Since when — I would appreciate an exact date — have our bureaucrats stopped feeding themselves at the great banquet that has been our political system until now?'"

When I asked how he felt about the *ad hominem* attack he defended himself more substantively. "Fascism is designed to stop people from thinking. That's what Hitler and Stalin were about. And that's what Ishihara does, our Japanese version of Joerg Haider. He uses his great gift for language to rev people up, but is he provocative in a constructive way? Does he inspire people to think for themselves? I don't think so. I speak as colorfully and as appealingly as I can, my speeches are full of trendy catchwords, but everything I say is designed to stimulate people to think for themselves. That's why I never speak of absolutes the way Ishihara does, 'the absolute value of the state,' for example. I hate the word *absolutely* and never use it because it brings thinking to a halt. Personal style apart, that's the real difference between Ishihara and me!"

Tanaka's second victory was more decisive than his first: voter turnout was higher, nearly 80 percent, and he received many more votes than the first time around, 822,897 to Hasegawa's 405,559. With the stagy flamboyance that continues to provoke his detractors, Tanaka held his victory press conference on a ski slope in the resort town of Asahi near Nagano City. Tanned and smiling, he was conciliatory: "It is my modest hope to seek dialogue with the assembly. I think both sides, including myself, are responsible for the confusion that occurred." In private he was less generous. "I won because our political parties and the ancien régime and the Diet and assemblies have lost their functionality," he told me. "They were all defeated, and so was the establishment press, the national dailies and their weekly magazines, the *Yomiuri* and the *Yomiuri Weekly,* the *Asahi* and the *Asahi Weekly* and their magazine for intellectuals, *Aera.* They were all hoping I would lose, but it was they who were defeated."

To many observers, the election process was a disappointment. Critics felt that a rare opportunity to debate environmental and employment issues that would have had relevance across Japan had been lost as a result of the focus on Tanaka himself. According to Mineo Nakajima, former president of the Tokyo University of Foreign Studies, "The Nagano election may have been a waste of time and taxpayers' money. What happened up there is a painful example of the emptiness of Japanese politics." Tanaka doesn't disagree: "They were physically repulsed by me. In the end, this election was about 'Do you like Yasuo Tanaka?' No matter what good things I might have done, they couldn't stand me personally."

I returned to Nagano in September 2002, a few weeks after Tanaka had been reelected. The prefectural office was buzzing with reporters and TV crews following the governor around as he moved from meeting to meeting: the country was watching to see how he would fare in his ongoing battle with bureaucrats and assemblymen who were still committed to maintaining the status quo. Tanaka's aides had scheduled me for an interview at the end of his day, 5:00 P.M., so that I might have as much time with him as I needed. But his schedule had changed; he was leaving on a 5:15 bullet train for Omiya, on the way to Tokyo. I was invited to ride along and interview him on the train. It was after 5:00 when he dashed from the building with reporters trailing behind him and stepped into his car, where I was waiting. His aide handed him a briefcase, which he settled bulkily on his lap with his two cell phones; a Yasshi decal the size of a quarter was affixed to each. On the race to the station he placed a phone call to apologize to someone for canceling a meeting: "This is Yasuo Tanaka, in the employ of Nagano's voters . . ."

We stepped onto the train just before the doors closed and sat facing each other in the first-class car, which was half empty. If I had been with Ishihara, the other passengers would have gawked, but I couldn't be sure they even recognized Tanaka, or perhaps he was such a familiar figure on this train, which he used to commute between Nagano and Tokyo, that no one was surprised to see him. The train began to move. "I'm all yours," Tanaka said, smiling and leaning forward in his seat.

I wanted to understand what felt to me like a contradiction. In his personal life, Tanaka was ostentatiously extravagant. He traveled first class and stayed at the finest hotels (his favorite Tokyo hotel, the Park Hyatt, was among the most expensive in the city), he insisted on eating at the best restaurants and wrote rapturously about good food and fine wine, he dressed in custom-made Italian suits. How, I wondered, could a man who appeared to revel in the luxuries of life and who seemed so identified with an ideal of elegance and style be genuinely moved by the plight of a senior citizen or a merchant or a farmer? How could Yasuo Tanaka the epicurean elitist also be a man of the people? I knew I wasn't the only one aware of this apparent contradiction. Over Chinese food in Tokyo, Tanaka's close friend, the philosopher and cultural critic Akira Asada, expressed his surprise that Tanaka had lasted as long as he has: "Local politics is the toughest game. When he was elected I thought to myself, It will be a miracle if he sticks it out for a year — there are no restaurants in Nagano he'd consider decent. I imagine he's discovered that his real gift is for politics and not for writing."

Tanaka responded to my question with a look of dismay. "What an odd thing to ask me!" The rebuke was gentle, a caress of disapproval. "What makes you think I am an elitist? Because I eat well and dress well? The Japanese believe that a volunteer must dress in rags and do without eating. But a volunteer cannot exist without food or drink. A priest is able to serve others selflessly, to volunteer himself, only if he has a glass of red wine and some meat on his table. It isn't only a matter of spirituality as the Japanese believe. Just because a man dresses in rags and survives on stale bread and water doesn't mean he's a compassionate man. And because a man dresses well and lives a stylish life doesn't mean he's without compassion. The truth is, I am able to volunteer myself because I am able to live the life I do."

I pointed out what I had sensed and others had written, that the life Tanaka chose to lead, with its extravagance and the idiosyncrasy of his personal style, was offensive to many of the people he needed to bring around to his way of thinking. One of Tanaka's refrains was that people failed to understand him. And he complained that his opponents declined to engage him in substantive debate. Mightn't it be true, as the political scientist Kiichi Fujiwara had lamented, that "just looking at Tanaka makes people want to mock or revile him?"

Tanaka had been holding my microphone for me, as if he were the interviewer. He turned it toward himself and paused a minute — I had the feeling that his response was not going to be one of his familiar sound bites. "In Japan, even more than in the United States, we decide who a person is based on exterior brands and labels. What school did he attend and how does he dress? I critiqued that way of thinking when I wrote *Vaguely Crystal.* I am still critiquing it. I've designed my whole life to serve as a critique of that kind of thinking. Yasuo Tanaka dresses outrageously in scarlet shirts and lilac socks and writes about fine wine and flaunts his sexual conquests, but Yasuo Tanaka also weeps when he listens to an old granny talk about her problems. How can these things go together? You asked that very question. My whole life is a contradiction designed to make people think for themselves and to force them to see beneath the surface. I suppose you could say I am a trickster."

With four years ahead of him and the support of the electorate, Tanaka seems confident that he will achieve his Nagano revolution. He says he wants to create "the Sweden of Japan" with a "Swiss-style direct democracy" based on voter participation. Skeptics wonder how he intends to replace the revenue the prefecture will lose as a result of his curtailment of public works. He is already pressuring large construction companies to expand into reforestation; he claims that forestry could provide 10 to 20 percent of Nagano's annual income. And he has declared his determination to increase the national brand value of Nagano produce. In addition to its well-known Shinshu apples, Nagano is Japan's largest producer of lettuce, mushrooms, and wine. Tanaka recently appointed a sommelier who has become a television celebrity with a high national profile, Shinya Tasaki, as director of the government's agricultural department.

There is no question that Tanaka has been handed a popular mandate to govern as he sees fit, but the prefectural assembly's animosity has by no means been dispelled and there is certain to be more trouble ahead. Tanaka has pledged to withhold hundreds of thousands of dollars in annual taxpayers' money that has until now been available to assembly members. Nominally the funds are for use in overseas visits and policy research and have been unmonitored. He is also pushing hard for a new ordinance that will promote increased voter participation in the governmental process by facilitating plebiscites. Both these moves represent a threat to members of the assembly and are certain to inflame their antagonism.

The April 13, 2003, election eased somewhat the antagonism toward Tanaka personally that had resulted in the no-confidence vote a year earlier. Among the fifty-eight members elected to the assembly (thirty-two incumbents and twenty-six newcomers), six of the twenty-nine incumbents who had campaigned against Tanaka lost their seats, while avowed Tanaka supporters increased in number from eight to seventeen. Even so, the election was not a decisive victory for the governor: only three of the eleven candidates he had campaigned for were successful; and forty-one members — 70 percent of the total assembly — declared during their campaigns that they would be voting on the merits of the issues without regard to the governor's position. Tanaka may have a mandate from the voters, but he is hardly in control of his assembly.

Tanaka's advocates across the country are already watching for indications that he may be interested in a seat in the national Diet when his term as governor ends in 2006. He will say only that he is fully engaged by the task at hand. "What I have in mind for Nagano will take three to four years to achieve, and I'm having the time of my life," he told me. "The voters in this prefecture are supporting almost everything I'm doing and propose to do. I have never felt so fulfilled and gratified." Perhaps Tanaka is keeping his political ambitions to himself. But whether or not he decides to enter national politics, and his outspoken abrasiveness and quirky persona would make this difficult, there is no question that he has encouraged a silent majority of younger Japanese to express its dissatisfaction with the status quo and, in the process, provided impetus for a new trend in Japanese politics. Observing Tanaka's success at breaking the LDP hegemony in Nagano and including citizens in the process of government, younger voters have been electing growing numbers of independent prefectural governors and Diet members committed to emulating Tanaka's revolution in Nagano.

Nor is Tanaka's vitalizing influence limited to politics per se. His attack on the press club system demonstrated that a door could be opened to alternative reporting, and other prefectures are following his lead. His environmental reforms have inspired his supporters to take a more vocal stand. In fact, it is fair to say that Tanaka has single-handedly made activism in general fashionable for the first time since the student movement ended in catastrophe in the early 1970s. Oki Matsumoto, the founder of the brokerage firm Monex, a close friend of Tanaka's and typical of the resourceful mavericks who back him, would certainly agree. In October 2002, the minister of economic and fiscal policy, Heizo Takenaka, presented an aggressive plan for restructuring the bad loans that have crippled Japan's banking system. The LDP considered the plan too radical, and the national media dismissed Takenaka as a zealot. But Monex conducted a national poll, which showed that 87 percent of voters supported Takenaka, a finding that Matsumoto reported to his client base via the Internet. "Yasuo Tanaka is showing us that if we want a viable economy and an effective democracy in this country, we have to take action ourselves," he told me. "He is showing us the way to a brighter future."

Epilogue:
Outgrowing Adolescence

Japan's economy is stalled, but the society is in motion. Predictions about where precisely it is headed are best left to fortunetellers. But changes occurring in the national psychology are certain to affect the course of the country's history in the twenty-first century. In the context of this chronicle, the most significant are a growing disenchantment with the United States and the gradual rediscovery of an affinity with the rest of Asia in general and China in particular, which goes beyond economic interests.

Since the end of the war in 1945, the reality of Japanese life has been significantly shaped and colored by American foreign policy, by the dynamics of a marketplace controlled by the United States, and, in a variety of ways, by American culture. At the level of political leadership, Japan's junior partnership with the United States was engineered during and directly following the U.S. occupation by Douglas MacArthur's right hand in Japan, Shigeru Yoshida. The eldest son of an aristocratic family with close ties to the imperial house, Yoshida, who had been educated at Oxford and spoke fluent English, had bitterly opposed the Pacific War and was superbly equipped to deal with the Americans he served.

As prime minister from 1946 to 1947, and again from 1948 to 1954, Yoshida created a central government dedicated to ensuring that postwar Japan would function as an effective shield against Russia and China. In his choice of ministers for three consecutive cabinets, acting in accordance with Washington's insistence that the key to power was an alliance with the same conservative-reactionary elements in politics and business that had prevailed prior to, and during, the Pacific War, he brought prewar politicians — including a number of Class-A war criminals — back to power. In August 1951, Yoshida announced the government's desire that U.S. bases remain in Japan. He was speaking for the United States and for MacArthur, with whom he conferred closely. The following month, at the San Francisco Opera House, he signed the Mutual Security Treaty permitting a continued U.S. military presence in Japan. In 1954, he arranged a coalition among conservative-reactionary factions that became, and remains, Japan's ruling party, the LDP. By placing Japan under the U.S. security umbrella and by carrying out an undeclared rearmament (also in accordance with U.S. cold-war strategy), Yoshida hoped to trade accommodation to U.S. foreign policy in return for the opportunity to convert military defeat into economic victory. Both parts of his somewhat Faustian bargain would come to pass: Japan would build an economy second only to that of the United States. And the country — more properly, the government — would remain trapped inside a costly and often paralyzing ambivalence about its own sovereignty on the one hand and U.S. needs and demands on the other.

The LDP's responsiveness to U.S. interests and pressure — a disposition Shintaro Ishihara has derisively characterized as "fifty years of eager subservience" — is a genetic legacy of immovable power. In 1960, in the face of the most violent protest demonstrations in Japan's postwar history, Prime Minister Nobusuke Kishi, a designated war criminal, ordered the Tokyo police to remove the leftist opposition bodily from the Diet chamber to ensure renewal of the Mutual Security Treaty. During the Vietnam War, which most Japanese opposed, the government allowed U.S. warships to dock at Yokosuka and other ports without disclosing that they were armed with nuclear missiles.

Prime Minister Koizumi's support of the U.S. invasion of Iraq in 2003 is a more recent example of the government's reflexive response to U.S. foreign policy. In an attempt to answer critics demanding to know how he could support the United States in defiance of international consensus, Koizumi declared, "For more than fifty years since the war, our predecessors have made the judgment that damaging trust between Japan and the United States would be counter to Japan's national interest."

As long as the LDP maintains its hegemony, the central government cannot be expected to take an independent stand that may run counter to U.S. interests; there is no precedent for opposing the United States, and alignment is a response that has been conditioned across the fifty-year span of Japan's reemergence as a world power. But clearly the LDP's iron grip on control of the government is beginning to loosen. The failure to bring the economy out of crisis and ongoing scandals have brought the party to a postwar low in national esteem. And the LDP's majority control of the national Diet and prefectural assemblies is being steadily eroded by younger politicians running as independents and winning elections on campaign promises inspired by Yasuo Tanaka and others like him to free the country from the stranglehold of the LDP machine.

Regarding the hypersensitive issue of nuclear arms, even the central government is manifesting a strikingly uncharacteristic rebelliousness. Since early in 2003, the United States has been pressuring Japan to arm itself with nuclear weapons and tell the Chinese of its intention as a way of persuading Beijing to get tough with North Korea. But the government has flatly rejected the proposal. In March, Vice Foreign Minister Yukio Takeuchi told reporters, "No one in Japan, including the government, is seriously discussing nuclear armament."

That is not entirely accurate. An essay in the February 2003 issue of *Shokun,* a conservative opinion monthly, argues that Japan is naïve to expect the United States to place itself in jeopardy by defending Japan in the event of a nuclear strike by North Korea or China, and urges the government to develop its own nuclear deterrent of two to three hundred nuclear warheads on sea-based cruise missiles. The Japanese may be a long way from invalidating the significance of their martyrdom at the end of World War II by abandoning their deep aversion to nuclear weapons. But the debate is now under way for the first time, just as amendment of the MacArthur constitution is now a subject of serious consideration. Inexorably, as the political landscape of East Asia alters, Japan's heretofore unbending renunciation of war and the corollary refusal to consider arming itself will cease to be viable options. Certainly, nuclear weapons and a strike capacity would dramatically diminish the benefits to Japan of alignment with American foreign policy interests in East Asia.

The shifting reality of the global marketplace is also loosening the economic ties that have bound Japan to the United States since the end of the war. In March 1950, John Foster Dulles visited Tokyo as the head of an economic mission reporting to Harry Truman and, after two weeks of touring, informed an official at the Ministry of Finance that Japan's best option might be exporting cocktail napkins to the United States. But with the outbreak of the Korean War three months later, in June 1950, Japan's fledgling postwar economy received its first big windfall in the form of orders for supplies and services from the U.S. military known as "special procurements." Between June 1950 and the end of 1953, the United States purchased $2.3 billion in transportation and construction, trucks, steel, barbed wire, posts, metal drums, and other materiel. U.S. troops in Japan on R and R also contributed to a heady economic revival. In 1952, both the International Monetary Fund and the World Bank admitted Japan as a regular member. Between 1954 and 1956, new special procurements generated $1.75 billion in additional business, driving the stock market up 80 percent. Toyota Motors alone, supplying the U.S. forces with tanks, trucks, and other vehicles, appreciated 40 percent.

Between 1960 and the mid-1980s, the United States provided Japan with a marketplace for everything it produced and, into the bargain, offered an inspiring model for success. Nissan's Yoshikazu Hanawa was speaking for an entire generation of businessmen when he recalled nostalgically, "We enjoyed the security of knowing that if we produced quality products, we could sell them in the United States. Our dream was catching up and overtaking the United States, and having that market, which seemed unlimited, allowed us to feel that success was inevitable if we worked hard enough. And we did succeed."

Japan's postwar capitalism came gorgeously to bloom in the mid-1980s, under the closely linked administrations of Yasuhiro Nakasone and Ronald Reagan. In May 1983, Nakasone posed for a photograph with other leaders of industrial nations following a summit in Williamsburg, Virginia. The photograph appeared in the Japanese press the following morning and occasioned a glow of national pride that characterized the Nakasone years. The Japanese were accustomed to seeing their premier at the end of the line looking small and inconsequential. Yet Nakasone, tall and handsome, was at the center of the picture, flanked by Margaret Thatcher and Ronald Reagan. If the infamous MacArthur-Hirohito photo of 1945 was emblematic of the occupation years, the Nakasone photograph conveyed no less dramatically a transformed Japan-U.S. relationship.

Nakasone's campaign slogan was "Balancing the books for the postwar era." His point was that Japan had achieved its long-standing ambition to catch up with the rest of the world, and the time had come to set new goals. He vowed to rebuild Japan's financial base without a tax increase and to resolve the trade wars with the United States. But his principal emphasis was always "internationalization," by which he meant achieving parity for Japan with the United States. If he appeared to make dramatic progress toward this goal, it was due in no small measure to the "friend-ship" he forged with Ronald Reagan, a connection that was ex-ploited by both men to serve their political needs. The Japanese media in particular took pleasure in reporting meetings between "Ron and Yasu."

The export boom that transformed Japan into the world's sec-ond largest economy was enabled by Reaganomics. U.S. industry was unable to answer the demand created by Reagan's supply-side economic policy, and Japanese industry was primed to take up the slack in automobiles, appliances, tools, consumer electronics, au-diovisual equipment, and semiconductors. In the 1970s, semicon-ductors were the cornerstone of American entrepreneurial cap-italism. The industry was created by Americans, and its managers were the best and brightest. By the mid-1980s, these same entre-preneurs were losing their industry to Japanese companies like Fujitsu and Tadahiro Sekimoto's NEC.

In 1985, under increasing pressure from an angry Congress and the private sector, Reagan was forced to compromise Japan's com-petitiveness: the Plaza Accord, signed in September, drove the value of the dollar down and doubled overnight the value of the yen, which continued to rise subsequently, significantly increas-ing the cost of Japanese exports. Even so, Reagan continued to as-sure Nakasone that he would veto any protectionist legislation. Japan and the United States had been engaged in heated contro-versy about trade restrictions since the Nixon years. In the textile agreement of 1972, Japan agreed to self-limit export volume. In 1981, Japan acquiesced again to pressure from the United States and volunteered to limit automobile exports to 1.6 million vehi-cles a year. In 1986, after years of tense negotiations about semi-conductors, the Ron and Yasu administrations declared an un-easy truce. But the following year, simmering resentment in the United States exploded into rage when Toshiba Machinery was caught selling sophisticated machine tools to the Soviet Union in violation of international export regulations. The United States pressed charges, asking for a one-year interdiction against all exports from Japan. During the summer of 1987, U.S. congressmen smashed Toyotas and "attacked" Toshiba radios and laptops with sledgehammers on the steps of the Capitol. On July 21, over Reagan's veto, Congress passed a comprehensive package of trade laws aimed directly at Japan, including 100 percent tariffs on all Japanese laptops and color TVs and a specific ban on all Toshiba imports. This move effectively terminated the protective embrace that had allowed the sense of security Yoshikazu Hanawa had recalled for me, and he admitted, "As the eighties ended, we woke up, or were rudely awakened, to the reality that we were on our own. And I would have to say that with that realization we also lost some of our illusions, not just about relying on the United States but also our sense that we were united by mutual interests."

But realpolitik and economics cannot account entirely for Japan's obsessive focus on America since the end of the war. In a domain of the national psyche, which has little to do with economic and military reliance on the United States, Japan has been impelled to emulate American society and culture by a fascination with something the Japanese have perceived as the American mystique. This deep and enduring infatuation, for that is what it is, was engendered during the years of the American occupation, part and parcel of a process that the historian John Dower has characterized as "embracing defeat." Kenzaburo Oe has described his earliest encounters with American troops as they rode their jeeps into his mountain village: "We had been told they would torture or kill us and rape the young girls. Instead, they showered us with jewels, chocolate bars and chewing gum. I unwrapped a stick of gum and sniffed the silver foil. Its sugary scent was enough to make me dizzy. To my ten-year-old imagination, that piece of American tin foil stood for everything wonderful." In an autobiographical essay, Oe has evoked the Japanese expectation that the conquering Americans would teach them how to lead a new life:

Presently I was drawn to a vibrant young oak tree that soared straight up. The assistant principal's English training had not been limited to shouting "hello!" We had been told that when a young American loves a girl, he kisses her. And that we, too, would be imitating the Americans and doing some kissing of our own. But what exactly was a kiss?

Approaching the beautiful oak, I pressed my lips to the fork in a pliant branch.

Yet there was deep ambivalence. MacArthur humiliated the Japanese, describing them as "a nation of twelve-year-olds," and they hated him for it. On the other hand, when Harry Truman angrily relieved him of duty in April 1951, two hundred thousand weeping Japanese lined the road to see him off. He was a tyrant with awesome power. At Japan's most vulnerable moment, he was also revered as a benefactor.

In the decades that followed, Japan's emerging consumer class evolved an exalted vision of America that became a national obsession. The American way of life as it was conveyed to envious Japanese audiences through television and films set the standard for success and happiness. The Japanese studied and brought home every imaginable American style and manner, from crew cuts and health food stores to Christmas parties and retirement homes. American fads from Hula-Hoops and yo-yos to paintball guns and outdoor barbecue grills created giant marketing opportunities in Japan. When Sony's Akio Morita conceived the Walkman, he chose to market it in the United States before introducing it to Japan as an American success, a strategy that became known as the "boomerang effect." Japanese films played to mostly empty houses while people lined up around the block to see the latest Hollywood blockbuster. American movie stars, athletes, and singers were overwhelmed by the number and the ardor of their Japanese fans.

To be sure, American popular culture has had a trendsetting impact on societies around the world. But the earnestness of Japan's focus on the details of American life remains distinct. The Japan Travel Bureau offered annual tours to Nashville designed to allow Japan's proliferating country and western bands to hear live performances at the Grand Ole Opry. And the country's largest bartending school sent students to New York and Los Angeles so they could observe both East and West Coast approaches to icing margaritas and daiquiris in a silver shaker.

Until recently, the Japanese view of the United States as a paragon of culture has been colored by something close to reverence. I recall an example as telling as it is ludicrous, an advertising campaign for Kentucky Fried Chicken. When KFC arrived in Japan in 1979, there was resistance to the product, which was perceived as greasy. In 1980, a television commercial created by McCann-Erickson Hakuhodo overcame consumer resistance and established the company as the fast-food market leader. The campaign positioned Kentucky Fried Chicken as the traditional food of America's southern aristocracy! The original sixty-second spot opened with Colonel Sanders as a boy of seven baking rye bread in the roomy kitchen of his "old Kentucky home." "A lifetime later," the narrator intoned, "this same tradition of excellence was transferred by the colonel to his fried chicken." American executives who saw the storyboards were appalled: how could the consumer be expected to make the connection between a loaf of rye bread and fried chicken? What they failed to perceive was the powerful appeal of the implied connection between KFC and a venerable tradition, aristocratic no less, of the American South. The campaign was a stunning success. The following year, the company launched another outlandish campaign designed to persuade housewives that American families "traditionally" enjoy a meal from KFC on Christmas Day. Reservation order forms were printed for a Christmas meal with all the fixings, including twelve fried chicken pieces, mashed potatoes, and gravy, and the Japanese company recorded the highest sales volume in KFC history that Christmas week.

Today, Japanese consumers would laugh at this variety of flimflam. The point is not that the Japanese understanding of American society is more sophisticated today than it was in 1980. The truth is rather that the American mythos is losing its incandescence in the Japanese imagination. In 1998, the Japanese animated feature *Princess Mononoke,* an allegory of self-discovery in the fourteenth century, became the highest grossing film in Japanese cinema history; ever since, Hollywood blockbusters have been losing audiences to Japanese, Chinese, Korean, and other Asian films. Publishers are declining to pay the exorbitant advances demanded by writers like Stephen King, John Grisham, and Tom Clancy: bestseller status in the United States is no longer a guarantee of success in Japan. The English-language boom is on the wane; some of the largest conversation schools have closed, and students are electing to study Russian and Chinese instead of English. Travel to the United States has also declined; tourists and students are choosing to spend their time in Europe, as they did before the war, or in Southeast Asia, or in China, which has become a mecca for backpackers and is attracting growing numbers of Japanese exchange students. The shift away from America is particularly evident in youth culture — in young fashion, with its new emphasis on creative uses of traditional kimono fabrics and national costumes from Burma, Thailand, and China, and in the environments that have become popular with the young. While Starbucks is still the preferred gathering place for young Japanese women after school or work, American hangouts like Tony Roma's and the Crazy Horse Café are often empty. The places to go in Japan's cities today are Vietnamese restaurants and authentic Chinese teahouses.

It is difficult to isolate the elements in what amounts to an ongoing process of disillusionment. Certainly Shintaro Ishihara's brand of neonationalism, with its emphasis on Japan's slavish acquiescence to American interests, has had its effect. At the level of popular culture, the cartoonist demagogue Yoshinori Kobayashi has played a role. The former stand-up comedian Takeshi Kitano, known as "Beat" Takeshi, may have been an even more influential source of anti-American sentiment (when Rush Limbaugh was introduced to Japan, he was described as "the American Takeshi"). At fifty-six, Kitano has been a dominant figure in Japanese pop culture for more than twenty years. He has written dozens of volumes of scathing commentary on Japan's fecklessness, starred in thirteen films, and directed ten of his own, all paeans to the macho, nihilist yakuza violence that his persona embodies. But he is best known for the talk and variety shows he conceives and hosts on national television, as many as nine at a time in one season. Takeshi insults and terrorizes contestants on his nightly game and quiz shows, attacking women, gays, and the disabled with an exuberance that recalls Don Rickles but is more virulent than Rickles ever was.

Takeshi's TV hallmark is violent abuse and disdain of anything held holy in Japan. In a perverse variation on *This Is Your Life,* his guests must endure surprise encounters with the people from their past whom they were most anxious to avoid, former lovers, ex–business partners, even disinherited sons and daughters. A similar twist on *Candid Camera* allowed audiences the pleasure of observing an unsuspecting senior citizen's terror when he was accosted on a deserted street by a yakuza gang employed by the producers. On a prime-time favorite called the *Takeshi Comedy Ultra Quiz Show,* he put forty entertainers in a bus and suspended it above a tank of water on a crane. When contestants answered questions incorrectly, the crane lowered the bus toward the water until it was submerged; an underwater camera was in place to record them clawing at the windows before they were hoisted to safety. On another episode, his producers placed a plastic bag over a losing contestant's face and shoved his head into a cage where he had to watch a mongoose battle a poisonous viper.

If Takeshi is a sadist, he is also a xenophobe with a pronounced distaste for what he views as American hypocrisy. On one of his longest-running shows, *What's Wrong with Japan?,* resident foreigners, including many Americans, are invited to the studio to voice their complaints about Japanese society while Takeshi ridicules their spoken Japanese in asides to the audience. Fifteen years ago, viewers would have been offended by a program designed to make a laughingstock of foreigners in general, Americans in particular. But the program's popularity is evidence of a significant shift in Japanese attitudes.

Japan's disenchantment with America was certainly deepened by the U.S. response to the terrorist attacks of September 11, 2001. The Japanese were gravely offended, with good cause in my view, by the widely promulgated and eagerly endorsed comparison between 9/11 and the Japanese bombing of Pearl Harbor in 1941, a military action aimed at the U.S. Pacific Fleet and by no means a terrorist assault on defenseless civilians. Beyond that, from the perspective of the widening distance between the two societies, the American interpretation of the Al Qaeda attack as the opening campaign in a war between good and evil struck many Japanese as intolerably self-righteous, not to mention hypocritical. Yoshinori Kobayashi disassociated from the Society for the Creation of a New History in November 2001, accusing his colleagues of "fawning acquiescence" to the American version of the incident. He titled his first of several "Arro-Procs" on the subject *American Imperialism Versus Islamic Fundamentalism*. "The Americans propose that this is an attack on democracy, on culture, on civilization itself," Yoshi-rin begins angrily. "Does that mean that Islamic fundamentalism is simply a cult no different from Aum Shinri, a pack of terrorists? I don't think so." In the panels that follow, Kobayashi creates a savage montage of what he calls the world's "most dissolute society": children shooting up their schools and being abducted or abused by their parents, plutocracy and materialism, pornography, racial discrimination. "The Taliban don't even see their women's faces until they're married," Yoshi-rin shrieks. "From their point of view, this is a picture of the dark side of civilization." He concludes with a strategic suggestion: "If

America has so much confidence in its culture, why not play its strongest cultural card against the enemy? Why not install large screens in the mountains of Afghanistan and project hard-core pornography twenty-four hours a day? Why not fight terrorism with ero-ism!"

At the opposite end of the political spectrum, Governor Yasuo Tanaka expressed his own discomfort with the American response to 9/11. Like many of the younger Japanese who support him, Tanaka has never felt drawn to the United States. His models are Swedish Socialism and Switzerland's participative democracy, and his affinity is for European styles and sensibilities. In fact, he shares the European's overall skepticism about American society and culture. At a press conference on September 12, he cited CNN and *USA Today* polls in which 87 percent of the Americans questioned agreed that 9/11 was "the cruelest and most tragic news they had ever heard in their lives." Tanaka said, "This gave me pause. Certainly this was a terrible incident, but I couldn't help wondering if those Americans who took it as the cruelest and most tragic news they had ever heard had any idea of what was going on, and has been going on, often as a result of U.S. interference in the affairs of others, in the rest of the world."

More recently, the Japanese have come to view America's professed motives with increasing uneasiness and skepticism. Since early in January 2003, Shintaro Ishihara has been referring to the United States as "the second Mongol Empire." This may be typical Ishihara bombast, but many Japanese are listening, and wondering uneasily if he may be correct.

If Japan is emerging from thralldom to the United States and the mystique of America, it appears that the Japanese are also reengaging with China on multiple levels. The most obvious has to do with business. Since the mid-nineties, Japan has been investing heavily in China. Toyota and Nissan are both producing cars and trucks in joint ventures with China. In September 2002, Carlos Ghosn purchased a half interest in the Dongfeng Motor

Corporation and began production of 80,000 Nissan subcompacts a year at an existing plant in Guangzhou. Nissan expects to be producing 550,000 vehicles a year by 2006 and 900,000 a year by the end of the decade. In March 2003, Sony announced plans to move its entire production of PlayStation 2 game consoles to China this year. Fuji Xerox is preparing to spend $300 million to expand its sales and service network in China, and the company plans to triple its sales of printers and copiers there to 700,000 a year and to double sales volume to $500 million a year by 2005. The recent surge of business activity on the mainland is increasing the Japanese presence in China month by month. In the fall of 2003, a Chinese pharmaceutical manufacturer will open a ten-story hospital for Japanese nationals in Shenzhen, the Chinese twin city to Hong Kong; the hospital will be staffed with Japanese as well as Chinese doctors and nurses and will employ a team of interpreters.

Japan's investment in China is beginning to pay off. While exports to the United States have remained fixed since 1990 at just under 30 percent of the country's total, Japan's exports to China during the same period have increased from 9.6 percent to 15.7 percent of the total, climbing 32.3 percent in 2002 alone. In the single month of December 2002, Japan shipped products to China worth $6.5 billion, two thirds of the total it shipped to the United States. It is likely that China will overtake the United States as the principal consumer of Japanese goods in the near future. Japan is also importing Chinese goods at an increasing rate: in 2002, Chinese imports outvalued imports from the United States for the first time.

A close economic alliance between Japan and China is a disturbing prospect for the United States for a number of reasons. Japan is the largest foreign investor in U.S. Treasury securities, and China is the second largest. Their combined holdings of $466.5 billion represent 40 percent of worldwide government investments in the United States totaling $1.66 trillion. Should a united Japan and China decide at some future date to apply pressure to the U.S. economy, they could easily devalue the dollar by withdrawing their investments. As such a move would result in a steep loss in the value of their own holdings, it is an unlikely, but not an impossible, scenario.

The growing interdependence of their two economies appears to be revitalizing a cultural bond between China and Japan that is deeply rooted in fifteen hundred years of tradition. Buddhism reached Japan from China via Korea in the mid-sixth century. Throughout the medieval period, there was constant cultural exchange between Chinese and Japanese monks, scholars, teachers, and artists. Beginning in the seventeenth century, Japanese society was regulated for 250 years by Confucian values adopted from China.

Language accounts for another enduring bond. While spoken Chinese and Japanese are entirely unrelated languages, Japanese is written with Chinese characters. Beginning in the eighth century, official documents in Japan were written in classical Chinese. During the Tokugawa Period (1600–1868), at the temple schools in their feudal domains, the male children of samurai families spent hours each day memorizing and reciting the Confucian classics in a hybrid Sino-Japanese. In view of the long tradition of Chinese studies, it is not surprising that the most important critical works on classical Chinese philosophy, philology, and literature have been and continue to be written in Japan by Japanese scholars. To this day, comprehensive literacy in the Japanese language requires an extensive knowledge of Chinese compounds and allusions, which color the Japanese lexicon as richly as Greek and Latin live on in English. The recent Japanese language boom, a reflection of the nationalist emphasis on reconnecting with the past, has led many Japanese to the discovery of the importance of Chinese in their own language and has stimulated interest in learning Chinese. In the past five years, Chinese-language schools have begun to appear in urban areas, and Chinese-language enrollment at Japan's universities doubled in 2000 and doubled again in 2002.

The vibrant cultural exchange that was interrupted in 1932 when Japan attacked Manchuria is gradually renewing. The first annual Japan-China Writers' Conference, cochaired by Kenzaburo Oe and his close friend Mo Yan, convened in Beijing in 2000. Government funding in both countries is being allocated to sponsor frequent meetings of scientists, doctors, environmentalists, and educators. Universities in both countries are actively recruiting faculty from each other, and the flow of exchange students back and forth is increasing dramatically: in 2002 for the first time, Chinese students enrolled at Japanese universities outnumbered Vietnamese, Malaysian, and Indian exchange students.

Tourism between Japan and China is also thriving. According to the Japan Travel Bureau, package excursions to China's major cities are now more popular than tours to the United States, with the exception of Hawaii. And Tokyo's hotels are packed with large tour groups from China's mainland. Walking on the Ginza today, you will overhear more Chinese than English: the Chinese presence feels pervasive in a way it never has until now. And the teashops are everywhere, crowded with young Japanese, offering dozens of varieties of Chinese tea.

There is no question that younger Japanese in particular are turning toward China with open curiosity and eager interest. It also appears that China's attitudes toward Japan are changing. China's new president, Hu Jintao, sixty-one, came of age well after 1945 and is unburdened by personal memories of Japanese atrocities during the Pacific War. In this respect he is like South Korea's new president, Ro Moo-hyun, who recently appealed to Prime Minister Koizumi for "future-oriented relations" uncomplicated by "the baggage of the past." President Hu has yet to reveal his approach to Japan, but it is unlikely that he will invoke or rekindle the animosity of the past as an impediment to improved relations in the future. As evidence of this, Japanese analysts point to an essay titled "New Thinking on Relations with Japan," which appeared in December 2002 in an influential Chinese magazine, *Strategy and Management.* Written by an editorial writer for *The People's Daily*, the chief organ of the Chinese Communist Party, the essay sharply criticizes demagogues and bureaucrats for continuing to promulgate defamatory images of the Japanese as "Asia's devils." Observes the writer, Licheng Ma, "When you fly over Japan and see how small it is and how mountainous, you realize what a feat it was to have achieved the world's second largest GDP. Japan is in fact the pride of Asia." Ma argues that belligerent nationalists like Ishihara are only a small minority, and he reports that almost all the Japanese he interviewed during a month in Tokyo were eager for friendship and cooperation. "The time has come," he concludes, "to let go of our own irrational nationalism and to normalize our relations with Japan." The essay represented a startling change in tone, and observers concluded that it could not have been written and published, particularly by an editorial writer for *The People's Daily*, without government approval.

None of this is intended to suggest that Japan and China are about to become, in John Donne's phrase, "one another's best." Hostility toward Japan remains ingrained in China. The horror of Tiananmen Square is still a vivid memory in Japan. Nevertheless, Japan is moving in China's direction, and beneath the rapprochement in progress is an affinity that is inherent and more powerful than the logic of mutual interest that has been advanced as the basis of the Japan-U.S. relationship. The truth is, notwithstanding the fantasy that Japan has joined the United States in confabulating since 1945, Japan and America are not natural-born partners. The notion of the "Asian coprosperity sphere" may be repellent because it invokes the militarism of the war years, but a communality among the societies of Asia constructed around a partnership between Japan and China makes economic and political sense. And it has a basis at the deepest level in a genuine cultural affinity that cannot be denied.

Still, replacing the American spell with a renewed dependency on China is unlikely to provide Japan with the self-certainty it longs for. Japan needs to grow up in the sense that an adolescent moves beyond the orbit of parental influence toward individuality. Natsume Soseki lamented Japan's failure to find its own way. Soseki's direct heir, Kenzaburo Oe, has his own vision of what is necessary if Japan is ever to heal what he calls "the wound of ambivalence." Oe has perceived and addressed the Japanese predicament with unique clarity and passion. For forty years, in twenty-seven major novels and countless volumes of short stories and essays, he has dedicated himself to a meticulous and tireless search for authentic moral purpose in the chaos of the postwar world. His voice belongs in any chronicle of Japan's quest for identity.

At the heart of Oe's greatest fiction is a poignant yearning for the belonging, consonance, and certainty that he experienced as a boy until the war ended in 1945 and he was expelled — he has often used the word *banished* — into a reality on the other side of a yawning discontinuity with his past. In his quest for reconnection to a utopian childhood, Oe became a mythmaker; from his reading of the cultural anthropologists Masao Yamaguchi, Mircea Eliade, and Claude Lévi-Strauss, he distilled a vision of myth as a web of connection folding every individual human life, past, present, and future, into a cosmic community. In a manner that recalls William Faulkner, he created an intricately detailed mythology of Japan's origins and prehistory, a peripheral alternative to the imperial mythology, centered in the village of his birth and a magical forest surrounding it on the remote island of Shikoku. It was to this place out of time and beyond history that his characters returned in search of self-knowledge and renewal. While his utopian socialism is antithetical to the neonationalist vision, Oe's attempt to transfigure the past through the power of his imagination is not unlike the nationalist commitment to rewriting history. In fact, Yukio Mishima's quest for a cause to live and die for was emotionally adjacent to Oe's longing for connection. And there is evidence to suggest that Oe understood the proximity of their needs, which may explain, at least in part, why he has returned continually in essays and fiction, however ironically, to Mishima's death.

When Mishima killed himself in November 1970, Oe was out of the country and used his absence as an excuse for remaining silent. Two years later, he wrote a one-hundred-page novella that is based unmistakably on Mishima's mini-insurrection and suicide, *The Day He Himself Shall Wipe My Tears Away.* The narrator, who maintains that he is on his deathbed in spite of what his doctors tell him, is reliving a moment from his childhood — he was ten years old at the time — when he accompanied his delusional father and a band of rebels on an uprising designed to rescue Japan from defeat. The date is August 15, 1945. When the father is gunned down during the travesty of an insurrection, his son beholds a sign that his death has been consecrated, a huge chrysanthemum (the imperial seal) that blossoms like fireworks across the sky.

On one level, this is a sardonic parody. In his preface to the novella, Oe wrote: "It is the writer's responsibility to place his imagination inside the shackles of the imperial system, in order to find some new means of escape from it." But this complex fiction is certainly more than satire. As the narrator reconstructs the moments leading up to his father's grotesque martyrdom, he receives objective testimony from his mother and others that should prove to him that his version of the story is exalted if not false. Yet he is undaunted, choosing to live not objective history, but a radiant myth of belonging in which history itself is annihilated. *The Day He Himself Shall Wipe My Tears Away* reveals that Oe understood intuitively the precise contours of Mishima's longing for the embrace of something transcendent and absolute. At the very least, it seems clear that he well understood Mishima's pain at living with the ambiguity that he himself had characterized as a condition of postwar Japanese life.

Between 1992 and 1994, Oe completed a trilogy of novels in which he explored the possibility of acquiring and sustaining "faith," even in the absence of belief in a Christian god, in the Christian promise of enfoldment and belonging. He titled the work *The Flaming Green Tree,* an image he borrowed from the Yeats poem "Vacillation":

> A tree there is that from its topmost bough
> Is half all glittering flame and half all green
> Abounding foliage moistened with the dew;
> And half is half and yet is all the scene;
> And half and half consume what they renew

In Oe's hands, this gorgeous antinomy becomes a metaphor for the paradox of faith, the fervent belief in something that cannot be experienced or known, and for the impossible polarity of modern Japanese life, the rending "ambiguity" that he described in his Nobel acceptance speech.

When I met Oe last, in November 2002, his meditation on faith as an agency of belonging had led him back to a focus on himself as an individual. "It's true that we have been severed from our past," he began. "But I have come to feel that there is value in being abandoned as well. I have no desire to return to a utopian time in the past, real or imagined.

"Our identity as Japanese has withered away. From the European and American vantage, we appear to be Japanese. But inside ourselves, who are we? What basis do we have for building our identity? In the past, we had awe and reverence for our fathers and our ancestors. This is still powerful in Korea and in China. But in Japan the family has come apart, and our sense of community has also disappeared. Now we have nothing but the reflection of ourselves we see in the eyes of the West. We are confused and lost. The response to that lostness is nationalism. People like Ishihara gather around them those who have no basis for identity and entice them with the power of the state. They tell us we are all the emperor's children. The state becomes a crutch for those who are no longer able to stand alone, like plastic implanted in a dysfunctional penis."

In place of faith in anything external to himself, Oe had focused on the path of the "upstanding man." He recited for me the lines in another Yeats poem, "The Tower," which contained a definition that suited him:

> It is time that I wrote my will;
> I choose upstanding men
> That climb the streams until
> The fountain leap, and at dawn
> Drop their cast at the side
> Of dripping stone; I declare
> They shall inherit my pride,
> The pride of people that were
> Bound neither to Cause nor to State.

"Yeats was talking about a kind of highly moral anarchist," Oe said, "an independent mind that relies on nothing outside itself. When I read those lines, I thought of Huckleberry Finn. He didn't have faith in anything. But he knew for himself, as an independent spirit and mind, what was right and what was wrong. Huck was an upstanding man, and that's what I want to be. I've come to realize I don't need a crutch of any kind to help me stand up, not a utopian past in my imagination and not faith in God. We have never had a God and never will, no matter how reverently we wait and watch and listen for faith to appear. But if we stand upright and alone and proceed straight ahead as individuals, relying on nothing outside ourselves, I believe we will each discover a basis for our identity as Japanese individuals within the multiplicity that is Asia. We will discover a credo. And I believe we will also discover the basis for a new morality."

Oe used the current debate on nuclear arms as an example of how the upstanding man might reclaim his identity and discover morality. He was planning an exchange of published letters on the issue of nuclear arms with the historian Jonathan Schell. He hoped that each individual Japanese citizen would step forward into a new morality by refusing to participate in the U.S. strategy of nuclear deterrence. That would mean insisting that Japan must step outside the protection of the U.S. nuclear umbrella. "I don't know how Japan could do that providently without creating its own nuclear capacity," he admitted. "But just taking the stand would allow us to feel genuine pride — not the kind Ishihara holds out — and a substantial sense of who we are as Japanese that would reflect our experience at the end of the war in 1945."

I said good-bye to Oe at the subway station at Akasaka-Mitsuke; it was before 9:00 P.M., but he was concerned about his retarded son, Hikari, and wanted to get home. I turned back, and as I stepped onto the Benkei Bridge, a tall figure moved toward me out of the darkness from the opposite side. It was Shintaro Ishihara. He must have been coming from my hotel, the New Otani. Perhaps he had also had dinner there, or maybe he had been swimming at the exclusive health club on the third floor where he was a member. I didn't ask.

I walked the governor back down the street to where his car was waiting. As we passed the police box on the corner, the officer on duty leaped up and saluted him. Ishihara asked where I had been, and I told him. "Oe . . ." he said reflectively. "I consider him a friend, but I know he doesn't think of me that way. That man has no friends. He's too perverse — all about himself." Ishihara's Special Police bodyguard was standing at the rear door of the car as we approached, and he eyed me coldly. Ishihara got in and drove away with an unceremonious wave of his hand.

I was stunned: what were the chances of running into the governor alone on the street at night, having just left Kenzaburo Oe! It was an unexpected, an unlikely, a somehow shocking coincidence, but it also felt symbolic. Both these extraordinary men had grown up during the war and had been recognized as gifted writers at the same time. The same critics and senior members of the literary establishment had acknowledged and championed them: they had shared a similar postwar experience. Today, notwithstanding Ishihara's sentimental impulse just now, they were implacable enemies. Ishihara saw Oe as a traitor to the state; Oe was certain that Ishihara was a fascist. Yet both considered themselves moralists, and both were driven by a quest for the substantial sense of self that has eluded Japan since the earliest days of modernization. Leaving one and encountering the other in the space of a few minutes, I felt that I had traveled between the poles of the ambivalence that continues to be a troubling condition of contemporary Japanese life.

Sources

The following are some of the individuals who gave me their time, often more than once, for interviews I conducted in Japanese on eight trips to Tokyo between May 2001 and December 2002. While the list is partial, it will give readers a good idea of the sources I have used in my research. Any factual errors or faulty interpretations in the book are my own responsibility.

YOUTH AND EDUCATION

Nobukatsu Fujioka, professor, Tokyo University, and co-founder, Society for the Creation of a New History; Shuji Fukumoto, principal, Keio University High School; Michael Furlong, professor of education, University of California, Santa Barbara; Yoshio Furukawa, director, Juvenile Division, Tokyo Metropolitan Police; Masao Ishii, Kunitachi City School Board superintendent; Ryoichi Kawakami, junior high school teacher, author; Ikuo Komatsu, director, Educational Policy Research Center, Ministry of Education; Kunitachi Elementary School No. 6, principal and teachers; Kunitachi Junior High School

No. 2, principal and teachers; Machida High School, principal and teachers; Thomas Rohleen, professor of sociology, Stanford University; Yuko Sano, Juvenile Division, National Police Agency; Noboru Sato, Juvenile Division, Tokyo Metropolitan Police; Tetsuji Suwa, education critic; Junjiro Takahashi, dean, Keio University High School; Minoru Yamaguchi, founder, Pass; Kunio Yonenaga, *shogi* grand master, Tokyo Metropolitan School Board.

BUSINESS

Carlos Ghosn, president and CEO, Nissan Motors; Yoshikazu Hanawa, chairman, Nissan Motors; Pina Hirano, founder and CEO, Infoteria; Nobuyuki Idei, chairman, Sony Corporation; Joi Ito, venture capitalist; Yotaro Kobayashi, chairman, Fuji-Xerox, Inc.; Minoru Makihara, chairman, Mitsubishi Corporation; Oki Matsumoto, founder and CEO, Monex; Tomoko Namba, founder and CEO, DeNA; Tadahiro Sekimoto, chairman emeritus, NEC Corporation; Masayoshi Son, founder and chairman, Softbank; Hiroshi Takahashi, president, Yusen Air and Sea Service Co., Ltd.; Hirotaka Takeuchi, dean and professor, Graduate School of International Corporate Strategy, Hitotsubashi University; Motohiro Uezumi, founder and president, WayStation, Inc.

GOVERNMENT

Joshua Fogel, professor of history, University of California, Santa Barbara; Akira Iriye, professor of political science, Harvard University; Shintaro Ishihara, governor of Tokyo; Daniel Okimoto, professor of political science, Stanford University; Andrew Saidel, vice president and chief financial officer, Dynamic Strategies Asia, L.C.; Yasuo Tanaka, governor of Nagano.

CULTURE

Akira Asada, philosopher and critic; the Denda family; Kazuya Fukuda, author and critic; Naoki Inose, author and critic; Satoru Ito, senior editor, Shinchosha Publishers; Mikio Kato, executive director, International House of Japan; the Kawatani family; Takeshi "Beat" Kitano, actor and director; Yoshinori Kobayashi, cartoonist; Tetsuko Kuroyanagi, actress and TV talk show host; Yukio Matsuyama, adviser to the editorial board, *Asahi Shimbun;* the Metsugi family; Shinji Miyadai, author and critic; Ryu Murakami, novelist; Susumu Nishibe, author and critic; Kenzaburo Oe, novelist, Nobel laureate; Toshiaki Ogasawara, publisher, *Japan Times;* Donald Richie, author and film critic; Otoshige Sakai, Noh actor, living national treasure; the Otoshige Sakai family; Tatemi Sakai, literary agent; Tetsuro Sakuragi, editor in chief, Sun Publishing Company; Atsushi Sonoda, editor, Sun Publishing Company; David Spector, TV commentator; Mayumi Ujioka, editorial writer, *Asahi Shimbun;* the Yano family; Akio Yamaguchi, president, Iwanami Shoten, Publishers; Tadanori Yokoo, printmaker, painter, and critic; Banana Yoshimoto, novelist.

Index

ACKNOWLEDGMENTS

This book is based largely on extensive interviews. I would like to thank the following individuals for their invaluable help in providing me with access to the people I interviewed at length and for coordinating their impossible schedules: Yoshinori Otsuki, Nagano Prefectural Office; Hideki Takai, special political assistant to the governor of Tokyo; Shigeru Miyazato, Tokyo Prefectural Office; Ai Nakamura, editor, *President Magazine;* Kanae Murayama, Fuji Research Institute Corporation; and Izumi Koishi, International House of Japan.

I completed the writing of this book on leave from the University of California, Santa Barbara, as a Guggenheim Fellow. I wish to thank the university and the John Simon Guggenheim Memorial Foundation for their generous support.

I owe thanks to my editor at Houghton Mifflin, Eamon Dolan, a demanding reader who challenged and encouraged me constantly to look more deeply beneath the surface of what I observed. I have benefited in particular from Eamon's uncompromising insistence on clarity and continuity.

Finally, to my wife, Diane, whose support I have relied on in all things, my love and gratitude.